Harry N. Abrams, Inc., New York

Wilhelm Boeck

Jaime Sabartés

Printed and bound in Japan, in association with W. Kohlhammer,
Stuttgart, who also planned and produced the book.

The plates are the work of the engravers Haufler & Wiest, E. Schreiber,
and G. Krämer, all of Stuttgart, and Meisenbach-Riffarth, Berlin.

Milton S. Fox, Editor

The cover design was made especially for this book by Pablo Picasso,
July 1955.

The total number of reproductions is 606.

Of these:   38 full page color plates.
    2 double spreads in color offset.
    4 pages in color offset.
  136 reproductions in black-and-white halftone.
  278 small reproductions in black-and-white halftone.
   95 reproductions in black-and-white offset.
   53 line cuts in the text.

Drawing on page 1: *Musical Faun* 1952

# Contents

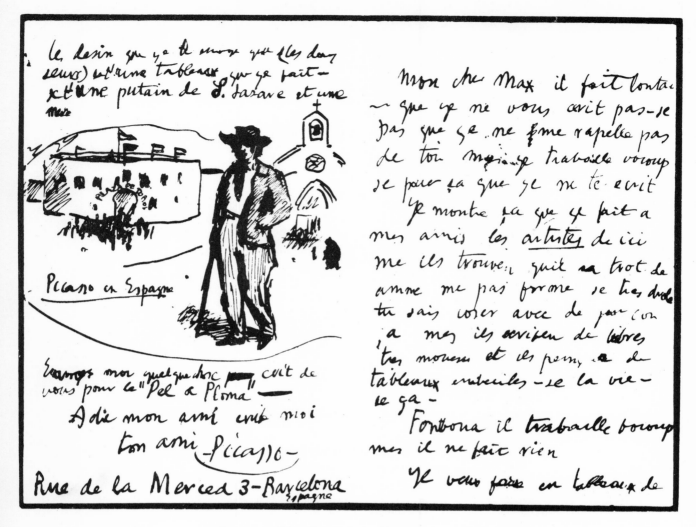

Letter to Max Jacob from Barcelona 1902

## Preface

*"We all start out by understanding and enjoying the artistic production of our own time. That, at least, is the normal, healthy, and natural way to start."*

*Max J. Friedländer*

Picasso's art is one of the forces that have shaped our era. Today it no longer matters whether we approve or disapprove of his achievement; we should understand its historic significance. This book attempts to interpret the works of Picasso by means of a method of interpretation that has been developed for the great works of art of past ages. Its aim is to demonstrate that the creations of a living master can be judged by these same standards.

The *œuvre* of Picasso, as it stands today, is so vast and so varied that it would be presumptuous even to attempt an exhaustive presentation in a single volume. Many omissions have been necessary despite the large number of individual works reproduced and commented on here. On the other hand, our emphasis on certain aspects of the master's work may help to clarify the bewildering wealth of his artistic production, and thus to make possible a deeper understanding of it.

In this book the attempt has been made to establish the closest possible correlation of text and reproductions. Thus it is suggested that the reader would be well-advised to study the reproductions in the order in which they are discussed in the successive chapters.

This monograph presents Picasso not only as a painter but also as

**7**

a draftsman and printmaker, as a sculptor and ceramist. It could not be my aim to treat exhaustively of every one of these fields of activity, especially since some of them have been discussed in specialized publications. Thus the writings of Bernhard Geiser on Picasso's graphic work make it unnecessary to enter into a discussion of detailed technical aspects of this side of his art.

The personality of a living artist is best interpreted by close friends. It is therefore a particular gain for this book that Jaime Sabartés—the intimate of Picasso longer than anyone else—has taken on this important task. His essay is to be supplemented by the literary documents printed in the appendix. In selecting these, I have taken account of previous publications and have tried to choose the less well-known pieces. Inasmuch as the documentary significance of the published verbal utterances of Picasso is under dispute there is no need to strive for completeness here. The bibliography has been selected and arranged from the standpoint of convenient use; an exhaustive Picasso bibliography would require a separate volume even today. Jaime Sabartés and Karl Flinker, Paris, have been good enough to undertake the task of devising the Classified Catalogue.

It would have been impossible for me to gain my knowledge of Picasso's work without the pioneering labors of others, especially of Alfred H. Barr, Jr., of the Museum of Modern Art, New York. I am also greatly indebted to Daniel-Henry Kahnweiler, the historian of Cubism and outstanding Picasso connoisseur, for help and advice. The sympathetic understanding and helpful interest of my wife, from first to last, made possible the completion of this book. Finally, I must thank Picasso himself who has expressed his interest in this publication by contributing the cover drawings.

*Wilhelm Boeck*

## Thoughts about Picasso

*"Art follows life as the shadow follows the body. Art points to the meridian and measures the passing hour."*

*Alfredo Panzini*

⟨Whenever the word "art" occurs in the course of my thoughts, I think immediately of Picasso. No matter what problem he has to face, or what question to answer, Picasso always solves it in the light of his art. For art is his personal and undisputed sphere.

"Art follows life." Picasso lives in his painting. What does it matter that the shadow slips away once its mission is fulfilled, marking in its own way the passage of time?⟩

"The day will come," I heard him say, "when the sight of a painting will ease the pain of a toothache." Picasso was speaking in parables, perhaps thinking of the effect a combination of colors might produce on a man who knows how to contemplate or has learned to see "with his whole soul"; that is to say, with nothing interfering with the trajectory of his gaze. It would be necessary that the observer's mood coincide with the mood which governed the artist's strokes, in order to establish the indispensable rapport with the artist's idea and state of mind at the moment he was painting a picture, in order to open the way to an adequately sympathetic response. It would be necessary that the very being of the observer be attuned to one color or another, for circumstances to work the miracle which now depends almost exclusively on medical remedies.

*La belle qui passe*
**1904**

The problem of Picasso is not the same as that which life presents daily to the man who strives to twist his path in a direction opposite to his destined one, in pursuit of something for which he will prove unworthy. Picasso must have been born to paint. Of what sense is it to say that he came into the world on October 25, 1881? This is merely a detail heading the series of biographical data that can be found elsewhere.

In these lines we wish to establish Picasso's position in the world of art. The fact that he was born in our time holds great importance, but what interests us most is that he has been permitted to follow unerringly the path of his own destiny. For Picasso (Pablo Ruiz) appears to have been born with a pencil in his hand. His father was an artist and his father's brother and sister were amateur painters. An uncle who was a doctor was also known for his artistic flights, as was his paternal grandfather. Before we get lost in the tangled branches of the genealogical tree, we will stop with this grandfather who was given to painting. He was reputed to have a bad disposition, perhaps because he saw or fancied himself obliged to give up his calling in order to keep the family alive—for in Spain at the time to be an artist was to be nothing. However, Pablo came along and proved the opposite. For him there could be nothing else in the world, nor can anyone imagine him in any other light. It might be said that he was born to demonstrate that art has its own prerogatives, and that by his accomplishments he showed that the artist, if he really is one, has his right to a place in the sun so long as he does not falter in the face of the demands of art.

Pablo, Pablo Ruiz Picasso, showed his inclination toward drawing at an early age by examining external forms, and by expressing himself through images. He did not sketch a head as a more or less deformed circle placed upon a somewhat elliptical body mounted in its turn on two sticks serving as legs, but he tried to draw lines similar to the outlines that his voracious gaze continually seized upon. His childhood way of seeing must not be considered as that of an ordinary child. Rather, one might say that he gave the impression of seeing as an adult. The Picasso phenomenon began to reveal itself at a tender age, as if he had been born in order to challenge everyday reality, for even in his earliest scrawls he tended to do the opposite of what might be expected.

The only reason or explanation that can be given to clarify this is that Picasso's eyes were made to see and that he had the faculty of knowing how to use them freely, applying them undistractedly. He looked with the burning desire to see, with an exclusive yearning to scrutinize, to focus, to register the value of a form, any form, in order to visualize it correctly, to fathom what merited attention. Surely he must have looked at the imitative sketches by children his age in the same way that he fixed his gaze on actual forms; and he must have compared them with the idea of reality that he was gradually forming for himself, and from his own viewpoint. For this reason and because his instinct led him to trust more in his own eyes than in his neighbor's or, better still, to trust in his own above all, the things that he now does present a view of reality that differs sharply from what many imagine reality to be. By this I mean that he did not need formulae, because images sprang to the demands of his vision without having to be mediated. He was interested only in seeing, and did not speculate on the possibilities of finding something better or prettier, or trouble himself with what people might think or say about him. From childhood, Pablo's thinking has been in his seeing. And then, as now, he always works on what is "his own." I mean by this that when he surrenders to his art, all feelings that merely are incidental to his rapture seem to fade away before the gaze that ceaselessly nourishes his mind.

If one believed in fairies the phenomenon of Pablo Ruiz Picasso could be explained by attributing to them the credit for granting him the most adequate gift—that great gift which brought to fruition his

*Family with Monkey* 1905

11

yearnings and his vision. We will do no more than suppose that these mysterious powers came to some agreement, coordinating their ideas so that none of the gifts that they had decided to bestow on the new-born child should stand in the way of the best of their intentions. Pablo might say at this point, "Putting this into the sphere of painting, which is my realm, I can understand what you mean: this is a mere supposition, because when anything is capable of upsetting a single intention, everything goes to the devil when you try to compose the totality." All of Pablo's fairies were quite lucky in reaching such an agreement—this consensus in itself was a phenomenon.

Pablo's paternal grandfather, Don Diego Ruiz de Almoguera, very much wished to be a musician and painter, but it remained a desire. His obligation of supporting himself and his family directed him elsewhere. This was probably why he ended an embittered man. The same thing happened to Pablo's uncles, Diego and Salvador, and to one of their sisters, before the magic wand marked the destiny of Don José, Pablo's father, making him the first artist in the family and changing his hobby into a profession.

The fairies, or perhaps sorceresses, compelled Pablo, their favorite son, to dedicate himself to his art, and to that alone. He learned to read, to write, and to use numbers, because this cannot be escaped. He does not dislike either letters or numbers; letters and numbers have their own forms, just as a table, a chair, a pencil, and everything that has its place in the visual world. What troubles Pablo is that numerals do not go higher than ten and letters of the alphabet are also limited, and that the slant of the strokes which regulate handwriting in school notebooks is repeated endlessly, with no hope of variation. To form syllables, compose words, and arrange them according to grammatical rules is something that far from enchants him. Pablo's eye demands variations, difficulties of execution, unlimited means of composition, and, above all, freedom. Pablo was very young when he began to sketch. To capture the movement of the lines traced in the air by the shake of a burro's tail, for example, is more difficult than to write a letter or add numbers. The inanimate object which presents itself to his sight also holds interest because of the variety of points from which it may be viewed; but with the visual form of a numeral nothing can be done, and there is no way of making it change. Whether one looks at numbers from a distance or from close up, from in front or from the side, they never change. Numbers can be written by anyone; they are always the same, and everyone writes them in his own manner. In fact, lack of imagination is rather advantageous for the task of lining them up correctly. On the other hand, without that inspiration engendered by creative genius—or producing it—it is impossible to suggest the image of a gesture, to harmonize two lines, or to lock an idea within the line that is used to limit a space.

Pablo understood all this from his earliest childhood. On opening his eyes to the light of reason he must have known his destiny. He had a world before him, a world pregnant with varied forms, susceptible of eternal variation. What better plaything could there be for one who enters the world prepared to contemplate it? What delicacy could more fully satisfy the frenzy for seeing, contemplating, and noting down what was offered to the wonderment of his gaze?

Therefore, in these early years his skill at cutting out paper figures
for the joy of pleasing his little cousins was unrivaled. And when he
went to school he was permitted to do just as he pleased, so that he
never suffered contagion from the "bad example," as he never gave
it heed. So peaceful was the atmosphere that Pablo found himself
free to sketch whatever struck his fancy: the handle of his father's
cane entrusted to him, a brush, or the dove that was to serve as his
father's model.

The voracity of Pablo's eyes is infinite, and so he must from childhood have known how to amuse himself endeavoring to discover the
mystery of form. What did it matter to him if he took only one object
into account—cane, brush, or some other thing—if a mere part of

that one object can engage the implacable striving that we discover in him while watching him work? Since childhood he must deny to himself speaking and singing in order to maintain or augment his powers of attention.

Let us say then of Pablo, the Pablo Ruiz of the early years, that his capacity for abstracting perceptions, combining them, arranging them, and fixing them at the point where he rivets his attention, must have revealed him just as we know him today. Perhaps, however, he would have been revealed less incisively, since the constant sharpening of that faculty by the years is firm proof of a redoubtable will, of a determination which he has displayed from the time he first opened his eyes to the light of day.

Since then he has become fascinated by seizing upon difficulties and coping with them: drawing foreshortenings, pursuing the characteristics of a gesture through the outline of a muscle in action. He tries to note the aspect of something in different positions without shirking any effort or eliminating any difficulties, because to him complication is more of an incentive than an outright obstacle.

Picasso's memory of what he studied aside from his art is dimmed: I could never figure out what he did in La Coruña, apart from what is told by certain drawings and paintings of his school years, and apart from the recollections of his surroundings drawn from the streets and especially from his home—for it is there above all, in the secret recesses of intimacy, where he reveals himself. It is precisely in the home that he came into his own most successfully, satiating his desires as a hunter of images, under the protective shadow of a father who, as he watched him, discovered gradually that what might have been considered a mere bent presaged an overwhelming passion.

One can imagine—although the exact details may escape—what must have happened in Don José's mind as he came to realize the degree to which his own importance was diminishing, or how his own qualities were being eclipsed as Pablo's personality began asserting itself. He must have felt that the shadow projected by his son was blotting out his light, little by little. This must have led him to pass his brushes on to Pablo, so that when he took possession of the tools of his father's trade he must have gradually come to realize the importance of his mission. Today Picasso knows that when he took his first steps in the realm of painting, Don José's own ambition as an artist began to decline as the sun on its journey toward the west.

Pablo works tenaciously, from morning to night, without rest. Work is an obsession. The first faltering steps were taken in La Coruña. We shall not speak now of the sketches sent to his family as illustrations to his letters, which he transformed into little newspapers, but rather of a multitude of small paintings, some of which he offered to Dr. Ramón Pérez Costales, and of the portraits that he still keeps in his studio.

The little sketches of the year 1895, *Awaiting the Turn (Esperando la vez)* and *On the Way to School (A la escuela)*, which were reworked much later in serious works, confused those who could not appreciate them in their time, that is, when Pablo was only fourteen. It was only because of his youth that works we admire today did not win the confidence of critics in those early days.

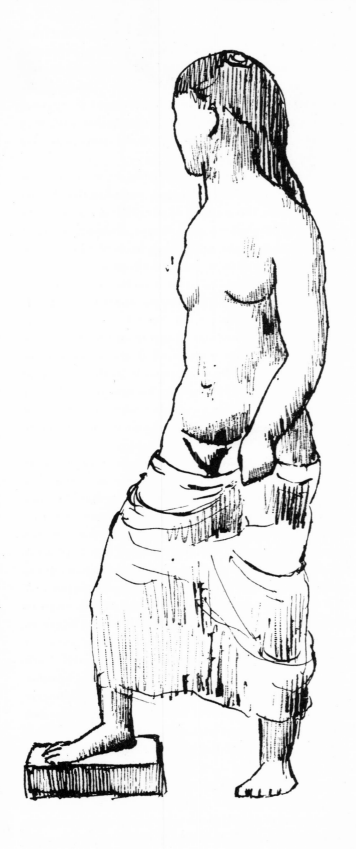

*Study* 1906

15

That lack of critical appreciation was fate's first blow. But I imagine that he did not pay much attention to it, since the idea of offering his work to the public was not his. The only thing which could have affected him in 1895 would still affect him, even today: that something might keep him from working and from doing as he pleased. Meanwhile he was satisfied to devote himself entirely to his little sketches.

The magic forces that welcomed him at birth continued to protect him. There was no opposing his whims. Had it not been so, somebody would surely have rapped his knuckles to remind him not to try to grasp beyond his reach. After all, there are rules for everything. Pablo, however, had the good fortune to be able to ignore many of them with impunity, for a rule lacks visual appeal and Pablo, absorbed in his work, had become all eyes.

One must see him in his schoolboy sketches: copies from plaster casts, rough sketches "from life" in which it is easy to observe that already in early adolescence he had a passion for precision. Details, no matter how minutely done, were always subordinated to the unity of the whole, their place maintained in accordance with their significance, then as now.

In his sketching he always seemed to ignore the value of certain objects, but his scrutinizing eye divined them even if it did not expose them to view. It weighed and measured them rigorously, evaluating their importance with a serenity more befitting a judge than a child, pampered by fortune, who no longer looked upon sketching as a game.

If, when he was fourteen, he could paint the *Portrait of Aunt Pepa*, it is because he was all eyes to see what was before him. Doña Josefa Ruiz Blasco resembles the portrait painted by Pablo because the presence of his aunt did not dull any of the powers of the nephew. Pablo did not look at her as a member of his family, but impersonally, thus achieving the subordination of all his other senses to that of sight. The only thing which could preoccupy Pablo at that time was that his model might tire before the work was finished.

During the period from 1895 to 1900—which ended in his first trip to Paris—Pablo's existence registers hardly any changes, although La Coruña, Málaga, Madrid, Horta, and Barcelona introduced him to various aspects of Spanish life. His eyes were opening to the spectacle of life, while his mental faculties offered him the opportunity to make comparisons. Madrid, seen in passing in 1895 while in the company of his parents, might be described as a purely ocular experience. In 1897 Madrid becomes more significant in his life. He goes there alone and is guided by a purpose which, if not entirely personal, in effect, moves him deeply because he feels, supposes, or is made to suspect, that his future depends entirely on this trip. It is most probable that Pablo made the journey without being convinced of anything of the sort; despite the importance which his family ascribed to the trip he derived consequences totally different from those imagined by them. Madrid for him meant escape and adventure, leaving the ordinary and discovering the unexpected. Had he acquiesced in the reasoning which lay behind his first departure from Barcelona, Picasso would not have ceased, suddenly, being like any other Pablo Ruiz, with a fixed salary and official distinctions, and suffocating in an atmosphere that eventually would have become deadly.

*Female Nude* 1907

Pablo's triumph in Madrid was as brief as his stay there. The moment the doors of the Academy of San Fernando are opened wide to him, he loses any desire to start painting and sketching within its four walls. The Prado Museum inevitably attracts his attention, and he prefers it; but he cannot spend his life looking over and over again at what others have done, for once he has seen what he looks at, it is certain that he has seen it well and will remember it.

A mild case of scarlet fever, which causes Picasso to return to Barcelona, is a convenience in that it makes the family realize that his stay in Madrid is now onerous to him. It is only by coincidence that his return to Barcelona marks the end of an adventure that has ceased to interest him.

A will such as his admits no obstacles. Picasso discovers his right and his will to be free. It is discussed with him and he himself is discussed in the family circle. So much the better: it is proof that he exists at least for someone. In the future they will have to pay attention to him. Now he will know how to take advantage of opportunities to break the ties joining him to family conventions. He has stored up so many images in his mind, seen so much, and so many friends believe in him that soon he will be finding himself more at home in the streets than in his own house.

Once cut off from the family atmosphere, he had no choice but to run. Had he remained he would have gone on painting and drawing as others in Spain painted and drew, scarcely knowing why, with little hope and few illusions. But he chose to improve himself, at the risk, naturally, of finding himself worse off, in which case one might be blamed for deserting the known for the unknown.

He could not think of Madrid in the way that others wanted him to. It would have been like looking backward. That was impossible for him. The frontier was two steps away, and he had to cross it. Picasso's life lay beyond. This he knew with certainty.

Some months before his trip to Madrid, on a summer vacation in

*Construction* 1912

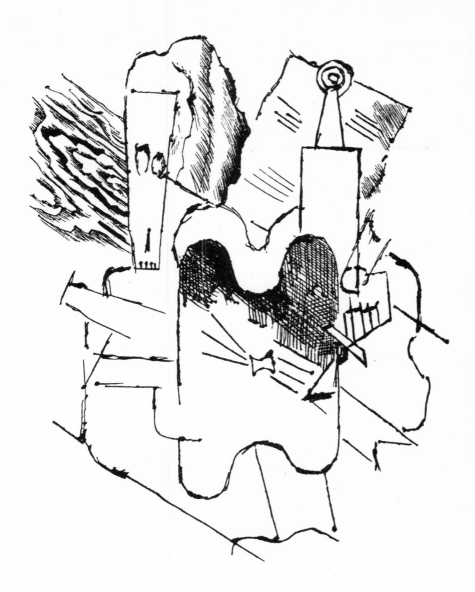

Málaga, the family had new illusions. Aiming to keep Pablo on a proper
road for the future—by strictly Spanish standards, that is—they hoped
to marry him to a cousin they supposed he loved. Whether he were in
love or not mattered little. But Pablo was not to be seduced from his
art, his only real passion, by the charms of this tender feminine beauty
from his own land.

Once more in Barcelona Picasso withdrew into himself. Perhaps it
was not in vain that the wing of an illusion had brushed him. Madrid
had been a healthy interlude, in spite of the illness which shortened his
stay. The bustle of a city such as Barcelona probably made him forget,
if only for an instant, whatever might have been preoccupying him. At
any rate, Pablo saw his life more clearly because something else opened
his eyes even wider. As he began to practice the language of his adopted
Catalonia, the ruggedness of the land revealed to him the truth in the
daily struggle for life, of some against others, of man against animals
and the earth.

The stages in Picasso's life following his nineteenth year are entirely
European in character. His journeys from Barcelona to Paris and from
Paris to Barcelona set up a rhythm of which he made fine use for weigh-

*Harlequin* 1918

ing impressions, establishing ideas, and maintaining the equilibrium of his physical strength.

The raptures of the amorous side of his life never fail to be recorded in his work, because Picasso, impulsive by temperament, cannot keep his own secrets. Incapable of depending on anyone or anything, his eager desire for freedom induces him continually to exteriorize his feelings without forethought or reflection.

His destiny, which is to all appearances an impetuous force imposed by duty in the guise of heredity, may actually be the end-product of a sum of artistic inclinations piled up by time in the shadow of the family tree. In order not to be led too far astray seeking uncertain clues, we shall not go beyond the grandfather's penchant for painting and music. Diego, the eldest son, inheritor of the grandfather's Christian name, also had a bent for painting. One of the sisters was well known for her competence, and we have already discussed the abilities of Pablo's father, Don José. The grandfather, Diego Ruiz de Almoguera, would have preferred to let his inclinations lead him into art, but that was impossible. Duty, that hovering shadow of the necessity to earn his family's bread, clipped his wings. The first one allowed by fortune to use the inherited gift in a profession was Don José. But it was only Pablo's arrival which supplied the daring to perform the miracle of changing a trivial talent—what the family atmosphere and the mores of time and place had regarded as a mere pastime—into a passion.

By saying "family atmosphere" I am guided by the desire to indicate up to a certain point the way of feeling and appreciating things in the milieu in which the Ruiz Blasco-Picasso Lopez family moved. An atmosphere like the one shared by the greater part of the Spanish middle class in the latter part of the past century. The Spanish painters of this period, even those whose fame is established, came up from nothing. However, the average family living in middle-class obscurity had no interest in artistic practices or problems.

*On the Beach* 1920

One cannot imagine how, except by magic powers, secret forces of the most powerful idealism could have been fused in a genius so compelling that it showed itself from Pablo's earliest childhood in a manner that might be called diabolic. It is incredible that so many attributes, virtues, and defects can form a unity or even coexist. As if he had nothing more to do than to obey a mysterious mandate, Pablo paid no attention to advice nor did he heed any demand foreign to those of his destiny.

It is certain that his being a boy and the first-born of the Ruiz Picassos justifies our saying that he was spoiled, or indulged at least by fate. Pablo was a thoroughly self-willed child—which was not entirely his fault—and exceedingly stubborn. Because he was accustomed to his father's tutelage his father accompanied him on his first trip away from home. It was agreed that Pablo should attend school only as long as he was willing to do so. Don José had to paint to earn his living, and it seemed

*Conversation* 1920

27-5-20 — Picasso

*Reclining Woman* 1920

reasonable that Pablo should be in school like other boys. But he could not yield to this type of reasoning. He could not accept norms merely because they were agreed upon; the authority of custom meant nothing to him. This perhaps reveals his character. Here is the proof that Picasso knew his own strength. Let Don José give him the dove he planned to use as a model if they do not want him to stay around. Or if not the dove then something else indispensable, the brushes for example, which could bring his father's work to a halt. Don José is torn between the duties of his profession and that of doing the impossible so that his son may learn something—and he sacrifices his work to the whims of the child. After winning this first concession Pablo had things his own way. Don José did not let his vocation offer resistance to his son's will, and Pablo began to fulfill his destiny. It was so written.

It may be said that fate manifested itself in Pablo as in no other child. In his home there was no wavering. He came into the world destined to paint, and painter he would be, at all costs if necessary. Painting meant for Picasso explaining himself by signs, expressing himself through a plastic medium, communicating what his glance registered and what was reflected in his brain. The means of doing this meant little.

We have already mentioned how he amused his cousins by cutting paper artfully with a small scissors—because it was scissors and not crayon or brush that he found at hand at the moment he happened to feel like demonstrating his skill to the two little girls. "Do you want a little horse? Here it is." In fact, in less time that it takes to tell it, Pablo astonished his young relatives by handing them the cut-out image they had just asked for. Picasso did not consider this important, nor did he even remember it when I told him that they had written me of it in a letter. However, his cousins will never forget.

I do not wish to take this occasion to comment, in the capacity of critic or historian, on Picasso's painting. What I have to say about it will come later, to illustrate the outstanding phases of his life. What concerns us here is to make evident the degree to which his role as an observer set Picasso apart from the rest of the world. One who has not seen him cannot imagine the intensity of his gaze, which is always in ambush for surprises. Even lying down with his eyes open or closed, when one would imagine him basking in the pleasure of doing nothing, he seems to be following some thought, pursuing an image perhaps seen in his dreams, ransacking his memory and imagination. One might say that, drowsing in a kind of reverie, he is gathering his impressions, or that he is working with his ideas as plastic elements, imagining how they might be given appropriate form. He can go on in this way indefinitely. His couch, rather than a place of repose, becomes for him somewhat like the waiting room in a railway station. It is a question of waiting, and he takes advantage of the situation by thinking and isolating himself as much as possible. The longer the train is delayed the better it will be.

*Three Bathing Women*
*1923*

23

I believe that his way of seeing life must differ from our own, but it has the advantage of not differing in every respect. He knows how to see within us and within himself. He infuses the most commonplace reality with a lyricism which is natural to him, and easily distinguishes truth from fiction. He can contemplate life better while lying with half-closed eyes than others can who seem to be on their toes, for his state of reverie affords him greater tranquillity.

It is said that the difference between a horizontal and a vertical line is that the latter signifies action and the former repose. For Picasso this is not valid. Two parallel verticals enclose a square when they meet two parallels going the other way. For him this is the only thing which matters. The limited rectangular surface of the paper or canvas before his eyes is a space adequate to receive his plastic elaborations, his poetic images, and his lyricism offered to the public in his current style. When he begins to paint or draw, this becomes his only means of expressing himself, establishing contact, and relating his visions, since the images that he seizes upon in the outside world, as he continues looking fixedly within himself, are exactly as he renders them.

I shall give one example from the thousand—not to use his own phrase "among thousands of millions"—which a close study of Picasso's personality affords every day, and I shall speak of what he is able to do with one ordinary object out of all those which the world constantly offers to his vigilant eye. The form of a log may remind him of one seen years before. Or, better still, it may be the oval of a cherimoya fruit just received from his native land which reminds him of an owl. Observing the fruit before him, Picasso sees the exact position of the eyes and the bill; as he observes the fruit from the side, the image which comes to his mind is confirmed. With his finger he follows the curve of the fruit, which then suggests: "The little feet here and the bill here." So strong is his conviction that he effortlessly remarks to whoever is with him: "Even the feathers, you see?" And indeed, even the feathers; it is enough that *he* sees them for *us* to see them. If the cherimoya brought him memories of his native land only in passing, the impression produced by it stirred up in him different ideas. His brain apparently received the poetic emotion which, in the service of his own feelings, produced a version of the bird much more telling than truth itself. For his artificial owl is the product of an imagination "in a state of grace."

What can we say of the illusion of a burning cigar that he received once, in Royan, from a broken stick? It was about the middle of 1940, and the German Occupation had brought scarcity in its wake. The tobacco supply was exhausted from one day to the next. I was vexed. Picasso, who saw me constantly, knew that I was not the same without a cigar between my teeth. This was enough to cause him to envision the image of a cigar in a piece of wood. A few strokes of oil paint performed the "miracle" of suggesting the cigar I lacked. Had not the imagination of Picasso intervened, the little stick would have been thrown forever in the fire or on the trash heap. Something memorable had been created.

Passing up many other illustrations of this sort which could be mentioned, I shall refer to the following example which is still more closely related to me, as I always have it before my eyes. It is a human form in outline, so to speak, constructed of some fragments of straw which

Picasso happened to notice during one of our meetings. I cannot recall the exact time or place. As soon as he found the little straws between his fingers he had to create something, as he cannot conceive of life in any other way. By knotting these straws, he joined them in places, forming the body of a long, slender, masculine figure with arms outstretched, legs dangling, the head in place, and the rest in perfect detail. It might be described as a sketch which is detached from its background, with the advantage that when you hold the little man between your fingers he moves by himself, even though your hands make only the slightest movement. It is neither drawing nor sculpture, but partakes as much of one as of the other, being superior to both in its graceful movement, which gives it the warmth of a caress. This is partly due to the pliable material, which is both smooth and extremely light. But he first had to discover it, to foresee how it could be used, to be capable of receiving inspiration and creating.

Picasso is destined to work on and on without respite. "My only rest is to fight," says Don Quixote. Picasso battles continuously. His thoughts are a substitute for Sancho. The equilibrium we see in his work comes as a result of this. Therefore what he once told me is still as true as it was always. I have spoken elsewhere of his being affected by a landscape "with little cows in a meadow" displayed in the show window of a picture dealer in the Rue la Boétie. Unless the significance of his words is understood, who can believe this suggestion of his that he cannot paint "as he would like," knowing that he does not lack the

*Still Life with Fruitbowl, Bottle, and Guitar* 1925

*Athlete* 1925

possibilities to do so? He said then that he would be delighted to paint something of that sort, with little cows and all of the details. It is difficult to explain what he meant and even more difficult to make it understood: to paint a meadow with cows and a background of trees does not mean that one must paint the landscape and the little cows, perhaps achieving an obvious, even trivial effect; but one must be capable of thinking of how to do it and to do it after having thought. In Picasso action and thought go hand in hand; his ideas are winged and his hands are swift; his thought is transformed into work, and if it does not take the lead he does not pursue it.

To say that he would like to paint one thing or another is to speak in parables, for it implies the rapture of surrendering himself to the contemplation of a landscape, and then comparing the effects captured by his sight with those which would be necessary to put the creation on canvas. It implies the sequence of emotions he might receive if, instead of being the painter of that landscape, he were merely a contemplative spirit capable of dreaming and working within a limited imagination. But no, Picasso cannot paint such a landscape as the one which momentarily attracted his attention. The time he would need to spend dreaming of the impossible, and the distance between his mode of being, seeing, and feeling and the other painter's, would be too great.

The type of premeditation which underlies the approach of the more or less academic painter who makes the landscape his battlefield is foreign to Picasso: the academic painter knows beforehand the effects that can be obtained through a given type of composition, and in accordance with the lessons he has learned, he obtains a result which was not unforeseen. This is the labor of a craftsman, perfectly calculated and controlled. It has nothing to do with the heart of Picasso's thought when he says that he would like to paint that landscape or one like it "if he had the time," for to have the time is something else again. Having time, for Picasso, means that there is a possibility of going backwards, of being born again, and of coming into the world in another form; of being capable of spending hours and hours before a canvas transcribing emotions; of being able to go on to think of something else; and of being able to confront the *motif* directly, tranquilly, in order to do as one pleases.

Picasso is all action, at times even carried away by a creative fury. If we liken him to a volcano in constant eruption, imagining it a constant eruption, in the human body, we will have the equivalent of a state of anguish and anxiety, worry and restlessness of the evolutionary process that leads either to a state of grace or to one of delirium, because for him suggestion and gestation go hand in hand. It is for this reason that he cannot be subjected to any determined plan, and premeditation is impossible for him. Ideas follow one another in his mind in proportion to the number of sensations that he is capable of receiving and the observations that he registers. The surface area that is to be filled is the immediate problem offered to his imagination, for its mere presence is enough to engage his thought. When he is not mastering the paper or canvas or whatever it may be, the material holds no significance for him: he can wholly possess it only while he is filling in the destined forms. The canvas, paper, or whatever he is using is then no longer just any paper or canvas. His mind stops an instant while preparing to take possession by infusing with warmth the still inanimate body of the beckoning surface. When it is still empty it is as vast as the primordial chaos, yawning like an abyss, fascinating as an unfathomable mystery: all of which is well calculated to incite the urge for adventure which fires Picasso. Everything depends on the first stroke, on the first impulse, on the initial line drawn spontaneously by the grace of God, on the unsuspected intention that guides his hand. It is comparable to the dive of the swimmer which cracks the mirror of the water in order to open the way to an enigmatic fate; once the starting

*Reclining Woman* 1925

point for the adventure is reached, the swimmer closes his eyes and his subsequent movements will depend upon the action as it occurs.

Picasso's creative adventure is similar: once the clean, unmarked surface of the canvas or paper has been deflowered, the lines or brush strokes which follow are only results of that spontaneous gesture which holds in itself the inspired but unrevealed secret. Thereafter, the main thing is not to drown. What does it matter that there are tides and reefs? Difficulties and dangers abound: there they are at the moment of the plunge. What would the game be without them? Without difficulties to conquer, without enigmas to solve, without mysteries to be penetrated, nothing would interest Picasso. Facile achievements disgust him, and his impulsive temperament rejects them.

Will what has been said suffice to prove that Picasso's work, as reflected in his life, is undertaken with an all-consuming longing for adventure? It is impossible to imagine him enclosed by a frame of conventions and commonplaces, fixed ideas, memorized lessons, and calculations of academic probabilities. Taking him as he is, we shall leave it established once and for all that he was more than right to say that he would like to paint a landscape with little cows grazing in a meadow, because a long time prior to the herd's appearance his thoughts would have led his brush elsewhere, perhaps far from that scene.

His childhood, which ended as he moved from Málaga to Galicia with his family, has left scarcely any impression on Pablo's memory. He was scarcely ten at the time. La Coruña became his real elementary school of experience. Matriculating in the Da Guarda Institute was an extraordinary event, as much so for the child as for his parents. Pablo was now no longer the spoiled brat from Málaga, the inattentive or indifferent student we knew in that famous examination, taken hastily and with repugnance, which gave him a promotion to the next class thanks to the insight of the examiner and the child's inclination to do nothing counter to his will.

One must suppose that the trip to La Coruña was of great importance for Picasso, leaving behind his native Andalusia and taking his first step toward the North. If he were not capable of suspecting the bearing of that trip upon a future as distant as it was unpredictable, the comments of the family which he had to listen to must have given him a hint— even though it were only that he must learn to weigh the content of certain words uttered in complaint or lament, and to compare them with what he remembered from better days in the house in Málaga.

The trip was difficult and very long for the adult members of the family. Pablo, however, hardly noticed it. Everything after Málaga was new: life on shipboard from Málaga to Vigo and the trip by rail from Vigo to La Coruña. Even today Picasso cannot understand the cause of the boredom which weighed upon the others. He, of course, had the advantage of being young. If the idea of going to school did not fill him with enthusiasm, something was to make him sense that—in spite of the Institute and what it might mean for his spirit—he was under obligation to attend classes that were unimportant to him, and to learn whatever he must.

La Coruña was, indeed, a step forward although it may have appeared as a stumbling block. It is true that the child was not then capable of perceiving it. Something, however, must have occurred in his mind,

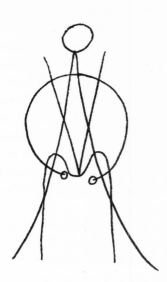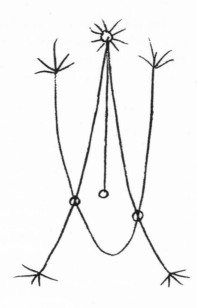

perhaps in unconsciously comparing the complaints made by his family
with the ray of joy that was beginning to penetrate his own soul, and in
discovering the possibility of a change in his life. This feeling, as a
source of curiosity, was his own property and, being his own, held the
importance of a secret.

At this moment Pablo ceased, as far as he was concerned, to be the
spoiled child of the house. Life was revealing itself to him in a way
which was to become familiar: in a kind of artistic expression which
promised him personal rights, and only rights, for now it was fate which
was spoiling him. The proof is that "he matriculated in the school of
arts and crafts" of La Coruña (September 20, 1892) with the serenity of one who follows the path of his destiny. By destiny I mean his
immediate destiny. The eventual scope of his powers was not yet con-
jecturable.

Pablo's adolescence unfolded in Barcelona. Barcelona is for Spain a
window onto Europe. The youth's personality grew along with his
physical development. The capacity for action came with him from
La Coruña; it was there that he had been immediately recognized as an
outstanding student of fine arts. The conquest was twofold, as he won
the admiration of his father as well. This was sufficient to make him
realize the moral responsibility which was conferred upon him, and
to understand that that responsibility gave him the right to certain
liberties.

He matriculated in the Provincial School of Fine Arts of Barcelona
(La Llonja) because it was indispensable, just as it is indispensable for
apprentice matadors to face bulls. Besides, his family, as well as the
majority of those who deemed themselves versed in the subject, could
not yet conceive of a professional artist without a diploma.

Picasso, let us say Pablo, or Pablo Ruiz, resigned himself to passing
the examination for admission to the advanced classes in life drawing
and painting. He won the entrance certificate in no time, and with it
the esteem and enthusiasm of his classmates.

It was only a step from there to the streets. Needless to say, Pablo
Ruiz began to stroll along them with his Catalan friends, who were glad

to enlarge his circle of acquaintances. In this manner Pablo entered upon his youth, growing in the admiration of his companions.

It was in Barcelona also that Picasso, Ruiz Picasso then, began to think about more distant horizons. France was next door, and Paris crowned the dreams of the young intellectuals of Barcelona.

The trip to Madrid in 1897 is an important event in Picasso's life. The competitive examination for admission to the Academy of San Fernando was another spectacular triumph. This victory alone removed any desire to go to class: it had been too easy for him. The Prado Museum was far more alluring. He became quite homesick. He was ill and had to leave Madrid, thus destroying the plans made for him by his family. Barcelona still meant "a warm bed and good food," as they say, and of course friendship—Pallarés, at this period; and through him, Horta de San Juan [also referred to as Horta de Ebro—*Editor's note*], the little town whose name passes into art history with Picasso. Horta de San Juan and Pallarés, Pallarés and Barcelona, they are responsible for Picasso's understanding of many aspects of the mode of being, appearing, living, and thinking in Catalonia. This knowledge permeated Picasso's personality, doubtless influencing him, because at that period of his life Pablo, his soul undecided, was ready to respond to any demand of the senses.

The first trip to Paris in 1900 marks the beginning of the great adventure. In Barcelona people talked about nothing but the Great World Exposition. Ramón Casas, Santiago Rusiñol, Miguel Utrillo, and others who went to Paris returned to tell of marvels. Art was on the other side of the Pyrenees. In the cafés everyone was talking of the same thing. In Els Quatre Gats it was all you heard. Barcelona had by now no more fuel for Picasso's aspirations. The idea had come to him to leave Spain and there was nothing else to do but carry this plan to fulfillment. Paris was the heart's desire for the long-haired youth of his time. Some went and others came back each in his turn. Picasso made trips for three years; the fourth journey was forever. Subsequent trips are only escapades made out of curiosity, for a change of scenery, or to see old friends.

During a few months of relaxation in Barcelona in 1903 and immediately upon his permanent return to Paris he made the sketches which he burned to keep himself warm in the winter of 1903–4. One of those which escaped the fire reappeared a short time ago. Among the few that were saved should be mentioned those that fill the free spaces in a copy of the book *Noa-Noa* (Morice-Gauguin), for this volume was Picasso's substitute for a sketchbook.

On his first trip to Paris Picasso had met Max Jacob, French poet and true friend: a good person to keep in mind, as compensation for the disenchantment of his return. Apollinaire came later to complete the lyrical triangle. Picasso needed the inspired magic of poetry and literature to maintain his spiritual flame constantly burning. The friends who kept visiting served to fill out the picture. Durio, the celebrated Paco Durio, a Franco-Spanish Basque sculptor, was also among Picasso's first friends. Paco knew Gauguin and Charles Morice (art critic for the *Mercure de France*), who was perhaps the first to sense the greatness of Pablo Picasso.

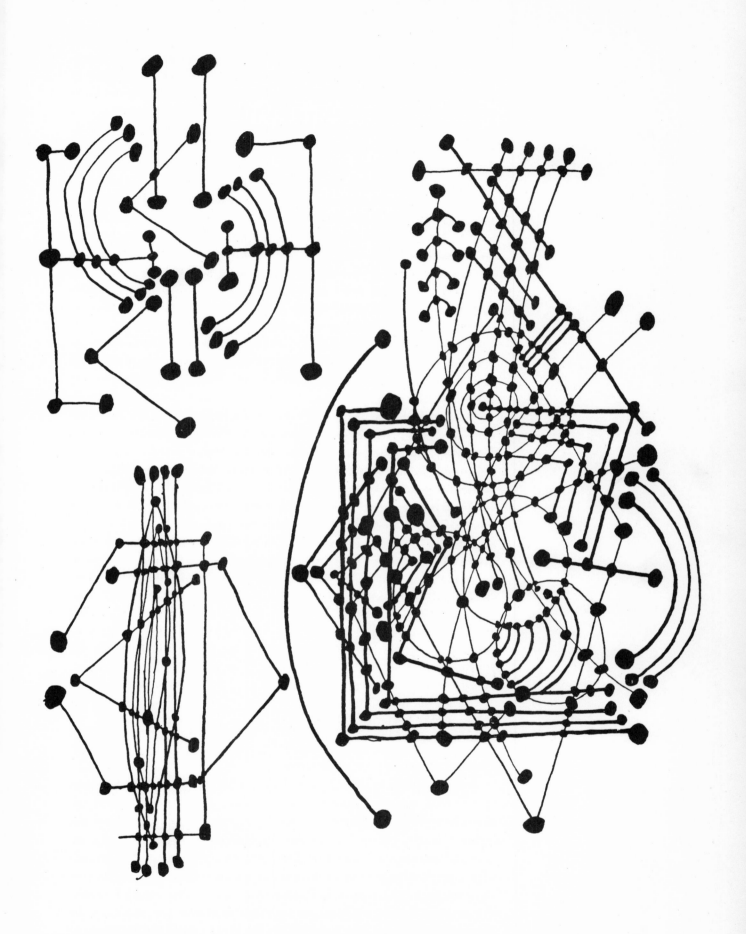

*Figures* 1924

In noting the names of Picasso's friends I am stopping to list the first ones that come to my memory, for they open a path through the tangle of recollections owing to their importance in forming the nucleus of his friends. They founded the intellectual family which provided the basis, sustenance, support, and starting point for the movement which gave rise to the great artistic adventure in the center of which we find Picasso.

The presence of Guillaume Apollinaire was significant for his culture, imagination, and intelligence, three virtues essential to the milieu which suited Picasso, and to the tide of spiritual revolution that was gathering. Max Jacob was an example of perennial promise. Picasso's brain was the fire and his head the crucible in which were fused the rarest and most refractory alloys.

Each one of Picasso's trips back and forth between Barcelona and Paris marks a step in the evolution of his artistic expansion. If nothing in this world comes of itself, neither is there anything nor anyone capable of carrying something to its utmost development by himself alone. All depends on the capacity for observation, on a sum of possibilities and presumptions: on the strength of will required to put to the test one's ever-continuing observations, day after day without resting or faltering. To test and test with the unusual intention of noting for oneself every aspect of each phenomenon, analyzing it without regard for one's immediate or future personal benefit. This requires unlimited constancy and will power, plus much intelligence and capacity for working without resting. Picasso found all of this in the Pandora's box which the bad fairy Carabosse had left him while looking surreptitiously at her sisters who, in the guise of Minerva, overwhelmed him with their gifts of grace and talent.

While in Barcelona Picasso had scrutinized what was most characteristic in the sketches of Steinlen through reproductions in the popular foreign magazines of the time. He sensed the human qualities of Toulouse-Lautrec, whose power lies in his exceptional way of seeing, feeling, and understanding what exists in hidden depths of the human being. For Lautrec did not conform to the accepted styles of his time, nor was he capable of using the pleasing mannerisms that served as a means of exchange in dealings over the cultural bargain counter. It was in Paris that Picasso appreciated Toulouse-Lautrec's true merit. It was here that his talent granted him an understanding of Lautrec's *raison d'être* and of his work, which was conceived in the torment of physical deterioration, in a state of spirit undermined by deformity which served to sharpen his senses and carry his vision to the extreme of embitterment.

Picasso's sensibilities, by now highly developed, were on the *qui vive*. His material resources were at their lowest and success seemed remote. But his capacity for comprehension was as unlimited as it is now. For that reason it is astounding that his considerable insecurity was not enough to put out the fire of his enthusiasm, calming his temperamental restlessness. Picasso afforded us an extremely important example in those days as we watched the waves toss him from one side to another without ever managing to engulf him. Out of all this, out of his restlessness, that is, which was also characteristic of the times and was caused by the circumstances under which he was struggling, we could foresee

*Hobbyhorse* 1926

the change coming. This change, which caught our attention as carefree youths, was the course his expression was taking in the sketches that he brought from his first trip to Paris toward the end of December, 1900.

What was perhaps most surprising to us who were incapable of following him or doing the same, was his tendency—at the very time one began to adjust to his way of seeing—to change his mode of expression so as to make us understand just what he was *then* feeling, once it had been sifted through his perceptions into the form of a sketch or painting. Each going and coming showed some new tendency, each one of his fluctuating movements reflected a new aspect of his spiritual anguish, a surprise captured in passing, owing to the fact that at the end of each journey he found an unexpected emotion. "Emotion" is here intended with the connotation of superficiality, for when it is only illusion that inspires the quest for new horizons, one frequently encounters only deception.

Nevertheless, bitterness is also necessary as a fitting restraint for indecisiveness. What is phenomenal, if not monstrous, is to begin to measure the exact scope of reality in its starkest form. Each of the

33

apparent transformations that helped Picasso to externalize his constant flow of impressions through his art is a true reflection of his way of seeing, of appreciating, or of feeling these same impressions, captured through a rare perceptiveness, or through a state of being that we could call "a soul in anguish." Without a keen enthusiasm for style, which he certainly had, the appreciation of real merit or infinite truth is almost inconceivable. Preconception or bitterness no doubt approaches pessimism. To accept everything, to doubt nothing, would annul one's critical judgment, and without this there would be no way to establish the indispensable contact with the visible world. Dreams are no less necessary, for with them the flame of illusion is kept burning and it is that small flame, above all, which motivates our enthusiasm.

I would not dare blame El Greco, as some have, for the change in Picasso's painting when he abandoned the bright colors which blazed in his mind on discovering, in 1901, the lighting effects of the footlights and the colored spotlights used in cabaret spectacles. These cabarets, the Moulin Rouge, Moulin de la Galette, or any other, which recall the tormented visions of Lautrec, were rendered by Picasso during the short period which elapsed between the beginning of his second stay in Paris and the latter months of 1901 in the Boulevard de Clichy studio which he shared with Mañac.

Picasso had just left three disillusionments behind: the first in Málaga, caused by his friend Casagemas and by his own family atmosphere; the second in Madrid, when he found out that to struggle in that city was not worth the effort; and the last of the series was perhaps in Barcelona, for it is very seldom that happiness awaits us at the station when the imagination is being blown by the winds of doubt—and Barcelona, especially from that time forward, was no longer anything more than a way station for him.

The grayish tonality with a tendency to blue seems to be a natural consequence of the irresistible need to penetrate to the inmost recesses of form, in order to bring out to the surface of the skin what lies hidden in the stillness disguised by pain or misery; of the need to explain what happens in each case in accordance with the narrator's sensitivity, measuring coldness by one's own lack of warmth, revealing one's solitude by the poet's own isolation. If we said that this was the most profound way of expressing an intimate sentiment, it would take only a few words to describe the impression we receive, even now, when looking at a painting of that era. And even if the blue tone were only typical of the time, and not in the spirit of Picasso himself, we would still have to agree that there is no reason to reject the means of expression that it offers us.

The truth, nevertheless, must be even more exact. Picasso feels the necessity to explain himself by contrasts, and no one could better meet this requirement. This he did in spite of that general tendency of all times which inclines us to lend ourselves to ready-made means of expression. How much better it is that Picasso's inclination for contrasts is intelligible to the spirit of the epoch.

People began to be favorably affected, became interested in, and were inclined to pass favorable judgment upon the externalized forms of Picasso's sentiments. So as to be understood in few words, we might

*Jupiter and Semele* 1930

call the style "Picasso à la Toulouse-Lautrec," or perhaps "Lautrecism à la Picasso."

And this is how the public would think of him. But then, carried away by his natural boldness and without stopping to consider the immediate consequences of an abrupt change, he transformed the grievous appearance of life decked out in tinsel, and restored its aspect of misery, tarnished by worldliness, shallowness, and the grimaces of empty pleasures, in an expression which was profound, melancholy, and at times truly painful. This was a secret he had recently discovered in the obscure depths of his environment, intimately reflecting a vision taken from the round of Picasso's ordinary activities and from within its narrow limits.

One may firmly maintain that the Blue Period is a testimony of conscience. The spectacle and tumult of the night life carried on for the benefit and diversion of foreigners greeted him on his return from Spain. It influenced him to go on boisterous sprees and to express himself in suitable language. As soon as he took a rest, however, and came to his senses by seeing through the whole ostentatious show, he understood perfectly that what he had just seen had nothing to do with him, nor he with it, because real truth is to be found only in silence.

Picasso had a world of creation before him then, as he does even today. He knew, just as he does now, the core that he could expect to find in everything and everyone, in what a person is and what he does. He saw the accumulation of sadness and misery that dims the eyes of the unfortunate. He touched that reality with his own fingers, saw it with his own eyes, for the phantom of poverty was not some kind of abstract threat but a latent possibility that took him by the hand.

The blue which gave a unity of tone to his color in this period came to be the gleam of a little illusion or hope. At times he speaks of this blue with great enthusiasm, describing it in a phrase like a prayer uttered in a sigh. Why? Because in his paintings blue shows itself as an aspiration to sublimity in the midst of desperation or sadness.

Max Jacob and Guillaume Apollinaire, two poets contemporary to Picasso's youth, were the most brilliant spectators of this great lyrical performer on the stage of art. Apollinaire's poetry, and the jokes, sallies, and witticisms of both of them, became for Picasso, or better still for his work, murmurs of approval, echoes of applause, commentaries at times, and sometimes a cause for controversy. These reactions benefited the impetuous temperament of the young Spaniard, who was a poet among painters, a painter among poets, and a human being above all.

Apollinaire and Max Jacob took advantage of the sparks of Picasso's lyricism by applying them to their respective means of expression. They used them to enliven their verse with verbal acrobatics; what for the one was pyrotechnics was a source of inspiration for the other and was exalted in fiction and fantasy. One might say that the ball, bouncing from hand to hand, went from one to the other, stopping with no one. However, the exercise was advantageous to all three.

One day love, let us say "a new love," announced its presence and Picasso's amorous passion hovered around a new illusion, in the form of

*Vertumnus and Pomona*  1930

a woman—not a rare occurrence. Now, we know that success in sexual matters only temporarily calms his restlessness, without satiating it. The state of mind which gave rise to his inquietude transformed itself after a period into a sort of transient calm which had the power of modifying Picasso's outlook. About this time, it seems to me, the roseate tonality began to appear in Picasso's art, and the shadows that had darkened his azure vision gradually faded away.

A little glow of light like the dawn of a new day illumined his palette. Picasso painted and sketched small slender forms, languid gestures. The color was soft, the outlines fine, graceful, and delicate. The pain had not passed, however; humanity reposes on a couch of bitterness. But now the characters, nearly always sickly yet at times smiling, seem to accept their fate. Disillusion, often accompanied by physical suffering, is now followed by the extreme horror of material misery—the poverty or indigence which obsessed Picasso for a period of three or four years.

If one were to reconstruct Picasso's itinerary step by step, it would not be difficult for a careful observer to appraise the extent of anguish or hope, of peace or tumult experienced by him at each stage.

We would discover in his work the record of his spiritual vicissitudes, the blows of fate, the satisfactions and annoyances, his joys and delights, the pains suffered on certain days, or at a certain time of a given year.

Picasso, like all mortals, has been ill several times. He underwent the usual childhood illness of his generation. Some hardships are attributable to a pattern of life which he was obliged to live out, against the grain of his environment, or else may be ascribed to some excess doubtless originating in the extreme curiosity which characterizes him: a curiosity which, as Balzac says, is indispensable to the good observer.

Picasso is, in reality, eminently curious: curious about food and drink, curious about amorous adventures, curious about reading, plays on words, plastic ideas and expressions. His curiosity rivals and even outstrips that of anyone else. He is curious about everything in life, curious about dreams, curious even beyond all of the usual bounds of curiosity.

It is in his work (drawings, painting, sculpture, and writings) that we become aware of his faculty for observation and the range of curiosity which lies behind it.

How easy it is to suppose, no matter how little one may know about it, that Picasso had relations with a certain laundress, once we feel the emotion that emanates from that painting of his (Collection Tannhauser, 1904) which, if it does not hold the key to the Blue Period, at least marks its end. It is not at all necessary to specify—in the event that one could not verify it—whether this amorous rapture was more than what we might call a momentary caprice, a brief encounter. On excellent grounds we may suppose that it was just this and no more. But that part is of little importance. What matters is that it undoubtedly requires more than a little time to observe movements belonging to some kind of work not ordinarily experienced by a painter. Picasso must have spent hours and hours, in many sessions, watching the laundress at work. I can imagine his scrutinizing gaze studying her gestures, following the lines which revealed each movement, cal-

culating the force of the arm by the weight of the body inclined over the ironing board, following the play of the lines in a cycle of movements continuously repeated.

*Playing on the Beach 1932*

One can imagine what might happen next, what Picasso might find at the end of each adventure: the surprise of surprising himself, of returning to himself, of thinking about himself in relation to his fellow man at any given instant. There would be a pause sufficient for the act of contrition needed to set things in order before he threw himself again into his career.

Adventure is Picasso's reason for being; if he does not seek it, still he does not flee from it. He is indifferent to the risk when it fails to elate him, and sexual adventures have never given him the highest ecstasy. His art is the only passion of his life. It dominates him, it excites him, it imprisons and frees him at the same time. He is filled with emotion and enthusiasm by it and is overwhelmed by it, because art above and beyond all else is his great adventure. It means nothing to him that the public has become accustomed to one or another of his manners of expression, that it is beginning to understand him, that it is merely ready to believe in him, or on the contrary, that it is piqued and exasperated by him. He works exclusively for himself, seeking no applause and conceding no importance to fashions and manners. A mode of expression, like a word cast to the wind, is of ephemeral value. What is important for him is idea, and an idea, according to Picasso, cannot be explained identically each day if one tries to speak from the heart. The content of each thought cannot have the same meaning at different moments; a change of light is enough to alter the appearance of an image, and the luminous intensity changes in proportion to the distance which separates it from something opaque. With ideas it is the same: those which come from dreams do not withstand the exigencies of day. On being brought to light they suffer from obstacles encountered in their path; they are affected above all by the hard and present aspects of reality.

In the case of Picasso we observe that an idea becomes fresh because he expresses it in a new way. His extreme curiosity forces him constantly to verify his own propositions. He suspects—because he is an unceasing critic of himself and his performance—that what makes much of the work of fellow artists difficult to swallow, may affect his own work. The necessity of explaining some idea to himself, using his own means of expression, imposes on his mind the duty of experimenting endlessly with line, color, and contrast. If his annotations and comparisons do not lead to foreseeable conclusions, they cause him to discover new doubts and unexpected questionings which, far from quieting him, egg him on to explore countless probabilities.

Therefore even if the struggle for life in the material world were less harrowing, thus endowing the spirit with a hitherto unsuspected freedom, the longing for the ideal would be even more insistent. When one pursues the course of an idea for the sole reason that the idea has presented itself, the necessity of clarifying one's position becomes ever more obvious. The pressing need to see ourselves more clearly obliges us to keep wiping the glass of the mirror in which we are looking.

Picasso had just emerged from a youth spent in walking the tightrope of financial worries. It was most creditable to have eluded the specter of hunger without having lost one's mind, to have heeded the advice of all-wise counselors, to have forced the escape hatch by cunning stratagems.

I do not claim that it was because of this or similar difficulties that Picasso and his fellow excursionists on the endless path of creative exploration were forced to state anew the problem of art, wiping the slate clean of all conventional attitudes: for aesthetic reasons it was necessary to analyze form in relation to space, to observe the distortions caused by the effects of light, to note the influence of color and the danger inherent in permitting oneself to be carried away by sentimentalism. They had to subject idea to the enormous necessity of reconstruction and composition, building scrupulously and conscientiously. They had to explain themselves by suggestions and suggest ideas in consistent plastic combinations. They had to seek out the relation of images and to harmonize equivalents. The fundamental work of this period of incipient reconstruction was achieved in 1907 in the painting [now known by the less provocative title *Demoiselles d'Avignon—Editor's note*] which was called *The Brothel of Avignon*. Why "brothel," and why "Avignon"? Who knows! It must have been the first thing that came to his mind as the possible reason for having painted a group of nude women. After he had

Paris, Winter 1948/49

**41**

The Artist's Father (1895)

The Artist's Mother (Pastel 1896)

42

Pablo Picasso in 1897

Pablo Picasso in 1904

43

Picasso in the Studio of Braque (1910)

Summer at St. Raphaël (1927)

44

The Studio at Vallauris (1950)

In the Paris Studio (1950)

45

In the Paris Studio (1950)

In the Paris Studio (1950)

On the Staircase of the Paris Studio (1952)

The Studio at Cannes (1955)

48

painted the canvas in question he began to consider (as he told me on several occasions) the likeness which he was discovering in each of the women of his imaginery brothel. "This one is Max's mother, this one ..."—I don't recall.

His fantasy leads him to discourse or ramble along like this, just as in the course of conversation when he is submerged in his own work he is mentally holding dialogues with himself. This is one of the most patent proofs, in my judgment, that the motive force of his activity derives from impulse. I mean that although he is impulsive by temperament Picasso does not appear so when he is painting, or better still, he differs sometimes, or almost always, from what his presence leads us to expect. Appearances proverbially deceive.

"It is so that I would not throw myself out of the window, I said not long ago," he once told me while trying to explain or make me understand what it was that obliges him to work in the incredible way that he does, supposing that I would not be able to comprehend it otherwise. "So that I would not throw myself out of the window. ..." Does this mean or allow us to think that he acts out of desperation? I do not think so. It must be, I tell myself, to get rid of certain preoccupations.

It is true that to exclaim "Let's see what comes out!," as I have heard him say when he is about to start a canvas or a sketch, may be like closing his eyes to life so as to look only within his self; as though an idea equivalent to that of throwing himself from a dizzying height had passed through his mind. But the fact is that "what comes out" suggests to him a series of new ideas, for the thought of "doing" causes him to relive, if not to create, a vision, and this vision is the beginning of a whole sequence of suggestions which overflow a single paper or canvas to inspire an infinite number of drawings and paintings. What defies ordinary imagination is the incredible number of modifications which each line or brush stroke suggests to him.

The great adventure continued as unpredictable as ever, and he gave himself to it with ever more enthusiasm. The outcome always retained its mystery, almost until its highly hypothetical end. I mean, until the moment that Picasso, because he had passed on to something else—sometimes a variant of what he had just done—would leave the former work aside, always with the firm intention of going back to it and developing it, along with himself, more fully, but never with the idea of finishing it. The verb "to complete" has no meaning for him. If ever it occurs to him he gives it only the most fatal meaning. Thus, instead of "throwing himself into the void," he prefers to keep living in his work; instead of finishing anything, or letting it come to a "bad end," he decides to permit his work to live in the illusion of attaining a still higher state.

Picasso's struggle in his work reminds one of the hero's battle with the dragon. We know that this fabulous combat must end with the dragon's overthrow and that the dragon's death is the hero's glory. But the legend always retains its mysterious power. It still surprises us, just as Picasso surprises us each time we see him jauntily sally forth from the mysterious adventures of his continual combat.

What does Picasso gain in these struggles? The answer is: nothing and everything. He wins transient peace or a little tranquillity, which for a moment alleviates the ceaseless unrest caused by the abiding need to produce, thinking of nothing else. Picasso's struggle is one without quarter. He is an experienced and dauntless warrior who wins battles which bring him, if not the right to relax, at least more and more experience, that is, greater knowledge of the art of fighting and the means to continue the struggle.

If Picasso feels attracted to women, it is not because of their features; whether the nose is large or small matters nothing to him. The shape of the face leaves him indifferent. Whether they are light or dark, whether the hair is blonde, brown, or black is all the same—although as a contrast to his own image he has a greater penchant for blue eyes, white skin, and golden hair. He is not interested in women for their separate features but for the total effect, and for something more which, being in the realm of sensibility, cannot be explained. What we commonly call "beauty" has very little to do with the sensual attraction which is known in English as "sex appeal." Picasso's sensuality is without doubt very powerful, but it does not respond to the attractions determined by official canons or academic definitions of feminine beauty. What is set apart as "his own," or what might be called his concept of beauty, is something which, with its primary roots in the senses, achieves its growth through the probability of being transformed into a friendship, with no excesses of ardor and without strong convictions as to the permanence of the sentiment. I do not know if I am explaining or complicating the matter. For clarity's sake I might say that

Illustration for
*Lysistrata* 1934

Illustration for
*Lysistrata* 1934

a woman for him is form, line, and color that are worthy of study—in short, an object that he might fasten upon in the realm of plastic composition, yet having the additional capacity to satisfy his senses. If in the course of his purely intellectual exercises the optical effect coincides with the compelling demand of sex, the woman can become much more, can become the whole world in fact, in an instant. Mistress of his senses for a brief interval, she may become whatever she wishes while his uncontrollable fervor calls out for her: an ideal woman who will immediately appear in his work as one of the elements required for the artist's communication with the external world, and for as long as his feelings make the presence of a given feminine form indispensable.

We may say, then, that "beauty" can mean "love" for Picasso and that love for him is more than beauty: it is the apogee of art, for this is what he values beyond all else. Let us say then, combining one idea with the other, that the sexual act in itself represents only the desire to satisfy a necessity that in him above all is an urgent one, a physical necessity that makes him close his eyes to the temporary suspension of his work. For the game of love is not identical with, but similar to, the adventure of art. Picasso's constitution—that is, his physical strength, and his endurance—enables him to approach love in the same serenity with which he faces the thousand and one perpetual difficulties that, in spite of endless, unexpectedly arising complications, he must grapple with if he is to get on with his life and art. It is not that these complications and many others beyond imagining come themselves or that he seeks them out. Rather he attracts them by the magnet of his curiosity and they fly to the call.

Curiosity is one of Picasso's most notable characteristics. He is more curious than a myriad of women. Instead of shying away from risks, he attracts them, provokes them. When, therefore, he gives us the impression of getting to the bottom of a given problem relating to his art, he is always going farther. The difficulties which complicate his existence—proceeding at times from sexual contacts which, on the occasion of each new adventure, he does not permit to preoccupy him in regard to their probable, eventual, predictable, or inevitable consequences—do not change him or worry him with calculating the pros and cons of every contingency. He gives himself to his passion impetuously because his temperament will not be reconciled to following the course dictated by what might be called foreseeable convenience; nor is he happy in following the path of comfort and routine.

On the other hand, Picasso is completely impressionable in the sphere of artistic expression. A smell, a word, a sound, or the mere fact of his eyes meeting an unexpected sight surprises him, fixes his attention, carries him on to think of something else. But his surprise is more intense than what we are generally able to conceive; for which his vision mounts guard in a state of alarm at the gate of his imagination, his sensitivity suffers a shock and registers the incident, however trivial it may be or seem, and automatically touches off the flight of a new suggestion.

Someone once asked me if Picasso had ever been in Italy; I have many times wondered the same thing. As for "being"—in the way that he *identified himself with* France—I do not think he has "been" there. He went there in 1917 at the insistence of chance, his friendship with Cocteau, the convenience of Diaghilev, and as a matter of curiosity. Picasso was then thirty-six. To abandon Paris, to leave France but not to return to his own country for the time being, did not stand for adventure but for something less than an interlude in the unrelenting passions of his life. The war of 1914, which had scattered the nucleus of intimate friends which had formed around him, continued its course without its being possible to predict an early end. Paris, subjected to the discomforts of the terrible conflict, seemed to him deserted.

Leaving the country of one's choice, especially under such conditions, becomes an obligation to kindle the wish to see it from afar, which in turn has the obvious function of stimulating the desire to revisit it. Picasso went of course to Rome and Florence. He visited the museums and studied the paintings with the same interest he is capable of putting into his contemplation of a picture displayed in a shop window, if it really attracts his attention.

What he saw in Rome and Florence served to refresh his memory and enabled him to make comparisons with what he remembered having seen of each painter, first in the Prado and then in the Louvre. The eagerness of his gaze was the same, but its ability to discover qualities attuned to his own criteria was superior.

For Picasso the Rome of 1917 was a completely indispensable change of locale in that fateful period of uncertainty. He knew Italian painting from what he had seen of it in Madrid and Paris and from books and magazines, photographs, and engravings. His long walks through the rooms of the Vatican and Borghese galleries, through the Uffizi and Pitti museums, became a visit among old friends, apparently forgotten yet encountered again with delight after many years. In fact with much more delight, for often his glance fell on paintings which reminded him of Paris.

13 janvier
XXXVI.
picasso

*Minotaur and Maiden* 1936

When he returned to Paris, with Florence and Rome fresh in his mind, he attempted to harmonize what he carried from Italy with his own ideas. He wished to see to what extent it would be possible to communicate simultaneously with past eras, overlooking differences of style and of place. This attempt responded perfectly to Picasso's temperament; I mean that he felt inclined to establish comparisons between his own work and what others had done, examining himself through the relation of his current to his past undertakings.

At this time Picasso, well advanced along the intricate paths of art, and of his own in particular, carried his painting to a higher point than he himself probably imagined. This was owing to the accident of his meeting Olga Koklova, far from Paris and outside of the milieu which had been created there. The meeting changed the entire manner of the life he had been accustomed to. The love affair of 1917 led to matrimony the following year. The intervening period was spent in sounding out the possibilities of living together. It was important to see if Olga would adapt herself to his personal setting and if he could fit in with the way of being, appearing, and feeling, of longing and living, of this woman who was monopolizing his attention. In such a state of irresolution, harmful to his art, it would be difficult for him to live or keep on working. Is this why he married? It is believable.

What is most essential for Picasso is composing a harmony—not creating one existence out of two congenial beings, or contriving the lie that is so often seized upon to patch up a mere family difference; rather he must harmonize contrasts, balance plastic values, seek correspondences. As I have already said, for him there is only one problem, that of art, since Picasso has the power to coexist with anything that can share in the atmosphere created when he is at work on a painting. With life it is not the same. If at times instead of harmonizing he causes discord, he is not to blame, for he does it inadvertently. In art, however, he is marvelous in arranging that each thing, in each case, assume its proper appearance, or the one which most suits his intention. He makes form and color blend, subduing the violence of a line with the caress of proper light, or else by combining it with a contrasting shadow in a play of carefully deployed colors, to achieve harmony from the dissonances.

If life does not offer him the same possibilities, the fault is not his. A human being is not simply a composition of line and color, but rather a bundle of caprices, contradictory impulses, false illusions, and opposing desires—but Picasso does whatever he can to recast the individual he comes into contact with. He attempts to place the woman who, by chance, attracts or interests him into the framework of his own environment, especially at the beginning, since thereafter the effort becomes merely one of the consequences of the first cause. In order for his "beloved" to enter the composition of his world, he takes her everywhere with him, especially during the brief period of incubation for his plans of mastery, which we might call the grand parade of his conquest, when he sometimes appears to yield to the outside will in a number of purely surface concessions.

Lines intertwine in a composition because the artist wishes them to do so; in conformance to the demands of a plastic conception, he causes them to seek and find each other. But, unfortunately for him, the great

13.6.38. Picasso

*Portrait of a Woman*
1938

problem of living itself is the only which cannot be resolved in accordance with ideas or intentions.

It is perhaps because of this difficulty of finding a solution that the problem of life, particularly of everyday life—for his problem, ever unresolved, follows him willy-nilly *come l'ombra segue il corpo*—continues to matter to Picasso almost as much as his art. It matters, because for him a difficulty is an incentive rather than an impediment.

Picasso's art satisfies and surprises us, nearly always fulfilling our aspirations or opening new horizons to us, giving us new hopes, carrying us away, or causing us to long constantly for something beyond, which our own imagination cannot conceive. For him, however, his art is something else. What we feel to be an end-product of the plastic problem which his art continually sets, he utilizes only as an antecedent, as nothing more than a datum, a mere point of departure for setting up the lines of a new problem: the problem that one day or another he will resolve, time permitting.

Be that as it may, it is clear that the sexual problem as Picasso sees it is not the one that best lends itself to solution in marriage, for a woman

*Old Woman* 1941

56

5 juillet 46

*Head of a Girl* 1946

ceases to be a wife for him almost immediately. It is as a *woman* that she is able to manage for as long as she fits into the picture that his imagination is forever arranging. She need only encroach too far upon his privacy to begin obstructing the composition of his purely personal type of life. But if she is out of place here she would be even worse in another picture than the one which he has been creating in accord with his imaginative demands for release from an obsessive idea.

From what has been said so far one might believe that Picasso obeys only the impulsive mandate of his temperament, but if we stop to consider his qualities and defects, we shall easily agree that what at first seems like rapture is sometimes no more than obedience to the demands of inspiration. The proof of this is that—outside of his commonplace acts, which are almost always performed in an atavistic rhythm—things which most directly concern him are usually contingent upon purely casual circumstances: time and place, his state of spirit, and above all demands relating to his personal activities.

Thus, a painting or a sketch made by him bears his own seal, irreplaceably and unmistakably. Even when the painting, sketch, sculpture, or whatever it may be is done with the deliberate intent of copying Poussin in his *Bacchanale*, for example, or Delacroix in *The Women of Algiers*, or Courbet in his *Demoiselles des bords de la Seine*, he translates them into his own spiritual language. Although we recall the originals perfectly—and sometimes more clearly or profoundly—we are led to speculate more about Picasso, the translator, than about the artists who inspired him. His interpretations were made from his recollection of the impression that he had received on whichever occasion he saw the painter in question, and wherever it was that his eyes really discovered him. The reality of the original work advantageously fuses with the concept suggested by Picasso's inspiration at the moment when he carries to conclusion what has been preoccupying him for so long, and what has thus been blocking him as far as what we might call "the picture" of the thing, its image or memory, is concerned. For when the image fuses in the fire of what we can call Picasso's inspiration, he translates or transposes it in his own fashion for us to understand. The appearance of an image is usually a result, not the cause, of the necessity to mold a suggested form which has disappeared from the field of vision. In Picasso's case, however, it is this immense necessity to free himself of an obsession which obliges him to reproduce the image in one way or another, wherever it may be. Once he is free of the obsession which was impeding his spirit, we often find that he repeats the process day after day in drawings, paintings, lithographs, and engravings, changing lines and transforming the composition while the flame of the idea burns itself out by penetrating the depths of the memory. The result may depend upon some immediate necessity that is related to the plastic importance accorded by Picasso. The gradation, transformation, or distortion which we can observe depends upon whether the image, as his continually effervescent state of spirit passes it through countless sieves, tirelessly registers the atmospheric changes of his own artistic restlessness, reversals of humor, or affective inclinations—for his soul can be influenced by any of these, or sometimes by all of them together along with something more that defies supposition.

Picasso is for me the most disconcerting of all artists. He is a painter by vocation, an innovator by nature, a gainsayer by temperament. He creates epochs with his various "periods." To make and to unmake seems to be his destiny. To make and to unmake, so that he will always have something new to make: to paint or sketch, obsessed by the passion to construct, like a sculptor or architect—more of the "artisan" than of the "artist." Picasso denies importance to *theory*, but he does not reject it. At bottom he is convinced that the greatest merit of the whole world of existence is rooted in the very fact of *existence* itself. Existence is all that matters to him. Thought or object, man or woman, flora or fauna: all are the same for him, as much in real life as in the life of his works. The appearance of merit or importance in one or another form depends solely upon the interpretation which he gives it in the course of his artistic digressions—or, in other words, he receives each thing as a simple element.

The difficulty encountered by those who consider Picasso from a distance is that his period of creative gestation is so short. And the strange thing—so as not to say good or marvelous—is that the brevity of this period does not drain or tire him; on the contrary, one might say that

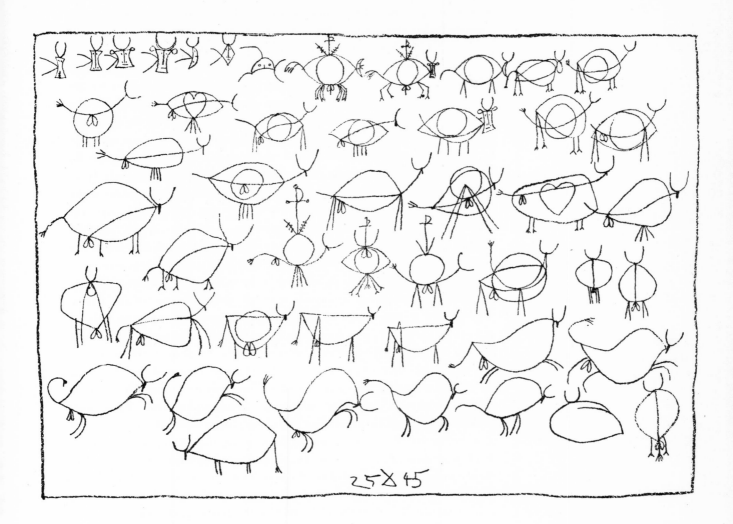

*Sketches of Bulls* 1945

it is precisely the constant, repetitive hammer blows of his creating that ignite the spark of genius in his mind, as steel and flint ignite tinder.

Picasso's style of expression is of no more than relative or secondary importance. If in the midst of a so-called period of "distortion" he should decide to explain himself, like a proper fine arts scholar, he might say that the phase as he sees it is no more than a kind of note, jotting, *aide mémoire*, or what you will, that intervenes parenthetically in the development of a progression which is unplanned—or, if you like, established with no formal aims—and which answers the need of explaining himself *to* himself, or of elucidating an idea. It may be that he is guided by the inclination to clarify some concept which—owing to his listener's occasional difficulty in understanding him—he may be led to believe, with excellent reason in most cases, is causing the attention of the person who is following, observing, and studying him, to wander.

The step from one mode of expression to another—painting, drawing, sculpture, lithography, etching, and much later the literary form—does not indicate a change of temperament but rather the urgent necessity of employing a language adequate to what he is saying, of expressing himself better and more clearly so that what he conceives assumes the weight of the irrefutable.

To be concise, clear, correct, explicit, precise, or exact is Picasso's great longing: to be clear to his own self by the conciseness of correct expression. Brevity or the glibness of the vernacular is not sufficient if naturalness and spontaneity are left out of account. This is the reason why he changes his idiom in accordance with what he proposes to say.

*Guernica*, conceived in the horror of a tragedy which affects him intimately, is the synthesized image of the martyrdom of an innocent, defenseless people who are flesh of his flesh, terrorized and in pain. A photograph of the crime would scarcely have given an idea of the disaster; it would be a diffuse image of an occurrence, a disorganized mass of abnormality and brutality. Episodic documentation lacks the interpretation of a human response. *Guernica*, that great painting of Picasso's (an oil painting on canvas, not a fresco, in spite of what writers and critics still say), is a frenzied, graphic poem of horror. It would have been necessary to feel the tragedy as deeply, as intensely as Picasso felt it in order to weep in such a way. It was necessary that the pictorial expression itself inspire horror, that the lines be a sob, that the color—with the color itself washed out—be pain and that the total effect be a piercing, gripping, strident, and everlasting shriek. This could not be done in prose.

*Family of Centaurs with Doves* 1946

60

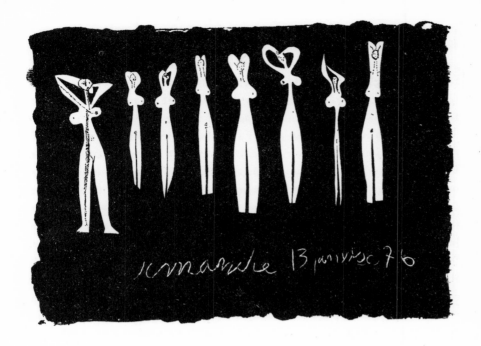

*Eight Silhouettes* 1946

If we wish to contemplate Picasso's paintings with the "cutting edge of the soul," we must look at them as he saw them within himself, without preconceptions or bias. The title of a work matters little; it was given after he had completed it, and it was not he who gave it. Godparents are usually the ones to give baptismal names. I believe that in art what counts or what ought to count is the impression we receive of the work before us. I realize that I cannot contemplate a group of musicians in actuality, in the same way, for example, that my eyes are startled by the *Three Musicians*, painted by Picasso at Fontainebleau in 1921. Such is the suggestive power of this work, at least to me, that, once one has observed the expression of the emotion experienced by Picasso when he conceived it—to pass it on to others—one feels his lyrical abandon and the degree of his rapture in that period. The climate of Fontainebleau is known for its soothing effect. Someone close to Picasso must have needed this tonic for his nerves, justifying the stay in Seine-et-Marne which produced the emotion which we receive in reflection from the *Three Musicians*. Painted there upon this occasion, the picture conveys a sense of stridence standing in relief against a background of infinite solitude. In this way he is accustomed to rendering the darkest grief or the most blissful happiness, surprise in despair or in hope: a chill that shakes the nerves, its intensity measured by the seconds it takes to run up the "thermometer" of the spine. *Guernica* electrifies, shivers the nerves, agitates, and distresses. But it does not explain itself, because the atrocity it commemorates is unprecedented.

Between *Guernica* and *War and Peace* (1937–42) Picasso gave us the nocturnal panorama of fishermen, the immediate significance of which is obvious. The theme or scene, however, unfolding in the dead of night is like an omen. Begun in August 1939, at the end of the interval of peace which followed the first war, the canvas had to be rolled up immediately because of the explosion which everyone feared was about to occur. It seemed as though Picasso, seeing the fishermen hidden in the blackness of the night near the port of Antibes, had premonitions of the apocalyptic tragedy being plotted across the border. He painted the canvas in frenzy, struggling against time, as though driven by a magical force, as though the fishermen's lanterns portended the great catastrophe for him who could read their signs. Picasso kept on painting, seeming to fear that his message would not arrive in time.

*Massacre in Korea*, painted in Vallauris in 1951, is an episode of cruelty in action during the conflict in the Orient. Here Picasso explains himself in simple terms, and not for the first time. Throughout his career on many other occasions he has seemed to stop for a moment to breathe —we are reminded of the returns he made to Barcelona to bask in the warmth of the family circle. Picasso speaks to us here in familiar language, a language which, to distinguish it, has been given the name "classic." He realizes that at times it is necessary to be more intelligible: the man in the street does not always understand readily.

The panel *Massacre in Korea* is an obsessive evocation of war. The war of 1914 had impressed him very deeply. It had scattered his friends, destroyed a good part of his illusions, and surrounded him with unexpected loneliness in the midst of nearly total confusion. He saw it making a clean sweep in the very area that he considered of most promise for developing his activities, putting his ideas into practice, and satisfying his longings.

The horror of war gives no immunity against its terror. For Picasso that horror and that fear are an obsession. Consequently, *War*, the first part of his larger composition, and a companion to *Peace*, becomes the latent proof of his state of alarm. Between 1951, when he finished his *Massacre in Korea*, and 1952, he was haunted by this theme. He threw himself into the study and analysis of it as the source of his deepest and most abiding concern, producing hundreds of sketches in the process: the human beast in the form of an eagle, voracious, fierce, savage, terrifying; weapons of destruction, tongues of fire, demoniacal scenes, ferocious faces, unnerving gesticulations, the armored tank of tomorrow, the thunderbolt of always—and all of it more horrifying than ever.

At the same time his spirit delights in harmonizing bucolic scenes of peace, full of grace, seemingly observed in the strange calm of an impossible dream—children's games which idealize in his own way those that are seen daily in certain streets, and which he sketches in different ways as if wishing to unlock the secret of the joy of movement. Finally one day the continuous "war against war" waged by his pencil came to the threshold of paroxysm, and he crossed weapons on the battlefield of contradiction, war against peace, peace against war. He put aside the mountain of rough sketches and began to paint on a surface of one hundred square meters, placing *War* on one side and *Peace* on the other and bringing them together at the apex of an arch. It is an admirable composition which hardly reminds one of the experimental sketches on loose paper and in notebooks.

When he starts to paint, Picasso knows how to place himself in a state of inwardness. What he brought forth from within himself, transferring it onto the paper, was indispensable to the process of gestation. That is natural, for if one carefully considers what passes through the mind in the course of intellectual creation, it turns out to be merely the basis or foundation, made up of mental remnants, surpluses, or excesses;

*The Birth of the Last Centaur* 1947

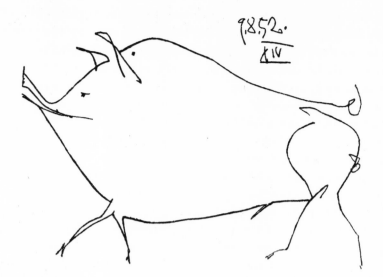

*Boar* 1952

images which come to the memory in answer to a momentary need; shadows of impressions or feelings; or symptoms of emotions—in short, all manner of things which had to be cast out so as to purge himself of every preoccupying vanity. True inspiration comes later in the contortions and pain of creation. The placenta does not belong in the child's cradle.

In the normal round of his being and doing, and apart from the habitual and ever-turbulent activities of his revolutionary art, Picasso is the most routine person I know. He goes to bed late because he works until the small hours of the morning. Once in bed he reads until he drops off to sleep. If no urgent necessity requires him to be up at a certain hour he stays in bed as long as he can. Whatever happens far away matters little to him as long as it does not affect him. What goes on nearby may bother him if it exposes him to enough distraction to take him away from his concentration.

If he goes to bed with the foreknowledge that he must get up at a certain hour he makes use of an alarm clock without trusting it, entertaining a vague illusion that he will not have to depend on its startling ring. The spiritual excitement afforded by his art is more than enough to keep him from requiring other stimulants. He may or may not sleep, as happens with everyone under such circumstances, but by trusting to the mercies of a machine he achieves the illusion of being tranquil. If he does not awaken it will not be his fault. Not believing oneself to blame is as important as ignoring the blame or as innocent as blaming something else.

Picasso in ordinary life is capable of doing the same thing without variation. When he leaves the house he prefers to go where he went the day before and the one before that. He follows the path he knows as if no other could suit him. When he walks through the streets he seems to move with the vague idea that he need not look around, since he has already seen a thousand times what he might find along the way. Nevertheless, it is quite probable that in spite of seeing the same sight every day, each of the things appears different to him each time. In fact it is more than probable. He will never see a thing twice the same, for the reason that his vision changes in conformance with the ideas that occupy him. Nothing can seem the same from one day to another as long as one does not allow prejudices to spoil the art of looking. When Picasso leaves his house he prefers to take a customary direction: along the same street, on the same sidewalk, and in the same way as every day. Routine is a denial of the effort required to direct one's will in the face of custom. It can be said then, without paradox, that when Picasso leaves his house he is not getting outside his usual orbit—nor, more important, does he get outside of himself. For even when he goes with others he never fails to be absolutely in his own company. It is probably because of this that he does not generally encounter new things capable of diverting his attention.

What might be called the backdrop of his everyday landscape, as composed by his routine, serves as a sufficiently neutral surface, best suited to a suspended state of spirit. Should something new present itself he will find no difficulty in observing it, and even without wishing to, he will take it into account since he did nothing to produce the phenomenon, nor anything to avoid it. The fact that he has neither

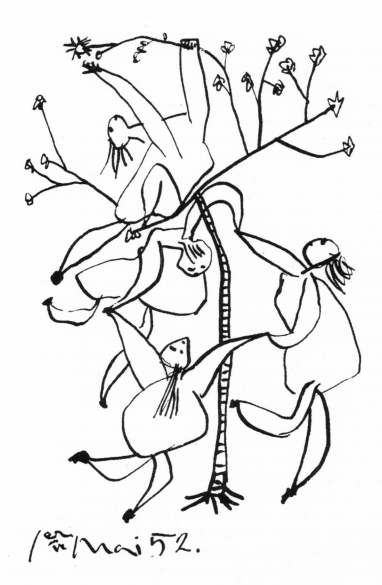

*Round Dance* 1952

provoked nor predicted it affords him the greatest tranquillity. This in turn acts upon his soul until the tranquillity becomes the medium favorable for appreciation, for contemplating close at hand that shaded effect of the landscape against the accustomed expanse of the background. So, when a decision to leave the house occurs to him it becomes, in relation to his surroundings, somewhat like the surface of a canvas (canvas or paper) available for painting or sketching, a screen which is to reproduce his own emotions in plastic form.

If it were once given to him to change his course or to modify the rhythm of his customary gestures, I am sure that his ideas would be obliged to take other paths, because for him change is an effort since he must first exert himself to imagine the possibility of violating his habits.

By saying what I have noted I am only trying to prove that Picasso feels no inclination to provoke unusual occurrences; he does not seek them out but neither does he reject them. He accepts them, if they come to him, as part of a number of natural occurrences. Therefore his retina and mind are always to be found in the best conditions for receptivity. Is it for this reason that his eye is always on the point of grasping an image? It may be. What cannot be doubted is that he receives it *in toto*, and that the absence of such interference as preoccupations or preconceived ideas allows him to record the vision simply and to pass it along to us with singular exactitude.

However, we must take care not to speak to him, not to make noise or walk around him when Picasso fixes his gaze on something which at times turns out to be the mere breath of a thought. His gaze from within to without, or vice versa, takes note of the external or internal vision which comes to distract him from his routine. To protect oneself against an emotion and mentally to convert it into the image which we are later to see demands the highest attention. For this reason we must be silent in Picasso's presence when he surrenders himself to his work. The merit of art lies in its power to eternize the fleeting passage of a vision. Picasso seizes upon the momentary impression in midair, spontaneously, without the least shadow of premeditation, as soon as the time arrives for him to cast out all which, if it remained within him, might deaden his faculties or be in his way.

Picasso has the gift of magnifying the image that falls within the focus of his vigilant gaze. He takes it from its ordinary place, makes it shine, and gives it relief. He dazzles us with the radiant reflection that has come alight in his poetic spirit, until he brings us to distinguish the image by what inherently sets it apart. At some unknown moment he himself distinguished it from innumerable others, at the instant when his elation blended into the sensory rapture of contemplating something which had surprised him by the very reason of its coming before him unexpectedly.

And so for this reason, which is the only one capable of carrying him away, Picasso is always prepared to capture what is offered to his contemplation. His eye is not clouded by the desire to take by surprise what comes into his ken. Such a desire would only frighten away any possibility of surprise. To plan the search impedes the chance of encounter. What one stumbles across under such conditions carries no surprise and what does not surprise fails to interest, to make an impression, or even to be noticed. It is an image of the imagination and nothing

*Balzac (II)* 1952

*Gardens in Vallauris*
1953

else. Of what need is it to go in search of the presence of the awaited, if the imagination has already furnished it in its own manner?

If Picasso should deviate from the itinerary of his routine it might be that he could change the course of his own destiny. To deviate might be to force the will of his tutelary spirits. Anyone can see better what is before him if he allows himself to be carried along the path of his destiny, rather than making an effort to look outside of himself. Picasso feels what he is able to feel, or he senses it, because he does not displace his capacity for feeling. I mean he sees spontaneously.

In regard to his art, Picasso is somewhat like a volcano in constant eruption. His activity—a sort of frenzy, or turbulence of latent revolt—is without equal. His capacity for work is constantly manifested in what he does. In Picasso, that is, the artist is revealed as a contradiction to the routine that we see in the image of the man. Let us add, moreover, that in his daily life he is a supreme conservative. He keeps all his possessions piled up around him. He does not part with anything. Whatever comes to him in one way or another, there it must remain, and no one may move it from where he left it or from where chance wished it to remain. The demand is for his own peace of mind, and it is by patiently building up this peace that he has what is needed for his spiritual expansion. During the process of his poetic gestation the least preoccupation would be enough to disturb him. But in the course of his daily life nothing upsets him. That there are mountains of books on the floor does not matter a bit. Papers everywhere and a thousand things in his way? He does not care. What does matter is that everything forever remain just where he left it so that his eyes may find rest in an unchanging environment. It is a visual necessity that no change should surprise him, so that whatever may appear on the scene may register its presence in accordance with the general disorder which has been strictly ordered by his mode of being and living, of yielding to or allowing himself to penetrate the disarranged life which circumstances have imposed.

"La puissance immobilisé" ("Power immobilizes"), says Paul Valéry in *L'Ame de la Danse*. Picasso's behavior purely as a human being gives new meaning to the poet's phrase. If Picasso could detain the course of time, all clocks would stop, the hours would perish, days would come to an end, and the earth have to cease its revolutions and wait for him to change his mind. And if it had really been he who had stopped it, the globe would wait in vain. Thus I found Picasso, and thus he must continue. It is necessary for the free pursuit of his destiny.

*Jaime Sabartés*

*Face* 1950

### Introduction I: Nature and Abstraction

Picasso's biographers have often voiced the opinion (occasionally endorsed by Picasso himself) that his art shows no development. Such a statement about an artist usually implies that he does not change. In the case of Picasso something entirely different is implied, namely, that no meaningful connection derivable from a personal core can be found between his extraordinarily different "periods." It seems as though by some inexplicable miracle he has combined many artists in a single person; and the inference is drawn that this person is not a unified personality. There is a good deal of evidence, however, that Picasso the man is a strong, well-defined personality whose manifestations on the most varied occasions are remarkably consistent. We must therefore conclude that we are still too close to Picasso to discern the unity of his art. The same is perhaps true of the development of his art, though here we may point out even today that his work of the last fifteen years is in many respects a synthesis of that of the earlier periods. The extremely varied character of Picasso's art, which baffles some critics, is regarded by many others as evidence of his unique genius and his ability to play all the instruments of his time with equal virtuosity. But neither the naturalistic nor the so-called abstract school —to take only the extremes—can lay claim to Picasso: even when he seems to observe the standards of nature he is by no means without other intentions, and even when he is non-objective he is not apt to lose sight of nature completely.

*"Documents"* page 503

Any artist's relation to nature is of basic importance; Picasso's cannot be reduced to any well-trodden formula. He does not paint "from" nature, in the naturalistic sense; nor does he create "like" nature, as the non-objective artists claim to do. He himself has said on occasion that he works "with" nature—meaning no doubt that his relation to it is personal, not objective. Nature has always been for him an inexhaustible source of inspiration; and "nature" stands here for environment in the broadest possible sense. It is not merely the optical appearance of things that fascinates and stimulates him, but the sum total of their properties graspable through form—something that might be called their "essence." For Picasso, art is a means of securing for him-

*"Documents"* page 504

Note 1

self objects in his environments, of taking possession of them by re-creating them. His ultimate aim is an "objectified stimulus," which attains an existence independent of the natural form of the object that has provided the stimulus. Through the mysterious co-operation of spirit and hand, many of his works give form to things he experienced in his encounters with the environment—form that is autonomous and bears the stamp of necessity. Seen in this light, the model is revealed as playing only a subordinate function, particularly when it is trans-muted into a schematic sign. Like artists of early periods, Picasso often strives to transform painting and drawing into a sign and picture language; but unlike those early artists, he does this on the basis of his ability to imitate the outward appearance of nature.

*The Owl* page 91

A particularly striking example of such a transformation of a natural object into a sign is Picasso's pencil drawing of the little owl (page 91) that Michel Sima gave him at Antibes in 1946, and that he kept for a long time as a pet and subject of studies. This small creature, which he reproduced in various media, is for him not so much a visual object as a personal experience, something that happens to him; he comes to grips with it, takes possession of it, and at the same time seeks to express it by a simple and meaningful sign. The result of this process is this striking drawing which embodies the owl as such in only a few lines.

Its abstract elements range from memories of things seen to geo-metric curves. An almost regular oval serves as the outline of the owl's body, while the three-quarter view introduces a perspective fore-shortening. Related asymmetric curves inside the figure denote the wings, the arched brows, and the beak. The unequal size of the eyes (the left one is larger) and the horizontal ledge that attaches the bird to the plane and gives it static support, enhance the perspective effect. The derivation of the almost symbolically simplified drawing from a prior illusionistic vision is thus unmistakable. All the elements contained in those few lines, such as the broad head, the form of the beak, the round eyes, the position of the wings, the inclined stance are also present in the photographs of the owl; Picasso often had himself photo-graphed with it. He seems to have experimented with an owl previous-ly, when he engraved its forms on a flint stone that had the character-istic oval shape "from nature."

*Studies of Owls* page 90

He did not regard the drawing of November 8, 1946, as a definitive solution, and early in 1947 resumed his work, evidence of which we find in one very revealing sheet of drawings (page 90). The two rapid sketches at the top of the sheet reproduce the older drawing with altered proportions; the perch that the bird grips with its claws is indicated by a horizontal line. This motif recurs in the other studies, which bring out entirely new formal elements overlooked in the older drawing. Certain angular breaks of the outline and the inclusion of the form of the tail lead to a completely changed, firmly articulated conception of the contour. The natural appearance of the owl has been broken up into its constituent parts: the hook-like beak has been moved to the profile view at the right and separated from the eyes, which are brought together in an area of their own. In the most finished study the owl is placed on a branch-like scaffolding which seems originally not to have been intended for that purpose; here the fascinating effect of the

*Owl* (1950)

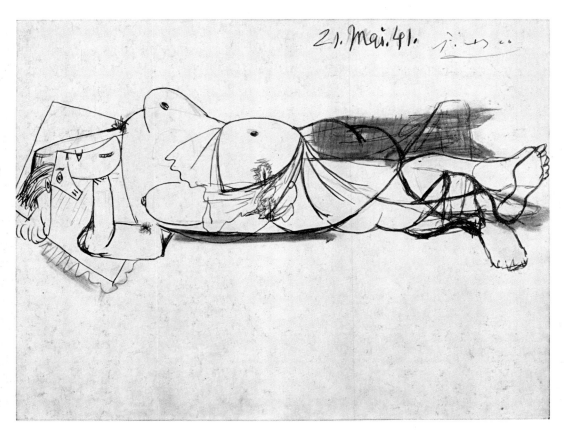

*Reclining Nude* (1941)

*Two Women* (1942)

*Aubade* (1942)

*Sleeping Nude* (1946)

75

*Reclining Nude* (1946)

*Still Life with a Guitar and Toreador's Sword* (1942)

*Pitcher and Bowl of Apples* (1919)

*Still Life with a Bottle and Bowl of Pears* (1922)

79

*Still Life with Casserole* (1945)

*Still Life with Dead Fowl* (1942)

*Woman with a Hat* (1935)

*Female Figure* (1938)

*Illustration for "Vingt poèmes" by Góngora (1948)*

frontally staring eyes is considerably enhanced by the stressing of their duality. (Closely related to the owl studies are the scattered drawings of human eyes, in which the relation of the round eyeball to a frame consisting of sharply intersecting arcs is similarly explored.) Faint lines indicating feathers within the planes—in contrast to the strongly rationalized figure as a whole—point to an effort to recapture the optical appearance. Of particular importance is the study at the lower right: it discloses an attempt, still in the groping stage, to combine the closed oval form of the older drawing with the more recent angular forms.

The desired synthesis is actually achieved in the lithographs of January 20 and 21, 1947 (page 92). Here, through the use of rich tones, the figure of the night bird again comes closer to natural appearance; moreover it is no longer seen as an isolated drawing, but as an integral element of a surface and space composition. But Picasso did not regard the lithographs as a definitive solution any more than the drawings: this is proved by the existence of still another, strongly divergent, variant.

More recently Picasso again treated the owl in ceramics and sculptures—needless to say, he also painted it—and in the process made it yield still other potentialities. Chinese potters of the Han period and later sixteenth-century European potters used the motif of the owl for decorative purposes. Picasso, starting from his drawings, arrived independently at the idea of matching the forms of the owl's body with specific vase forms. Thus, the head, shoulder, belly, and foot of the vase shown on page 447 are also the head, shoulder, belly, and foot of an owl. The bird's claws, wings, and feathers are indicated by stylized dashes, and the beak, eyes, and eyebrows are added as accents partly for the sake of vividness and partly for the sake of ornamentation. Here, the twin function of the object as a picture and utensil has replaced the more general twin function of image and symbol.

Picasso's constant search for greater reality finally impelled him to express his experience of the owl in ceramics (page 73). The elementary ovoid body is this time approximated to a horizontal position and poised on short legs. (The preliminary drawings [page 89] still show a more differentiated spatial form and longer legs.) The face with the deep hollows of the pupils suggests a disc or the round dial of a clock. The effect of plastic volume, of a continuous palpable surface, is deliberately weakened everywhere by groovings and by the coloring. Only a painter could invent this sculpture *sui generis:* it is one of Picasso's most significant accomplishments in the field of plastic arts.

Just as Picasso's successive owls record the conversion of a model into an artistic representation, so the eleven states of his lithograph of a bull, executed in 1945 and 1946, provide us with a truly classical example illustrating the process of abstraction. Since each state on the stone was obtained by alterations of and additions to the forms of the preceding state, the transitions can be followed step by step as in a slow-motion picture. In these lithographs, form as such is the subject of an epic portrayal, which parallels the dramatic sequence of drawings depicting a combat between two centaurs, which Picasso executed at Antibes over a period of time (page 99). To follow its progress from an almost naturalistic rendering to the final linear sign is a captivating adventure for anyone sensitive to form. Here we shall discuss the most important stages of this progress.

In the first rendering, the general features of the species are embodied in the bull's structure and stance. It is an instantaneous view: the brush, by means of subtle intermediate tones, reproduces the appearance of the animal in light and atmosphere. And then, a week later, when Picasso resumed work on the plate, he intensified the shading and transformed the domestic animal into a demonic creature with an oversized, formidable, threatening head (page 100). After a few days he proceeded from this expressive composition to the formal developments which begin in the third state (page 100) and result in the brilliant simplification of the eleventh (page 103). The time intervals between the various stages grow progressively shorter, reflecting greater creative intensity. The contrast between the heavy body and its upright supports, and the stressing of the flat elements and of the silhouette begin as early as the second state. There the artist also begins to use the pen; a more precise instrument, it is used predominantly in the following states. He proceeds to divide the surface structure of the bull into elements that have nothing to do with its anatomy. Some ridges are deliberately accented with swellings, and they define lighter and darker segments. The intermediate tones have not yet been eliminated, but a graphic technique—the pen is used to draw each hair—has replaced the soft modeling with the lithographic brush. The forms become perceptibly geometrized and new structural elements appear in the curve of the cheeks and in the drawing of the stylized ear.

In the fourth state the results of this process are fully apparent: incised sharp lines mark out a kind of geometric net which, together with the shaded planes, produces a Cubist illusion. The curved outline of the back now shows a hump, acquiring the shape of an irregular pyramid; the structure of the legs is also Cubist in character. The tail swung forward—a relic of the first naturalistic, instantaneous view—is now felt to be an alien element. The chest, articulated in detail, still reflects the multiplicity of the soft, natural forms in this area of the body. The head has been subject to the greatest alterations: while the horns and the ear are those of the previous state, the geometrically stylized face is now turned to the beholder, who sees its right half, including the nose and the mouth. The small left ear is placed directly next to the horn which was part of the old lateral view, and the eyes, one conceived differently from the other, are brought closer to each other. (The principle of multiple views applied here will be discussed later.)

In the next, fifth, state (page 101) Picasso proceeds still more radically: he discards the hind part of the back and thus eliminates the beginning of the tail that has become meaningless. The soft, non-structural parts—the swelling of the belly and the dewlap—are removed, and the tension of the body is made visible by a broad "line of force" that goes from the head to the genitals. The head itself is drastically geometrized, and the double presence of frontal and lateral views is stressed more sharply; yet at the same time the two views are merged by a deliberate displacement of individual features (the frontal eye is in the half face seen laterally, and vice versa). The frontal symmetric arrangement of the horns recalls a heraldic design. If there had been no earlier or later states, we would have been compelled to say not only that the bull shown on this sheet is fragmentary, but also that the means used to represent it are curiously heterogeneous.

The sixth state (page 102) is quite obviously a mere transition without independent meaning. Here the mass of the body is lightened by the elimination of the high hump and more of the belly, and the columnar, full-grown legs of the previous states are replaced by tapered, flat segments. The transformation is not yet complete: three forelegs are still visible. The original tail which has long since become incomprehensible is eliminated, and a new one is added to the hind parts stunted like the rest. But most noteworthy of all is the appearance of a second head, sketched at the end of the thin neck. For the old head with the perpendicular line indicating the nose has not yet been entirely eliminated, even though it seems now to be attached to a new humped form separated from the back. In short nothing here is definitive, everything is in flux.

At this point Picasso once again summons nature to his aid and rearranges some of the previously obtained forms within an extremely simplified contour. The elements thus retained consist of two groups of planes which are joined at one point; together they have the shape of a horizontal 8. The white "line of force" characteristically passes through the point of junction (eighth state, page 102). Even in the seventh state the genitals were reduced in size to conform to the new scale; in the eighth the forelegs too are disembodied. The shorthand indication of a head in the sixth state is bafflingly included in the head form with its pointed mouth: it has become the face, while the lines of the neck are now part of a new ear.

The next step marks the discarding of the chiaroscuro values of the planes in favor of a pure, weightless, linear drawing; also, the excessive length of the body frame is shortened by the removal of a segment of the hind part. Finally, after some intermediate solutions and further alterations there emerges the outline of the last state (page 103). The legs have become simple lines, a new delicately curved tail is sketched in, and the head and the genitals are added as tiny accessories. Nothing remains of the interior lines, but their most important tensions have been communicated to the extraordinarily elastic contour. Each of the few lines remaining in the eleventh state has its history, and that is why we have so attentively followed the uniquely instructive, successive stages of this lithograph. We can see that the final linear form of the bull, comparable to the drawing of the owl discussed above, did not spring in its striking precision ready-made from the artist's head. It was the felicitous final result of an extremely complicated process, which we should like to think was completed with the subtly animating accent of the asymmetric lines of the horns. But the *Bull*, like the *Owl*, retains traces of its birth from an experience of nature, namely, in the impressionistic rendering of the ground plane and in the wash of color inside the body and between the legs. This is in conformity with the artist's intention. However, we may assume a certain degree of spontaneity in the final state, since it is separated by an unusually long interval of time from the previous state.

On Christmas Day 1945, while working hard on the *Bull*, between its fifth and sixth states, Picasso executed a lithographic drawing

*The Bull VI* page 102

*The Bull VIII* page 102

*The Bull IX* page 103

*The Bull XI* page 103

*Studies of Bulls* page 59

showing a whole herd of bulls, each of which consists of only a few elements—the line of the back, the line of the belly, the head with horns, the tail, the genitals, four legs, plus an imaginary "line of force" and a circular line representing a transverse section of the body. These many variations on the theme "bull" display inexhaustible imaginative and inventive richness. A few strokes convincingly render a bull in profile, from the rear, from the front, at complete rest, or performing the most violent leaping motion. Even these shorthand symbols show clearly that the pictures draw their freshness from visual impressions and are controlled by them. These drawings contributed a good deal to the final success of the single figure in its linear perfection. But just as in the case of the owl, the shorthand symbol of the bull did not mark the end of Picasso's experiments. In April 1947 he returned to the theme, this time treating it in monumental form in a large litho-

*The Black Bull* page 106

graph (page 106) which may be regarded as a synthesis of the previous attempts on a higher level. The massive body, the taut outline, the pictorial black-and-white effect add up to a new design in which the curve of the back, ascending toward the neck, and the line of the powerful chest are combined with a symbolically small head, strong legs, and an expressively enlarged organ of reproduction. This time the figure is also related to its spatial surroundings.

Picasso's art has made many enemies because he has never shrunk from subjecting the human figure to principles of form that ignore its natural structure. There is really no reason, however, why the artist in the sovereign domain of his art should not let himself be inspired by the human appearance without being obliged to imitate or idealize it, provided that he observes a law of form which is for him the higher one. Picasso, in particular, repeatedly reveals his southern origin by the matter-of-factness with which he measures all forms, even those seemingly most remote from nature, by the proportions of the human figure.

*Reclining Nude* page 76

We may illustrate this by analyzing the large *Reclining Nude* (page 76) painted at Antibes in 1946, which represents an extreme instance of abstraction in Picasso's art. The painting is built on the contrast between the horizontal couch, which is delineated with Cubist straight lines, and the figure on it, which is raised on the right side and kept low on the left; it is developed spatially by the shading of the cubistically adjoining planes. The sensation of space suggested by these forms and by the couch induces the beholder to see the exposed surface of the wood panel at the upper right as a deep background element. On the other hand, it is this very structure of the grained-wood panel that emphasizes the autonomy of the surface that comes close to dominating even the painted parts. This very elementary and powerful tension between space and surface endows the painting with its strong vitality. In addition there is the tension between the geometric-abstract treatment and the natural appearance—here, that of a human figure. For the proportions of the figure on the couch suggest that it is human, and some conspicuous details turn the conjecture into a certainty: we recognize female breasts and buttocks, and even though these seem to be outside any familiar organic connection and perspective order, they compel us to interpret the left part of the figure as the abdomen and the grained-wood segment at the right as a space enclosed by upraised

25./2.49.

*Owl* (1949)  —  *Eule*

*Studies of Owls* (1947)

*The Owl* (1946)

91

*The Black Owl* (1947)

arms. Now we begin to notice everywhere soft contours reminiscent of a female body; and when, on the basis of linear indications of the eyes and of the mouth, we interpret the pointed triangle at the right as the head, we only confirm our previous insight. The value of the painting rests upon the large, clear relations obtaining between the elements of surface and of space—and here the color contributes to no small extent—and upon the fact that the figure convincingly suggests natural appearance, even though the world of the painting is not the world of nature.

The genesis of the *Reclining Nude* can be traced back in its various stages over a number of years. The immediately preceding version executed at Antibes a short time before (page 75) still suggests a reclining woman: the tapering waist, the swelling of the buttocks, the pairing of the legs from which the feet are separated as small triangles, the pairing of the breasts, and the more natural connection of the features in the triangular face which is framed in round masses of hair—all this might encourage the misconception that the artist intended to compete with nature, or even to portray a reclining woman. This is not true, although the further back we go in the history of the picture, the closer we come to the natural model; indeed, the series begins with strictly academic studies of a sleeping woman. Nature provides Picasso not only with the original impulse, but also with indispensable stimulation during the work. More particularly, the human body serves him as the secret measure of all things, even in the most abstracted form—a form that he transmutes into shorthand symbols.

*Sleeping Nude* page 75

This process of a continual, fruitful reconciliation between nature and abstraction is illustrated by the pen drawing of May 21, 1941 (page 74), which is one of the preliminary sketches heralding the large *Aubade* of 1942 (page 75). In the drawing the artist has not yet forgotten his model, as evidenced by the pieces of clothing, the pillow under the head, and the various body parts. Referred to the model in nature, these are rather disarranged, and present an unsatisfying transitional stage between nature and abstraction (for instance, the arm under the head is anything but naturalistic). Of particular interest to us in this context is the obvious experimentation with the perspective arrangement of the breasts and the position of the buttocks, which first pointed upward, but then came to be turned in the opposite direction (the correction was made by means of the shading on top). The feet too are changed. Thus we must once again regard the drawing less as a finished work of art than as a stage in a development toward a work of art. The path leading from this drawing to *Aubade* is by no means a straight one; as always in Picasso, the major work is the result of many currents that merge unexpectedly. For this reason we may say that it presupposed certain gouaches (page 74), done earlier that year, in which the figure and composition problems receive tentative solutions that are embodied in the monumental version.

*Reclining Nude* page 74

*Aubade* page 75

*Two Women* page 74

Another noteworthy example of the gradual process of abstraction has recently been provided by Picasso in the series of busts painted from a nineteen-year-old model at Vallauris in the summer of 1954. In the earliest variants the young girl (Sylvette David) is portrayed more or less naturalistically in grisaille. The individual character of the graceful girl is recorded in each of her features. The slender upper

*Sylvette* Cl. Cat. 229

body, the long neck, the face that is at once severe and lovely, the bushy hair above the forehead, and the light "horsetail" are retained through all the variations, which diverge from nature to different extents, sometimes tending toward Cubism and sometimes toward flatness. There is a long stretch of creative transformation between the modeled profile of May 3 and the geometrically simplified one of June 3 (page 333); the latter nevertheless contains all the individual characteristics, enriched by the bold coloring which combines azure blue, violet, and green in the clothing. It would, however, be erroneous to assume that the polarity of nature and abstraction is reflected in the chronological sequence of the more than a dozen Sylvette portraits. The artist's spirit obeys no formula; he chooses the given degree of abstraction according to the dictates of the moment.

*Sylvette XIII* page 333

### Introduction II: Range of Styles

Modern man has access to the art treasures of the past in an "imaginary museum," and the twentieth-century artist has the most varied, indeed, the most contrasting stylistic means at his disposal. Unlike the old masters whose formal language—for all their artistic freedom in regard to details—was the end product of various religious, social, and local traditions, and whose choice of means was largely predetermined, the modern painter has almost unlimited possibilities of choice. Weak natures are for that reason exposed to the great danger of learning numerous skills without truly mastering any of them. On the other hand, artists of the rank of Picasso, who change everything they touch into gold, are enabled to achieve greater scope and mastery than any artist of the past. As we shall see, Picasso has always made abundant use of all historical styles: he has often sought inspiration in the treasures of the past, motivated by an inner need of which he is frequently unaware. Otherwise he could not so easily have assimilated the accomplishments of others. To be sure, his own inventions in the realm of form far exceed his borrowings. But like all inventions, these were not created out of nothing. Whatever he discovered had always existed before him; but one had to have eyes to see it, and of course also the necessary imagination to improve it.

Picasso's virtuosity in the simultaneous use of completely different stylistic means is part of the essence of his art. The value of any of his works does not depend on its style: what matters is the experience captured in it. In each instance the artistic form is dictated by an actual experience, a contact with the outside world. In this chapter we shall illustrate Picasso's great range of stylistic means and his complete mastery of them by a comparative study of some of his works, beginning with still life compositions.

The oblong chalk drawing of 1919, reproduced on page 78, shows a pitcher, a dish of apples, and next to the bowl a single fruit on a table surface against a neutral background. At first glance the stylistic ideal embodied here appears to be one of extreme plasticity. The violent contrasts between light and shadow serve primarily to model the vessels and the apples. Particularly the squat form of the pitcher and the

*Pitcher and Bowl of Apples* page 78

compact proportions of both the pitcher and the dish suggest that the persons who use those things are full-blooded and robust. The space surrounding the objects is comparable to a narrow stage, and stresses their massive materiality: they take possession of it by the heavy shadows they cast. The top view of the opening of the pitcher and of the rim of the cup diverges from the traditional laws of perspective.

The oil painting of 1922 in which a similar subject is treated (page 79) embodies a diametrically opposed stylistic goal. Here the effect of solid space is avoided. The bottle with the white label at the left, and the bowl of pears and the single fruit at the right are presented as sharply delineated flat surfaces. The horizontal ground plane is not contrasted with the vertical background, nor is the background filled up to the frame. The geometric, differently treated and graded planes of shadow do not clarify the volumes of the objects, but fit them into a richly nuanced non-objective composition formed by overlapping transparent discs of varying density; indeed, the multiple outlines seem to express the profiles of these overlapping planes. While the older still life scarcely awakens associations of color, they are directly aroused here by the variety of graphic structures and tones. Thus the two works exemplify stylistic tendencies that are as different as possible in every respect, though each of them is consistently followed through.

As our next example we shall take two paintings of 1942, which are on a fundamentally different artistic level. While the two works just considered are more or less confined to the solution of a formal problem, the later works aim at strong expressiveness, and here again the means used differ in each painting. In the large *Still Life with a Guitar and Toreador's Sword* (page 77)—there is a red-handled sword in the lower left of the picture—the spatial elements are absolutely predominant. The space in this picture is not as in old art a segment of the common space in which objects are set; but the objects themselves create the space or help to define it. In a sense, objects and space are to each other as the positive is to the negative. Even the solid blue shadows of the mirror and of the guitar have a life of their own; they are not mere reflections. A kind of colored atmosphere fills the space, bringing the objects closer to each other. These are expressively enhanced by perspective devices quite different from "correct" foreshortening. The rising arched curve of the guitar is echoed by the spatially very effective distortion of the mirror with its pale golden frame, whose glass reflects a corner of the room. The fragile tumbler in front of the guitar on the round table also possesses dynamic vitality because of the intricate, asymmetric balance of its parts.

The *Still Life with Dead Fowl* (page 81) shows how Picasso achieves equally expressive effects in a flat composition. The actual space of the red-tiled kitchen and the table in it are entirely subordinated to the picture surface. The top and the legs of the table with their broad colored outlines form a system of diagonals within the picture rectangle. This abstract system is contrasted with the more naturalistic, organic forms of the bird and of the plants—the modeled upper wing which for once even throws a shadow, the open outlines of the claws and of the leaves, and the spiral lines of the green vegetable. The angular edges of the latter and the straight lines of the bird's tail are connected with the bottle. This bottle, with its combination of angular and round forms, and its rich green and violet tones, ties the whole composition together. The fowl is included in the system through its black contour. The jagged, broken outline of the lower wing connected with the head by a red, zigzag line and the unnatural arrangement of the crudely drawn eyes symbolize its cruel end. Thus we find that more significant expression is achieved by a proper combination of abstract and naturalistic elements than can be achieved by either in isolation. There is a possible analogy here with the modern confrontation of organic life and technology.

In the still life of 1944, which is shown on page 475, the stylistic means used are even more elementary. We have before us a tightly knit structure, in primary colors, formed by broad brush strokes. Its space is essentially defined by the terminating and summarizing effect of the broad, black border against the light background on top. As for the subject matter, the white-highlighted, red circles with black bands of rays on a green undercoating suggest something like cherries. With that in mind we may interpret the left-hand vertical form as a pitcher, the blue mesh pattern on white as a tablecloth, and the yellow segmented rectangle next to it as a sort of napkin holder. The longer we examine the picture, the more certain we become that the forms just mentioned denote objects, and that the sections above and on both sides of the black border are non-figurative foils. The light background in broken yellow adjoins a red triangle to the right, and a red and blue strip with a violet edge to the left. This latter color, which played an important part in the painting of 1942, and which is echoed by the orange tone at the lower left, here too performs a special task at a crucial place: namely, it contributes to the creation of a space, a background for the still life. But because the blue, a "receding" color, here appears chiefly in the foreground, while the "advancing" red occurs in the background, the space-forming energies of the colors are largely neutralized, and the general flat effect is preserved. The interplay of compositional values can rarely be calculated as exactly as we have attempted to do here. Needless to say, this magnificently simple painting is not thereby divested of mystery: a work of art is an equation that can never be solved by logic.

No less simple and magnificent is the effect, though here achieved by entirely different means, of the *Still Life with Casserole* (page 80) dating from the year 1945. It has more affinity with the *Still Life with a Guitar* of 1942 than with the preceding painting, but it carries further the "thing-like" isolation of objects, and thereby is comparable to the drawing of 1919 (page 78). But the method used here is quite different. Let us compare the pitchers in the two works. In the older one the vessel's surface is rounded on all sides; the vessel of 1945 shows firmly delineated light and dark planes, whose shapes combine into a schematic but unmistakable image of a pitcher. This pitcher is the outcome of a process similar to that which resulted in the bull described above (pages 100–103), and the casserole may remind us of the owl (page 90). Here too we are confronted with a synthesis of two contradictory forms—the roundness of the casserole and its rectilinear projection on the picture surface. Picasso achieves this synthesis by combining an enamel-blue and a dark-brown plane, without resorting to traditional modeling and without in the least sacrificing the purity

*Still Life* Cl. Cat. 181

*Still Life with Casserole* page 80

*Pitcher and Bowl of Apples* page 78

of the local color to the shadow. The fact that the same formal devices serve to represent living and inanimate objects (the bull and the pitcher, the owl and the casserole) surely helps to account for the animation of this still life: the objects in it—we have spoken of a "stage" in discussing the drawing of 1919—seem to behave like the protagonists of a drama. This is particularly true of the candlestick in the center, whose burning flame—again with a shadow that is as animated as itself—is in fact something alive. There are related works in which objects as animated at this brass candlestick are so obviously treated as "figures" that we may wonder whether Picasso has not deliberately introduced anthropomorphic elements into his still life compositions. Picasso does not distinguish between animate and inanimate objects, and a pitcher can occasionally be more interesting and more "alive" to him than a human figure. He does not recognize a metaphysical hierarchy of objects.

We have analyzed a few comparative examples, each of them showing that in works produced in the same year Picasso used diametrically opposite means to solve related problems. His versatility is even so great that he can live in worlds far apart on the same day. For instance, on April 22, 1947, he executed a series of lithographs representing a flower in a drinking glass. Among them is a sheet executed with a very dry brush (page 104); using the subtlest intermediate tones, he renders the transparency and the reflections of the glass, the white of the flower and the delicate gray of the background. He gives us a complete interpretation of the optical appearance of the object, such as Manet gave us in his still life compositions. Another sheet offers an almost ornamental treatment in vigorous black-and-white (page 105): here the model is almost entirely dissolved. The height and roundness of the glass are indicated in the form of a seal, and the flower between the leaves has vanished; instead, the form as a whole suggests an ornamental flower. Impressionist and symbolist treatments are at Picasso's disposal on one and the same day, and he does not feel them incompatible, for there are transitions between the two. The various stages of the lithograph of the bull (pages 100–103) can be interpreted as such transitions: the first state can be derived from naturalism, the second from Expressionism, and the following ones from the various phases of Cubism. All these potentialities of various origins are latent in Picasso, ready to be summoned at any moment.

He chooses his formal principle with the same freedom in treating any subject whatsoever, including the human form and even the human face. It is understandable that persons unfamiliar with modern art should be most easily shocked at this point. They feel that a frivolous game is being carried on with something that is most sacred—man's likeness to God. To do justice to Picasso in this matter—and after all the aim of any unprejudiced student must be to arrive at a view adequately accounting for the artist's intentions—let us repeat that in his metaphysics man occupies no privileged position. Consequently, the human form is subject to the same artistic laws as all other forms. On this basis we are justified in taking offense at only those works in which the distortion of the model has not resulted in an artistically coherent structure, but in a caricature. But where Picasso has attained his autonomous, formal goal, and where the suggestions of the natural

*Flower in a Glass* page 104

*Flower in a Glass* page 105

*The Bull* pages 100–103

*Combat of Centaurs* (1946)

*Combat of Centaurs* (1946)

99

*The Bull* (December 5, 1945)

*The Bull* (December 18, 1945)

*The Bull* (December 22, 1945)

*The Bull* (December 24, 1945)

*The Bull* (December 26, 1945)

*The Bull* (January 2, 1946)

*The Bull* (January 5, 1946)

*The Bull* (January 17, 1946)

103

*Flower in a Glass* (April 22, 1947)

*Flower in a Glass* (April 22, 1947)

*The Black Bull* (1947)

form have only symbolic significance, nothing should hinder us from following him in his explorations.

In the light of these observations it would be quite possible to find examples of human representations more or less parallel in structure to the still life compositions discussed above. We have mentioned the voluminous objects in a still life dating from 1919 (page 78) which suggest a definite type of person: at that time Picasso actually painted ponderous and vigorously modeled figures (page 184). Similarly, we have examples of purely flat structures not only in such motifs as checkered clothes or harlequin masks, but also in faces composed of geometric, colored planes. In the head of the *Woman with a Hat* of 1935 (page 82), the painter, strange as it may seem, is interested in portraying a definite person. But he is no less interested in defining the formal elements that account for the fashionable appearance of this woman with long hair and an elegantly decorated little hat, and in expressing them as concisely as possible. The "line" of the fashion is suggested in the patterns and the arrangement of the various planes, without indication of naturalistic details. The fascination of this portrait derives primarily from the contrast between the concave "slenderizing" forms, which reduce the mass, and the convex forms suggesting the abundance of the hair and richness of the attire. The head, with its hat, is daintily balanced on the neck, perched on it like a decorative bird on a pole. Despite this artificial equilibrium the effect is not one of instability, because—in addition to the fact that the static conditions are analogous to those of a figure—the forms are securely connected with the picture plane. Almost nothing here reminds us of the natural human appearance (the eyes and the mouth are indicated in symbolic shorthand), and yet the function of the head in relation to the upper body, and the fashionable look are aptly rendered in a valid manner—one of many possible manners.

An entirely different paraphrase of the "head" motif is shown in the painting reproduced on page 83. "Seated Lady with Hat" would be misleading if taken too literally as a description of this picture. To be sure, those familiar with Picasso's language will easily identify the protruding upper part of the "head" as the nose with two nostrils at the bottom and one eye on top, with the second eye at the center of the larger segment to the right. They will also identify the ears, the hair, and the row of teeth between the lips in the lower part of the face above the chin. But all these identifications contribute little to our understanding. What is artistically convincing in this "head" is the consistency with which it is developed from twisted forms coiled like ropes, in accordance with their own inner laws. What has come into being in this way is a mysteriously alive, monstrous creature of an unknown species, whose visible features suggest organic unity. The round parts of the body, modeled by shadows in a warm reddish color, are contrasted with the greenish jagged planes of the hat against a dull blue background, and with the angular segments of the chair. But these chair segments are related to the "head" through their spatial effect and the interior lines which parallel the forms of the head. They are also related to the violet-blue convex basis of the figure, which is excellently balanced despite the asymmetric arrangement of the planes composing it. We have before us a being which does not exist in the

*Harlequin* Cl. Cat. 78

*Woman with a Hat*
page 82

*Female Figure* page 83

nature we know, and which strives for its own perfection in accordance with a norm invented by the artist.

Picasso can also render facial expression even while disregarding the natural relationship of the features. In the *Guernica* studies (page 237) the large curved eyes with peculiar featherlike eyebrows diverge to such an extent that each must be considered separately. The upper eye glances upward with fear; the other eye looks downward with an expression of vague horror. The form of the eyes is repeated in a reduced scale in the nostrils, which are also arranged irregularly. The second main vehicle of expression is the mouth, whose bared rows of teeth suggest a vulnerable openness. The stunted forehead, ear, and neck suggest that the woman awaiting her fate here is exposed to the utmost physical danger. The curious straight lines ending with spherical drops cut into the living organism like sharp instruments. Some abstract drawings dating from the twenties, which had been used as illustrations for Balzac's *Unknown Masterpiece* (page 31), recur here, now invested with a fearful meaning: we are compelled to interpret the drops as tears. However unfamiliar the individual forms may be, here they clearly express intense human emotions.

The range of expression that Picasso achieves by pure linear drawing can be illustrated by two sheets in each of which he invents a special system. The faded, wrinkled face of a very aged woman (page 56) emerges from an tangle of curved and broken lines, seemingly thrown pell-mell like threads on the floor of a tailor's workshop. In this drawing as well as in the penciled *Head of a Girl* dated July 5, 1946 (page 57), the resultant form transcends the means used and leads us back to nature. An almost classically regular face suggested by a few sure strokes is surrounded by a graphic ornamentation consisting of long spirals, which the beholder's imagination comes gradually to interpret as a soft mass of hair. And we waver between this charming illusion and the temptation to glide along the harmonious, continuous lines which suggest the curves traced by a skater. The two possible ways of looking at this picture clash unexpectedly at the left, where one of the spirals cuts across the eyes and the eyebrows. If supreme mastery consists in achieving the maximum effect with the minimum of means, we may properly apply this term here.

## Early Years in Barcelona and Paris

Some art historians attach exaggerated importance to the national characteristics revealed in a given work of art; others dismiss them altogether on the ground that genius transcends national boundaries. It is, however, undeniable, as was shown by Jean Cassou and other writers, that Picasso's Spanish extraction accounts for some essential features of his art. Picasso was stimulated by old Spanish masterpieces and by contemporary Spanish painters; his Spanish racial heritage is an integral component of his art throughout its transformations. That is why his works are so clearly different from related French works, for instance, those of Braque. Although France has been his chosen homeland for several decades, although French art has influenced him more than any other, and although without it he would never have been what he is, he cannot seriously be classified as a French artist. Actually Picasso is a global artist; although he springs from a specific nation and remains bound to it, he has predominantly been formed by other forces, and by virtue of the universality of his art he belongs to the world as a whole. That is precisely why it is particularly fascinating to discover the national sources of his unique richness. For even in his very earliest works, he reveals not only his extraordinary gifts, but also his unmistakable Spanish characteristics which later recur in a thousand forms.

Pablo Ruiz Picasso was born in Málaga on October 25, 1881. His father was a teacher in the local art school (after 1901, Pablo used only the family name of his mother, Maria Picasso, as is often done in Spain). In 1891 the Ruiz Picassos moved to La Coruña in Galicia, and in 1895 to Barcelona. Only a few of Picasso's Barcelona paintings are known; among them is an oil of 1895, today in the museum of Málaga, showing an old couple in a kitchen. The theme is social, and the treatment naturalistic, but although the fourteen-year-old author is confined to the contemporary idiom, he reveals amazing technical skill. At that time the boy served as an assistant to his father who specialized in compositions representing birds and flowers; he would cut off the legs of a dead pigeon and pin them on a board, and Pablo copied them minutely. To this day Picasso has retained a love for pigeons, which he inherited

*The Artist's Mother*
page 42
*Portrait of Uncle
Baldomero Chiara*
Cl. Cat. 1

from his father, and he kept pigeons in his studio in the Rue des Grands-Augustins in Paris. The boy's sure touch and miniature-like accuracy in reproducing natural forms are particularly evident in his chalk drawings from casts. His drawings of arms and legs, for instance (page 353), are comparable to similar things by one of the greatest naturalistic draftsmen, Adolf Menzel: they disclose the same obsession with detail, which endows his representations of objects with a demonic animation. In 1896 the fourteen-year-old artist was so competent that he took only one day to pass the entrance test for the Academy of Fine Arts, Barcelona, although the regulations allowed a whole month for this task.

The half-length portrait of an old beggar (page 356) dating from that time discloses advanced technical skill. There is no doubt that in this as in other related early paintings Picasso was inspired by the great paintings of Velazquez, such as the famous *Water Seller of Seville*. That is the source of the magnificently realistic rendering of the shining skin, the tidy hair, and the coarse clothing of his model, as well as of the generous, broad brushwork vigorously juxtaposing lights and shadows, which stresses the momentary quality of the figure, and largely contributes to the serious concentrated expression. On the other hand, nothing in this picture suggests imitation, let alone copying: like Picasso's later works, even this youthful painting is characterized by the extraordinary intensity of his own effort. And like all his paintings inspired by historical models, this one reveals a mind that consumes the thing seen in the fire of enthusiasm and re-creates it from the ashes as something new that belongs to Picasso alone. It is therefore not surprising that he has often recognized his paternity of such early works by signing them later. The various extant still life compositions dating from 1895, which seems to have been a particularly fruitful year for him, display the same broad naturalism reminiscent of the old masters. The contemporary portraits of various members of his family (page 355) moreover display such profound psychological insight that we are deeply moved when we realize that their author had then scarcely emerged from childhood. Particularly striking is the expression of inner torment in the portrait of the father (page 354), who at that time pined for his native Andalusia and led a withdrawn life after handing over his brush and paints to his young successor. Picasso also used his father as a model for the figure of the doctor in *Science and Charity*, showing a doctor and a nurse beside a hospital bed. This conventional genre painting, executed in his first studio in Barcelona, earned him an honorable mention in Madrid in 1897. An earlier painting showing a bayonet fight, which caused a sensation among Pablo's friends, has not come down to us in any form.

Such great gifts were scarcely compatible with the academic teaching of the time, which confined the student to a secure routine. Thus we may presume that even if he had not fallen ill with scarlet fever, he would not have stayed at the particularly conservative Royal Academy of Madrid, where he was admitted with distinction in 1897. He spent a few months there in 1897 and 1898, and then returned to Barcelona. The following summer, which he spent as a convalescent in the village of Horta de Ebro, was particularly beneficial: during that time he entered into a close union with unsophisticated nature, which

became a constant source of energy for him. In that early period, however, he still needed the stimulation of friends and city life, which brought him into close contact with the passionate intellectual and artistic currents of his time.

Barcelona, jealous of its special position as capital of Catalonia, was at that time far more advanced culturally than Madrid. Its literary and artistic Bohemia, which was anything but provincial, maintained close relations with Paris groups, and through these was in contact with the great international Bohemia in other European capitals. Like the Bohemians of Paris, Oslo, Berlin, or London, those of Barcelona were attracted by various contemporary movements—ivory-tower aestheticism, mysticism, humanitarian socialism, and philosophic anarchism; the latter was also nourished by the Catalan aspirations for independence. As elsewhere, a new young generation was up in arms against the "barbarians," as the Philistines were called in Barcelona, and by its eccentric and irresponsible behavior conjured up the spirit of the world cataclysm that was lurking in the background.

When Picasso returned from Madrid to Barcelona, the artistic headquarters of the local Bohemia was the recently founded cabaret *Els Quatre Gats* (The Four Cats); patterned after the more famous *Chat noir* in Paris, it combined a bar, a restaurant, and a small stage. In 1898 the young Pablo, who still signed his name P. Ruiz Picasso, documented his close association with this meeting place of artists by a colored pen drawing for the restaurant menu, which is a typical early *Art Nouveau* production, and which reflects the young artist's interest in Japanese colored woodcuts. However, his friends of *Els Quatre Gats*, whose portraits he drew on the walls of the cabaret as early as 1897, led him also along other paths, more fruitful for the future of his art.

In 1891 two painters belonging to this group—the versatile Santiago Rusiñol, who also distinguished himself as a playwright, and Ramón Casas, had imported Impressionism from France. Ramón Casas was also a draftsman in the manner of Toulouse-Lautrec, who thus entered Picasso's line of vision even before his trip to Paris. For some time he associated with the painter Isidre Nonell; Carlos Casagemas and Sebastián Junyer were among his intimates. More lasting than his associations with these painters was his friendship with the writer Jaime Sabartés who, decades later, published a valuable book containing a vivid account of those early days. He tells us for instance about the tremendous passion for work that distinguished Picasso even then. He covered the walls of his and his friend's rooms with paintings, and produced drawings in such quantities that he could use them as fuel for his stove. Only a small fraction is preserved; among these, *Promenade*, a chalk drawing dating from 1897 (page 357), clearly reflects French influences: the subject matter is elegant and fashionable; the vigorous black-and-white, flat treatment combined with an illusion of depth suggests Manet, and the loose composition is reminiscent of Degas and Toulouse-Lautrec. Picasso's drawing most resembles Toulouse-Lautrec's contemporary lithographs. But a closer study of sheets in which Toulouse-Lautrec treats related subjects, and which are characterized by floating lightness, immaterial fragrance, and the dance-like animation and delicacy of intermediate tones, shows that

*Promenade* page 357

*Portrait of a Woman*
Cl. Cat. 11
*Nude* Cl. Cat. 14

Picasso is quite different: the sharp outline of the clothing, which has a hard and plastic quality, and the closed forms of the hat feathers are quite un-French. On the basis of such features Pablo's later Parisian works in the style of Toulouse-Lautrec can be distinguished at once from the latter's own.

In addition to fashionable society, two other frequently overlapping subjects fascinated the young painter in Barcelona—the everyday life of the street, and the relations between the sexes. Both were popular in *Els Quatre Gats* as generally among Bohemians. In his treatment of them Picasso was certainly influenced by French art, but here again a comparison clearly reveals his originality. As early as 1890 there appeared in Paris a two-volume work under the programmatic title *Dans la rue:* it contained texts by Aristide Bruant, cabaret star immortalized by Toulouse-Lautrec, and once famous for his ballads written in argot, and lithographs by Théophile Alexandre Steinlen, who had been connected with the *Chat noir* since 1885. Félix Valotton, too, a Swiss closely associated with the Nabis since 1890, portrayed Paris street life with its graceful trivialities and its frequent little joys and sorrows. To the unsentimental objectivity of these artists whose works were surely well known in Barcelona, Picasso added the spice of a truly unmerciful, sarcastic observation, particularly in his figures of women.

*The Divan* page 358

He reveals a similar ruthlessness in representing the importunate and greedy lover in the vivid drawing *The Divan*, of 1900 (page 358), and in portraying the skimpy furnishings—on the bare table a solitary bottle from which the man has drawn courage; over the sofa, next to the oval mirror, a half nude, displaying a pair of breasts; in the doorway, near the border, the blurred figure of the matron. The awkwardness of the couple that cannot elude their fate is seen almost with the eyes of Goya; the effective chiaroscuro is also reminiscent of Goya. Looking at this drawing we can understand why a short time later the young Picasso was nicknamed *"le petit Goya"* in Paris, while the Catalans referred to him as "the young Andalusian." One glance at Toulouse-Lautrec's colored lithograph *Débauche*, treating the same subject with a lascivious elegance, is sufficient to reveal the freshness of the eighteen-year-old Spaniard's realism. The inexorable young psychologist who penetrated into the dens of vice did not shrink from encounters with insanity, as we can see in the charcoal drawing of a madwoman with a vacant and hungry look in her large eyes, published in the magazine *Catalunya Artistica* in 1900. This drawing already heralds the so-called Blue Period.

Note 3

In 1900 Picasso also dedicated a sheet to free love, a favorite subject of the international Bohemia. It was published as an illustration to a poem by Joan Oliva Bridgman, in the Barcelona magazine *Joventut*. In the foreground is seated a sleeping girl with a nude torso and a veil-like cloth on her lap; from the dark background emerge the outlines of the head and the torso of a nude man. The girl's vision is intended to express the violence of her unquenched yearning. Here Picasso's world comes into contact with that of the great Norwegian Edvard Munch, who rendered the demonic side of erotic relationships in expressive allegories: at the turn of the century Picasso and Munch produced many similar pieces.

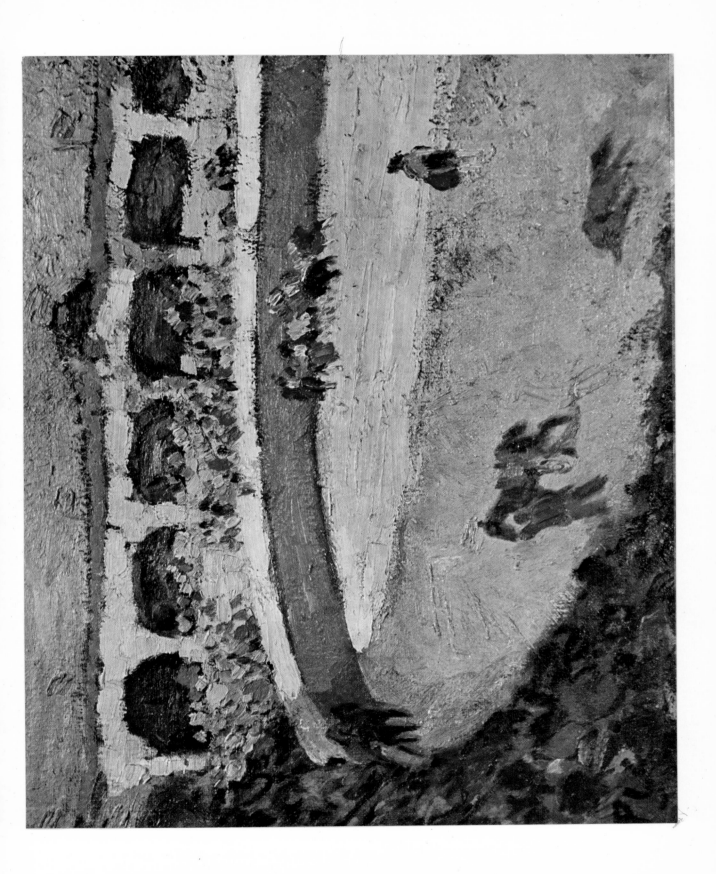

We find the most striking instance of this parallelism when we compare Munch's woodcut *The Kiss* in its various versions dating from 1897 to 1902, with Picasso's charcoal drawing of 1901, *The Embrace* (page 360). Both works show erect, embracing figures progressively merging into a single closed, dark form, and their faces into a single light spot. Picasso's drawing is the result of several preliminary sketches. These begin with a pen drawing of a pair, dressed in middle-class fashion, in intimate conversation in the street (page 359); then the scene is transferred to a popular milieu in a suburb, and the figures are shown clasping each other in their arms; the final sober drawing succeeds in conveying a sense of an unbreakable union, enhanced by the expression of momentary passion which, in conjunction with the dramatic black-and-white, once again reminds us of Goya's etchings. And, as is often the case with Picasso, a few years later he treated the same motif in different media—in the gouache, *The Embrace*, showing a nude couple leaning on each other (page 361), and then in the corresponding painting, *La joie pure*, both dating from 1903. Here too we are reminded of a Munch etching of 1895. Because the painting is based on old experiences, its earthiness is in striking contrast to the emaciated figures belonging to the later period.

*The Embrace* page 360

*Couple on the Street* page 359

*The Embrace* page 361

Further similarities might easily be discovered in the way both Munch and Picasso subordinate form and color to symbolic expression; but this affinity is probably accounted for by the cultural climate of Europe at that time. On the other hand, Picasso could scarcely be entirely unacquainted with the works of Munch, who was in close contact with the Paris artists. Cirici Pellicer in his book on Picasso's early years shows in detail that northern literature and art were well known in Picasso's milieu in Barcelona. Schopenhauer's and Nietzsche's philosophies, Ibsen's, Wilde's, and Maeterlinck's plays and poems, and Richard Wagner's music dramas—*Tristan* and *Siegfried* were performed in Barcelona in 1900—impressed the Catalan elite as much as did Rossetti's Pre-Raphaelite paintings and Burne-Jones' or Böcklin's ardent and mysterious mythologies; and *Joventut* even published a special issue in honor of the twenty-year-old Heinrich Vogeler, who settled at Worpswede in 1894. The Promethean and visionary qualities of the Germans were in particular accord with the anarchistic instincts of the young Spaniards and with their romantic predilection for the Gothic Middle Ages. As regards Picasso's development, one is inclined to think that his contacts with German culture yielded their richest fruit only in the Blue Period, after his eyes and mind had come to know the treasures of French art in Paris.

In the fall of 1900 Picasso set out for his longed-for Paris; the trip was paid for by his family, who did not tell him that they had used their last savings for this purpose. He was accompanied by his friend Carlos Casagemas, who a short time later committed suicide because of a woman. What Picasso painted and drew in Paris was not too different from his previous works. He found the fascinating decadence of Toulouse-Lautrec's world confirmed, and in his own Spanish way paid tribute to the great Impressionists with his *Moulin de la Galette*. On Christmas he was back home, with an unquenchable longing in his heart.

*The Ballerina* Cl. Cat. 9
*At the Café* Cl. Cat. 12

In the spring of 1901 he again tried his luck in Madrid, i. e., he attempted to inject new blood into the somewhat anemic Madrid Bohemia, for instance, by contributing drawings to the newly founded *Arte Joven (Young Art)*. This magazine ceased publication soon after Picasso left Barcelona for Paris in the summer of 1901. This time, as before, Picasso, who had not yet learned French, associated chiefly with congenial Spanish friends, among them the painter Sebastián Junyer-Vidal of whom he did several portraits, the sculptor Pablo Gargallo to whom we owe the excellent bronze portrait of the young Picasso, and Julio González whose wrought iron sculptures inspired Picasso much later. While forming his literary taste by reading Mallarmé, Verlaine, and Rimbaud, he diligently studied not only the Impressionists, such as Manet, Renoir, Degas, and Toulouse-Lautrec, but also Van Gogh and Gauguin, Maurice Denis, and Edouard Vuillard—in brief all the painters of the Paris school of the day—displaying his amazing gift of assimilation. His first exhibition at Vollard's took place as early as June. Its lack of success is understandable: at that time his uncommon artistic abilities had not yet become crystallized into a convincing personal idiom.

The technique of these paintings of 1901 shown at that first exhibition in Paris accurately reflects the corresponding phase of French painting, Post-Impressionism, which revels in color; Maurice Raynal characterized the efforts of this school as "mining exhausted shafts." In 1900, when Picasso encountered this somewhat tired art, it had behind it the experiments of Divisionism (splitting of colors) and Pointillism (technique of dots). The painters still avoided linear contours, but the larger patches of color again belonged unmistakably to objects, e. g., as the ornament of tapestries or fabrics; the selected colors were partly vigorous, partly sugary and stylized. That was, for instance, Pierre Bonnard's manner around 1900; it is also Picasso's in his bullfight pictures, and others such as the *Girl with Pigeon*, the *Attente*—a half-length figure of a rouged prostitute staring at the beholder—or the portrait of *Bibi la Purée*, as the model was known in the Latin Quarter (page 111), with its touch of caricature reminiscent of Picasso's earlier portraits of his comrades of *Els Quatre Gats*. Particularly fascinating from a coloristic point of view is the *Danseuse naine* who stands close to the footlights, à la Degas, in her cinnabar-red, green-belted ballet dress, her pale lavender stockings, and her high black coiffure above the repulsive smiling face. This figure is placed against a background consisting of a firework of broad, mottled dots.

Whereas here the artist's delight in exposing ugliness once again reveals the "little Goya," his original, un-French taste is manifested in other paintings only by his predilection for blue-green tones. Even in pastels executed with the Degas pastel technique and representing cabaret singers in the manner of Toulouse-Lautrec, the details unmistakably reflect the Spaniard's taste for sharp and harsh outlines and clashing colors. One of the paintings of 1901, most important historically—one which also suggests a comparison with Degas and the Nabis—represents the studio he then occupied on Boulevard de Clichy. This interior, with its bathing nude, is called *The Bathtub* or *The Blue Room*. The furniture with a rug and blankets, and the flowers on the table, remind us of the charming motifs treated by the "intimist" Vuillard;

the woman standing in the bathtub, and her surroundings evoke a typical Degas situation. The Toulouse-Lautrec poster on the wall showing the clown-dancer May Milton, which Picasso is said to have removed from a wall on Montmartre, points to Picasso's own experiments with posters. But even though this painting suggests familiar comparisons, it strikes a new note: the objects are rigid, the texture is cool, the figure seems almost deformed, the space lacks warm breath; the temperature is determined by the predominant blue tone. This painting stands at the threshold of a new stage of development, in which Picasso for the first time freely unfolded his energies as a master in his own domain.

## The Blue Period

The so-called Blue Period of Picasso begins early in the winter of 1901 and ends late in 1904. The relative uniformity of the works falling under this designation is all the more remarkable because the artist's life during those years was particularly unsettled: he frequently changed his place of residence, and was engaged in a hard struggle for existence. At the end of 1901 he returned to Barcelona; in 1902, late in the summer, he attempted to conquer Paris for the third time (in the interval other exhibitions of his work took place there). But he was soon again penniless, and was forced to share a small hotel room with his friend, the poet Max Jacob. Early in 1903 Max Jacob too found himself in straitened circumstances, and Picasso was forced to return to Barcelona. He worked there until the spring of 1904 when he went to Paris for the fourth time, finally succeeding in gaining a permanent foothold there. He moved to the famous *Bateau-lavoir* ("floating laundry"), a drab Montmartre tenement at 13 Rue Ravignan, now 13 Place Émile-Goudeau, where he lived until 1909 with struggling young writers and painters as his closest neighbors. Fernande Olivier has given us an account of those often desperately difficult years when his genius blossomed; she vividly evokes the small, vigorous, continually restless, and curiously fascinating Spaniard amidst his friends. At no other time in Picasso's long career was his life so closely interwoven with his art as in those years when he portrayed human misery in classical works reflecting his belief that art is born of sadness and suffering.

The typical works of the Blue Period are devoid of lively colors: they are almost in monochrome—cool, passive, earthenware-blue has supplanted all the more active colors except for an occasional ghostly oxide-green. The most various hypotheses have been advanced as to the origin of this infinitely desolate blue. It is sometimes traced back to influences of other paintings; sometimes physiological or psychological explanations are offered.

The main reason why Picasso at that time chose blue as his dominant color lies probably in its negative value and its otherworldly symbolism, which are in perfect accord with the expressive form of the paintings.

These wretched figures emaciated by hunger and vice are unthinkable in any other than this sorrowful tonality, which seems to be one of their attributes. The color in no small measure transports these outcasts to an idealized realm in which they are no longer beggars, prostitutes, or mental cases, and are surrounded by an invisible aura of martyrdom that restores their innocence. The painter has evidently been chastened by his own experience: his earlier irreverent and critical attitude toward society has yielded to one of deep compassion for suffering mankind. For the same reason, large individualized figures now dominate the foreground. The aim is to give heroic stature to a social class that previous art portrayed only realistically. A Degas laundress is a social type, an ordinary woman who does her work industriously; a Picasso laundress is a martyr of society who deserves respect. A Degas absinthe drinker is a sensual woman who finds a measure of happiness in her addiction; a Picasso absinthe drinker is a sufferer surrendered to mysterious powers, who cannot be judged by earthly standards. With such paintings Picasso became the heir of Van Gogh, whose *Berceuse* was also intended as a kind of lay image of a saint.

*Seller of Mistletoe*
Cl. Cat. 21

*Célestine* page 121

In *The Glass of Beer*, a portrait of Jaime Sabartés dating from 1901 (page 364), which is one of the earliest paintings of the Blue Period, the influence of Gauguin and Van Gogh is clearly discernible. The spatial effect is subordinated to a purely two-dimensional order; the ascetic absence of all pictorial attractions, the economy of means which enhances the expression of inwardness point directly to Van Gogh. As for the composition, particularly characteristic are the concentrated compact forms tied together within a closed outline, and the deformations which are partly caused by the absence of spatial perspective. These deformations, however, serve expressive purposes, as in the flexible, wristless hand holding the beer glass. The sober colors—the jacket is dark blue against a blue background, the hair is dull brown, the glass is gray—are entirely in keeping with the austere forms, and heighten the expression of genuine purity. Sabartés has told us how this portrait came to be painted. One evening, while waiting for his friends in the Café La Lorraine near the Musée de Cluny, Sabartés fell into a reverie, from which he was suddenly aroused by the voices of Picasso and his companions. It is that moment when he surprised his friend in the café that the painter later recorded in a canvas, which Sabartés describes as "the specter of his solitude."

*The Glass of Beer*
(*Jaime Sabartés*)
page 364

The humanitarian ethos and formal qualities of this personal style proved particularly suitable for a subject that Picasso treated several times in 1901 and 1902—maternal love. In portraying the union of mother and child he came closer than ever to sentimentalism and a kind of empty monumentality which, in contrast to the portrait of Sabartés, he also expressed with plastic means. It has been correctly observed that the style of these paintings is related to that of Jean François Millet, in whose works we often find a similar mixture of social morality and religiously colored feeling. The most characteristic canvas of this group is *Mother and Child*, 1901, from the Bernheim Jeune collection (page 363), showing a Madonna-like woman seated in a simple wooden chair on a beach, kissing a standing child on the forehead. The figure of the child is entirely within the outline of the mother's drapery and her

*Mother and Child*
Cl. Cat. 17

*Mother and Child*
page 363

inclined head; and the softness of this outline is stressed by the vertical forms of the dark chair. The child's long white dress roughly reveals the curves of her body; the mother's garment is articulated in a few wide heavy folds forming a kind of garland. The beach, the sea, and the sky, comparable to the color zones of Romanesque murals, compose the background; however, except for the flesh-colored figures, the beach, the brownish chair, and the apple held by the child, everything is in blue tones. Although nothing in this picture—not even the basket with needlework in the lower corner—forces us to give it a religious meaning, nothing in it hinders us from interpreting it as an image of the Virgin Mary.

*La Vie* page 366

It has been historically established that Picasso was for a time influenced by the religious symbolism of the Nabi Maurice Denis, who in turn had been influenced by Gauguin. Picasso also paid tribute to the secularized philosophical symbolism of the world-wide *Art Nouveau* movement in *La Vie*, a large vertical canvas dating from 1903 (page 366). A barefoot woman is seen standing at the right, her serious face in profile, with a sleeping infant in the folds of her draped garment. At the left stand the graceful nude of a young couple, seeking each other's protection as though suddenly frightened; the man is larger, with the high forehead of an intellectual, the tender woman is all devotion. They face the mother but their glance is turned inward; engrossed in their own destiny, they do not see her, although the index finger of the man's sensitive left hand points emphatically to the child. Behind the foreground figures we see two painted studies: the lower one shows a squatting nude lost in a reverie; the upper one, a seated couple whose attitude echoes that of the couple standing in the foreground.

Note 4

This composition has been variously interpreted. A psychoanalyst has related the "Paradise Lost" mood of the couple to Picasso's impending, definitive departure from his Spanish homeland to his Paris "exile." But Paris certainly had no such negative connotation for the young painter. Nor did his personal poverty contribute to the social attitude expressed here any more than in other paintings. The interpretation of the mother's sorrowful expression as hostility toward her undesirable offspring is refuted by the peaceful expression of the child and by Picasso's other paintings treating the subject of maternal love. What is undeniable, however, is that the picture reflects a pessimistic view of society: it stresses the opposition between the completeness of the biological cycle on the one hand, and the distortion of this cycle through the forces of civilization, on the other. The couple that longs for consummation in a child is confronted with motherhood as a social burden. This casts a shadow on sexual love, which becomes tainted by fear and a sense of rejection, by that terror before instinctual forces which also characterizes Munch's couples of lovers. The ghostly blue locates the allegorical scene in a far-off, shadowy realm.

Picasso's friends unanimously emphasize the extraordinary intensity, rapidity, and trance-like raptures that marked his work in the Blue Period: significantly, most of the time he painted at night. The following excerpt from *Picasso: An Intimate Portrait*, by Sabartés, may serve, as an illustration:

"I generally found him in the middle of the studio, not far from the stove, seated on a dilapidated chair, perhaps lower than an ordinary

*The Bath* (1905)

*Head of a Woman* (1905)

*Seated Woman* (1906)

*Head of a Woman* (1905/6)

128

chair, because discomfort does not bother him and he seems even to prefer it as if he delighted in self-mortification and enjoyed subjecting his spirit to tortures so long as they spur him on. The canvas was placed on the lowest part of the easel, and this compelled him to paint in an almost kneeling position.

"He filled up the canvas thinking only about freeing himself of what was seething within. He always hears everything that is said around him, sees what is going on on every side, and divines what he cannot see; yet nothing distracts him except that which is expressly called to his attention. He is never so wholly absorbed in his work as to become oblivious of his surroundings. In the midst of inspiration his spirit remains in a state of alertness. When his tenacious glance leaves the canvas it is only for an instant, and even during that interval he does not remove it entirely from what he is doing. Even when he is attending to his palette, he goes on contemplating the picture from a corner of his eye. The canvas and palette compete for his attention which does not abandon either; both remain within the focus of his vision, which embraces the totality of each, and both together. He surrenders body and soul to the activity which is his *raison d'être*, dabbing the bristles of the brush in the oily paste of color with a loving gesture, with all his senses focused upon a single aim, as if he were bewitched. So absorbed and so thoroughly wrapped in silence is Picasso when he paints that whoever sees him, whether at close range or from afar, understands and keeps silent. The subdued murmur which the distant street sends into the studio serves as a background to the silence scarcely broken by the creakings of the chair which supports the weight of his body, agitated by his creative fever. The ear can perceive the sound of the passage of the brush across the canvas."                    Note 5

The people of the Blue Period, their metaphysical essence and their formal stylization, reflect the deep influence of old Spanish art on the young Picasso. Even prior to 1900, his concern with Gothic sculpture manifested itself occasionally in his elongated, disembodied figures, and in his emphasis on expression; and he certainly knew the medieval Catalan frescoes now in the museum of Barcelona. He was thus naturally attracted by El Greco whose Mannerism springs from medieval roots and embodies the highest pictorial qualities. Picasso had an early opportunity to become acquainted with the works of this great Spanish painter, who was rediscovered not in Madrid or Toledo, but in Catalonia. Miguel Utrillo (adoptive father of the French painter), a critic who belonged to the *Els Quatre Gats* group, was the first prophet of El Greco's fame, and a monument to him was erected in the little town of Sitges as early as 1897. It seems, however, that only in 1901, when he saw El Greco's masterpieces in Toledo, did Picasso become genuinely interested in him. His enthusiasm for this magician continued far beyond the Blue Period. Even in 1912, an El Greco was hung in a place of honor in the Picasso room at the *Sonderbund* Exhibition in Cologne.

El Greco's programmatic significance consists in this, that his example encouraged the young painter to free himself from servitude to naturalism and to place artistic expression above formal "truth," Greco also helped him to disregard realistic coloring—this is one of the essential features of the Blue Period. The extent to which he was inspired by his great model as regards details can be seen in paintings such as the *Old Guitarist* of 1903, or the water color sketch of the *Madman* of 1904 (page 367). The gaunt forms of the tattered beggar are realistic. The ruthless deformations of the figure in favor of expressive effect in his paintings are even more striking. But the ascetic type and particularly the oversized sensitive hands and feet directly remind us of figures such as El Greco's *John the Baptist.* The fluid, soft light on the surface of the figure and the greater interest in psychological—in this case pathological—features, are further elements of affinity with the great Toledan.

During the first decades of the twentieth century El Greco became the patron saint of Expressionist and all non-naturalistic painting, and the tendency of the Blue Period can be roughly reduced to this European common denominator. It would not be difficult to compare a composition such as the magnificent etching of 1904, showing a blind man and his companion and known as *The Frugal Repast* (page 368), with Expressionist works by painters of various countries, and to discover that they have fundamental traits in common. But all this would not bring us closer to understanding Picasso's unique contribution. At that time he followed a solitary path: his degenerately fragile, morbidly sensitive, and dolefully knowing figures were seemingly outside the general trend of contemporary French painting. For instance, he paid no attention to the emergence of the Fauves in 1905 and their struggle for a new form. Still, we find Spanish analogies to Picasso which are not accidental. There is for instance the sculptor Carlo Mani, whose main opus, *The Degenerates*, falls within that period; and there is Antonio Gaudí, the brilliant builder of the Barcelona cathedral, who ventured a kind of Expressionism in architecture, and who is even said to have gone through a Blue Period of his own around 1906. Gaudí's artistic independence certainly encouraged Picasso in his solitary and dangerous path.

The *Frugal Repast* mentioned above perhaps gives us a better idea of the outstanding technical mastery Picasso had in the meantime achieved than the paintings whose tone- and light-values he perfectly transposed here into black-and-white. Only a comparison with Pisanello's drawing of *Luxuria* in Vienna, who looks just as consumptive as the female figure in Picasso's etching, will do justice to its great graphic excellence. The eloquent hands in this print perfectly illustrate Sabartés' sensitive description: "... the hands in Picasso's blue work seem to seek one another's warmth. Some are outstretched as if the finger tips wished to touch what they are reaching for, hands that denote fear and throb with anxiety; some timid, others frozen with cold, others astir as if to banish solitude."

## The Rose Period

What is usually designated as the Rose Period of Picasso extends
from the end of 1904 to his first Cubist experiments in 1907. The name
is evidently meant to suggest an analogy with the preceding Blue
Period, but the Rose Period cannot be demarcated as clearly as the
other (in fact, according to some writers it begins in the second half
of 1905) nor do the works produced during it display the same characteristic uniformity as those of the Blue Period. In his basic monograph
on Picasso, Alfred H. Barr, Jr., does not follow the usual classification;
and he deserves special credit for having distinguished the various
developmental stages within the Rose Period, most of them covering
no more than six months, and also for having established their correct
chronological sequence. We shall nevertheless retain the usual designation here, not merely because it has become customary, but because it
actually has a certain symbolic significance. In the first place, Picasso's
material well-being improved at that time, and as a result of his growing
success he began to discover the brighter aspects of life. The stimulating circle of friends from the *Bateau-lavoir* was enriched by, among
others, the young Spanish painter Juan Gris and the poet Guillaume
Apollinaire, who encouraged Picasso on his path toward self-liberation.
At the same time, collectors like the American writer Gertrude Stein
and the Russian merchant Sergei Shchukin, who bought many of
Picasso's works (these were later placed in the Museum of Western
Modern Art in Moscow), encouraged him by their interest and financial
help. Finally, the transition from the shadow-like blue to warmer,
positive colors also marks a change in the artist's attitude toward his
work. During his Blue Period Picasso had striven to express his inner-
most feelings; between 1905 and 1907, as his palette became neutralized
and acquired a more positive tonality, this subjective approach yielded
increasingly to objective expression. His effort to eliminate subjective
moods from his paintings led him gradually to Cubism.

During the last months of 1904 and the first half of 1905, Picasso
produced a group of works that are closely related even from a purely
thematic point of view: all of them treat the world of acrobats or
saltimbanques. They belong to what Barr calls the "Circus Period."

*also called "Circus Period"*

*Guillaume Apollinaire*
page 13

*Clown on Horseback*
Cl. Cat. 25
*Family with Monkey*
page 11

131

We know from Fernande Olivier with what enthusiasm Picasso frequented the Medrano circus at that time. Feats of physical skill which become an "art"—whether it be bullfighting, boxing, or the Russian ballet—have always stimulated his creative imagination. In addition the circus offered the illusionary reality of the footlights and the heady smell of horses and wild animals. But we cannot say that the paintings and drawings of 1905 convey much of this. They occasionally show an athlete lifting a girl high in the air, a child juggling balls, or a rider pirouetting on a horse, but by far the greater number of these works represent circus people in intimate attitudes reflecting their family life. Like the outcasts of the Blue Period, the acrobats are characterized by a slender, fragile physique, this time as a prerequisite of their trade, and by a melancholy seriousness, sign of a heightened awareness of their dangerous and futile occupation.

The central figure in these works is the harlequin with the two-cornered hat and checkered costume; he is usually represented as a passive onlooker with a gentle and doleful facial expression. This figure appears standing and watching a woman at her toilette or bathing a child (page 125), or seated as one of a group which includes a monkey with a noble and intelligent animal face. An acrobat's close friendship with a dog in still another picture expresses the sympathy obtaining between all living creatures, which is emphasized in this group of works. Only rarely do the figures enter into active relationships, even in the largest canvas of the group, *The Saltimbanques*, now in the National Gallery of Art, Washington, D.C. (page 369), which enjoys particular fame because Rilke refers to it in the fifth of his *Duino Elegies*. Because the figures in these paintings are self-enclosed or arranged in loose groups, they leave much scope for interpretation, and there is danger of reading too much in these groupings. At all events, as representatives of a humanity that has become insecure in its very foundations, the acrobats who escape from solitude only by trusting each other are of a deeply moving symbolism. These compositions, which seem to reflect Picasso's predilection for Puvis de Chavannes, mark the culmination of his tendency to linear expression, which was clearly marked even in his Blue Period, and which brought him into open opposition with his Fauve contemporaries, and their emphasis on color. At that time he occupied a lonely outpost, from which he was gradually to conquer unknown or forgotten realms of the line.

Among the compositions representing harlequin families, some take up again the subject of maternal love; the figures of mother and child now display a tender, moving humanity, free from the social anxiety and symbolic alienation of the Blue Period. This is especially true of a study dating from 1905 (page 371), showing an infant at the breast of a slender but earthy mother, who still has some of the physical characteristics of the women of the older period—a narrow head, angular shoulders, pendulous breasts, flexible hands, and long sensitive fingers. These features no longer denote morbidity, but a lofty, noble sensibility: in brief, their effect is positive. This is in no small measure achieved by the new coloring: the flesh has a warmer tone, which is stressed by the dull rose drapery covering the mother's arms and the infant's body. This color recurs with greater vigor in the pink flower and in the black, helmet-like coiffure where it appears side by side with a very strong

Picasso
1905

sapphire blue, whose radiant potency is no longer broken by decaying greens. The whole blue background, even where it is clouded, no longer relegates the luminous rose figure to a frosty inferno, but serves as a magnificent foil for her ethereal, humanly transfigured forms. In all the works of this period the warm tones break victoriously through the cool. This can be observed, for instance, in a marvelously delicate still life of 1905 (page 372). The horizontal canvas shows a table covered by a dove-blue cloth; the vessels on it, in a severe arrangement, are all seen in profile; a vigorously warm brown teapot is placed between a small jade-green cup and a violet-gray bottle. At the extreme right a blue box ornamented in a warm glittering gold stands next to white and light-gray vessels. Set off against the beige background we see a white drawing sheet and a small painting with a cool gold frame representing a woman in a dark-green and madder-lake Spanish costume. This description may suggest the subdued colors of the composition, which displays all degrees between coolness and warmth, and which, for all the differences in technique, is not unworthy of the similarly counterpointed mature still life compositions of the great Velazquez.

*Still Life with Picture*
page 372

In the summer of 1905 Picasso visited Holland. As a result of his contact with that country's naturalistic tradition his painting entered a new stage. The finest fruits of this period are the various studies for a projected large canvas, *The Watering Place*, showing nude youths and horses. The last, lingering vestiges of fragile overbreeding have now been eliminated from the figures: the boys are elastically built, energetically outlined, and sure of their movements. A healthy, hardened generation, with oval heads and clipped hair, and limbs that are robust rather than sensitive, is portrayed with great economy of means and effortless mastery; its solid earthiness is fully affirmed. The boys, who are themselves a picture of animal health, ride, drive, or lead their horses with noble tranquillity (page 370); there is none of the problematical quality of the blue figures. The horses, too, are vigorous; thoroughly trained but by no means overbred, they are no less sensitive than those appearing in the circus pictures. Here it is the plastic effect that the artist is primarily interested in; accordingly the color design is very simplified, in sharp contrast to the paintings last mentioned. But the warm tones of the flesh, of the dune landscape, and of the brown horses clearly predominate over the blue and gray tones of the sea or the sky. The gloomy nightmares of the Blue Period have been completely dispelled by open daylight; it is as though they had never existed. The beings created by the painter no longer feed on his blood, they have their own rich substance. They are self-contained, complete, "classical," as they have been called. Their classicism, their solidity and clarity, are quite original and naïve—they are the results of Picasso's inner development referred to above, not of an effort to imitate or emulate Classical models. It is a rare moment of harmony that was bound to occur in the creative history of even this master engaged in a continual back-and-forth dialectical movement.

*Dutch Girl* Cl. Cat. 27

*Boy Leading a Horse*
page 370

Picasso's summer journey of 1906, which took him to Gosol in the Spanish Pyrenees, marked another crucial stage in his development. The charcoal and chalk drawings of two heads, one executed before and the other after Gosol (page 128), bring the new change into sharp relief. The head with the shawl might again be called "classical," indeed

*Head of a Woman*
page 128

it seems scarcely possible that the draftsman has not sought confirmation of his accomplishments in the Classical Greek sculptures of the Louvre. Even though Picasso at that time often depicted women shawled and wearing flowers in their hair, and even though our drawing unmistakably reproduces the features of Fernande Olivier, the artist is now so clearly separated, so far removed from his model, that the figure portrayed is like an entirely self-contained, ancient draped statue. The form of the head, whose outline is visible even under the hair, the solid contours of the cheeks and of the nose, the almond-shaped eyes, and the lines of the eyebrows, the regular mouth above the strong chin, and the resulting somewhat rigid expression might be those of a Greek sculpture of the fifth century. Only the soft modeling of the hair, the graphic suggestion of the white of the shawl, and the indefiniteness of the area covered by it, suggest that this drawing is the work of a painter. It seems hardly credible that the profile drawing shown on page 137 was done by the same master only a few months later—so completely different are the formal ideal and technical treatment.

To account for this change we must mention the fact that in 1906 Picasso had studied the early Iberian bronzes of Osuna that had shortly before been made accessible to the public, and had been inspired by them. Even his Gosol compositions are stylized in a primitive sense, and the faces show the archaizing simplification and mask-like immobility that in the head shown here attain the magnificence of sixth-century Greek sculpture. Such heads are matched by massive, compact, and crudely articulated bodies whose unpleasant ponderousness is allayed only by the atmospheric chiaroscuro. Occasionally, as in a pen drawing of a standing nude (page 15), the broken outline and crude hatching remind us of woodcarvings. This sculptural tendency is paralleled by the predominance of pink and terracotta monochromes, in direct contrast with the blue tonality of the preceding period. The main work of that time, the portrait of Gertrude Stein (page 460), also reveals the supra-individual stamp of archaic form in the head, whereas the rest of the portrait obeys an older and gentler law, such as governs for instance the drawing dating from 1906, which is reproduced on page 127.

The portrait of Gertrude Stein is remarkable for still another reason. After forcing his model to sit for him eighty times in the *Bateau-lavoir*, Picasso wiped out the face on his return from Spain and replaced it by the new mask-like form. He dismissed objections to his alteration with the characteristic words: "Everybody thinks that the portrait is not like her, but never mind, in the end she will look like the portrait." From the point of view of the artist, a great step forward was made when he gave up the "classical" in favor of the "primitive." The far-reaching significance of this step will be discussed in the next chapter.

*Face in Profile* (1906)

*Face* (1907)

*Head in Three-Quarter View* (1908)

139

*Study for "Demoiselles d'Avignon"* (1907)

### Origins of Cubism

In the course of 1906 Picasso turned more and more resolutely away from subjective expression, and, as becomes fully apparent in the light of his subsequent development, concentrated on objective, formal problems. He thus shares in the general artistic current of those years, even though the path he follows is his own and unique.

Significantly enough, it was only then, shortly before the death of Cézanne, that the epochal importance of Cézanne's contribution to painting began to be realized. Ten Cézanne canvases were exhibited at the Autumn Salons of 1905 and 1906; the memorial exhibition of 1907 for the first time conveyed the overwhelming greatness of this painter who had repeatedly come to grips with the fundamental problem of representing the third dimension on the picture surface. The Fauves, who under the leadership of Matisse made their first public appearance at the Salon of 1905, also subordinated subject matter to form conceived as an end in itself, but they followed Gauguin in their one-sided concern with color and decorative values, and neglected the spatial problem raised by Cézanne. For that reason Matisse, whom Picasso met in 1906, did not influence him to any important extent. Picasso was interested precisely in discovering the laws governing the representation of three-dimensional form on the flat surface, whereas Fauvism with its fanatical cult of color was in a sense a continuation of Impressionism, which ultimately gave up any attempt to render volumes. Only Cézanne, who sought to combine the Impressionist heritage with a solid structuring of the picture surface, could be of possible use to Picasso—and Picasso realized this with his usual clear-mindedness. Picasso's hour struck when, after following a fruitful but somewhat isolated path, he assumed leadership of a movement that is justly regarded as the greatest revolution in painting since the Renaissance, namely, Cubism.

Like all great innovations, Cubism was prepared by intellectual efforts whose lasting influence no one could foresee, not even the directly participating artists. The best proof that Cubism has genuine historical roots is that various young painters associated with it—Picasso did not invent it single-handed—reached similar results though each of them worked on his own. On the other hand, it cannot be denied that

141

Picasso's development toward Cubism is more logical and inevitable than any other painter's. In his work Cubism occupies a central position. Perhaps only his fellow countryman Juan Gris, who died prematurely, is comparable to him in this respect; but Juan Gris joined the movement at a later date.

The first to recognize the far-reaching importance of the *Demoiselles d'Avignon* (*Girls of Avignon*, page 143), Picasso's main work of 1907, was Daniel-Henry Kahnweiler, the soundest theoretician of Cubism. But in 1907 even Kahnweiler, who began to frequent the *Bateau-lavoir* at that time, could only divine the revolutionary significance of this extraordinary painting: what this first attempt held in store for the future was still utterly uncertain. The history of the composition itself, which we can retrace on the basis of numerous preliminary sketches, once again illustrates the process by which form asserts its supremacy over subject matter. The earliest studies (page 140) show that the original seven symmetrically arranged forms included a sailor seated in the center; a student entering from the left, with a skull in his hand, introduced an element of allegory into the picture. In the following sketches the clothed male figures have been eliminated, and the females are rearranged in such a way that they fill the entire surface. Here nothing suggests a specific scene or locality—it was only later that Picasso's friend André Salmon gave the picture its poetic title, which refers to a brothel in Carrer d'Avinyó (Avignon Street) in Barcelona. A description of the painting could only record five nudes placed in a room bounded by curtains, and a still life with slices of melon in the foreground. The still life appears in all the studies.

Unlike the many-figured paintings of 1906, the *Demoiselles d'Avignon* shows no deep space surrounding the figures. Here the space is a relatively thin layer formed by the figures themselves; the space they occupy and the space they leave unoccupied complement each other as the positive and the negative. Partly bounded by simple planes —"as though carved out with an ax"—they constitute the picture; the same is true of the curtain segments, which are equally important in the over-all structure. Similarly, the textures of the flesh and of the curtain material show no fundamental difference in treatment, which could have impaired the homogeneity of the picture. In short, we can speak here only of the balance of the picture as a whole and no longer of balance within individual figures. What Matisse achieved in 1906 in his *Joie de vivre* through rhythmic treatment of the surface is achieved in the *Demoiselles d'Avignon* through a tight structuring. The formal conception embodied here is most strikingly disclosed in the faces: it is precisely these most individual details that are subjected to the greatest, indeed, grotesque distortions and dislocations. At this point we must mention a historical incongruity of the work: the three left-hand figures belong to a somewhat older stage than the two right-hand ones. As is often the case with Picasso, even the "definitive" state of the painting is evidently only one of many possible cross sections of a continuing creative process (Picasso himself considered it unfinished at the time).

What is common to all the studies is the general design of the picture (inspired by Cézanne's bather compositions, as well as by a certain influence of El Greco in the abstract breaking of the planes), and the

*Study for "Demoiselles d'Avignon"* page 140

Note 8

*Les demoiselles d'Avignon* page 143

(p. 143) *Les demoiselles d'Avignon* 1907
(p. 145) *Landscape* 1907

incontestable predominance of form over color, which, in the left part, still suggests the warm monochromes of the Rose Period. The archaic severity, particularly of the figure at the extreme left, struck even the first viewers as "Egyptian"; after Gauguin, this was not unusual in a Parisian painter. Equally incontestable is the primitivism of the two central figures, particularly in the forms of their heads, inspired by the pre-Roman Iberian bronzes, whose sober, compact expression had strongly influenced Picasso as early as 1906. On the other hand, the peculiarities of the two right-hand figures—such as, apart from the heads, the handle-like arm of the sitting woman and the enormous hand which supports her head—point to Picasso's acquaintance with Negro sculptures; we know that these even induced him to experiment with carvings in wood. There is some dispute as to when Picasso became acquainted with African masks, which had become popular among Paris painters a few years earlier. Presumably he first saw them only during his work on the large canvas so that the painting reflects both his short "Iberian" and "Negro" periods.

*Nude* Cl. Cat. 39

Note 9

The Negro sculptures radically abstract from natural forms: with their large noses protruding at sharp angles from the concave faces, they are the very opposite of everything Classical. Under their influence Picasso completely negated the natural form, for the first time in the *Demoiselles d'Avignon*. The doglike face of the standing figure at the right, and the unnatural arrangement of eyes and mouth in the seated figure, show his determination to use signs whose form can no longer be directly measured by natural standards. But the painting, particularly the head at the upper right, also discloses a new attempt to reconcile solid and flat treatment through the delimitation of volumes by measurable planes: we are actually witnessing here the birth of Cubism, so named only one year later. In painting this head Picasso still compromises between the use of local color and the use of color as a means of distinguishing between various planes: this accounts for the green and red hatchings executed with the brush, which appear also on the breasts. The head of the seated woman also shows hatchings, but here they are confined to the closed blue planes, which are contrasted with the terracotta-colored face; in this Picasso unconsciously anticipates his later works.

*Les demoiselles d'Avignon* page 143

With this painting, which was not understood even by broad-minded contemporary artists, Picasso entered a period of "horrible moral solitude." Kahnweiler testifies to this by quoting Derain who said that some day Picasso would hang himself behind his painting. Derain was mistaken: the *Demoiselles d'Avignon*, now in the Museum of Modern Art in New York with other epochal works by Picasso, became a landmark in the history of art of our century, and even though it was at the time accessible only to an insignificant number of European art lovers, it opened up entirely new horizons.

Note 10

In the course of 1907 Picasso produced a number of other works in which the style of the elongated, concave, and pointed Negro masks with their large convex eyes and angular noses is combined with broad hatchings and an expressive, angular composition; among these is the representative *Nude with Drapery* (page 374). Then he went to another extreme of sculptured treatment, characterized by a stable order of sharply defined volumes, for instance, of a head. The charcoal and

*Nude with Drapery* page 374

chalk drawing reproduced on page 138, beside which the "archaic" head of 1906 (page 137) seems almost naturalistic, clearly derives from abstract Negro sculpture, which for all its rigidity is anything but dead. It was precisely the stimulating, magic vitality of the exotic sculptures that aroused the enthusiasm of Picasso and his contemporaries and helped them to dethrone the academic concept of beauty.

The frontal head of this drawing, with its symmetric outlines, the delicately tapering chin, the noble mouth, and the vigorously protruding nose under the unseeing eyes are evidence of Picasso's deep insight into the religious, hieratic spirit of that so-called "primitive" art. The form is of an overwhelming, self-sufficient magnificence, which the artist seems merely to reproduce. Actually a great, if not the greater, part of this effect must be attributed to the draftsman's consummate interpretation. He contrasts the angular blocky frame of the hair with the delicate plastic transitions in the face; the nose and the mouth, which is clearly divided into two lips, are assigned a mediating function. He conjures up the swellings by means of freely drawn hatchings and faint rubbings, and through the lateral curves rounds off the section reproduced here into a compositional whole. Following this austere, plastically stylized figure, Picasso in 1908 drew a number of figures, whose structure, defined by intensive shadows, is reminiscent of woodcarvings (page 461). To some extent the same may be said of still lifes dating from the same year. Of crucial importance for his subsequent development, however, were above all the landscapes he painted in the Rue des Bois during the summer.

Landscapes lend themselves more readily to the clear delineation of volumes, which was the main objective of the first great phase of Cubism, than representations of the human body—particularly rocky landscapes stripped of organic growth, in which human figures, if any, are subordinated to the general organization of the picture. Such structures of crystalline purity were anticipated decades earlier by Cézanne's L'Estaque landscapes. In 1908, in the same L'Estaque, Georges Braque, who had met Picasso in 1907, painted landscapes very similar to Picasso's; this is another confirmation of the view that the evolution of art has supra-personal causes, for we have no reason to doubt that the two painters worked independently. It was also in 1908 that the self-explanatory term Cubism was used for the first time, either by Matisse in a conversation, or by the critic Louis Vauxcelles in a review of an exhibition of Braque's works. Later the expression Analytic Cubism was used to characterize the process of breaking down the natural appearance into stereometric elements. A culminating point of severe crystalline treatment is reached by Picasso in his austere landscapes painted at Horta de Ebro in 1909, with their hard, block-like forms of buildings (page 462).

In contrast with the dominant tendencies of the immediately preceding period, these works are essentially concerned with *form*, not *color*; against the claims of color the Cubists launched the slogan of "drawing for drawing's sake" (Raynal). The "return to linear discipline," for which Picasso had paved the way long before, gave an entirely new direction to painting, as Cocteau realized when he described Cubism as "a classicism opposed to the romanticism of the Fauves." Color was for the time being assigned a subordinate function—it was regarded as an

(p. 149) *Still Life with Gourd* 1909

obstacle to the solution of plastic problems. But it recovered its importance where the natural appearance had to be disregarded, and where the purpose was to create an autonomous "pictorial individual," for such a purpose could be achieved only by strengthening the picture surface at the expense of one-sided Cubist modeling. For this reason, Picasso, for instance in his Horta de Ebro landscapes, extended large parts of the colored surface beyond the system of the individual cubes, gearing together the element of the picture surface. At the same time he produced works of a pronounced coloristic charm, among them still life compositions with gentle curves and pyramidal structures (page 149), whose predominant color seemed to some critics a sufficient reason for speaking of a Picasso "Green Period."

In the course of 1909 the influence of Cézanne asserts itself with decisive effect. This applies not only to Cézanne's effort to reduce natural appearance to basic stereometric forms, but also to this technique of modulations, i.e., of constructing the picture surface by piecing together colored plane particles. In a head of a woman (page 139) Picasso, who is now concerned with plastic rather than pictorial values, resorts directly to the principle of modulations: he articulates the head into facets, splitting it up into small angular and spherical planes. The aim pursued here can be only partially achieved if the artist clings to his model: Cézanne had wasted his strength trying to solve this problem comparable to the squaring of the circle. That is why the face in our drawing is less abstract than the coiffure, the torso, or the hand. In the face itself, the mouth is naturalistic, the ear is completely geometric, and the eye is a little of each. As against the *Demoiselles d'Avignon*, this drawing marks a temporary regression: once again the autonomy of the picture is sacrificed to the static structure of the figure. The figure paintings of 1909 disclose the same one-sided concern with plastic effects, which is confirmed by the use of subdued colors (chiefly ochers and grays) in the modulation planes. The well-known bronze head of 1910 attempts to apply the principle of modulations to sculpture.

In 1910 Picasso made an energetic effort to restore the formal unity of the picture, which he had almost achieved in the *Demoiselles d'Avignon*. The figures surrender their solidity and spatial independence; they are flattened out and pushed closer to the background, which for its part, being formed of Cubist blocks, seems to come closer to the picture surface. In this way a homogeneous structure is secured; the painting produces the effect of a low relief rising gradually from the edges toward the center. In the beautiful *Girl with a Mandolin* of the Roland Penrose collection this formalizing process is still in an early stage, the figure still asserts its own rights, still retains plastic unity. The graceful feminine body and its movement are expressive even though they are not individualized. But at the same time its forms are embedded in the relief-like picture space, and the larger planes defining it are related to the picture surface, so that the half-figure can be the carrier of the artistic unity: the problem of the segment here is the same as that presented by the portrait bust which eighteenth-century painting solved ornamentally.

In the portrait of Wilhelm Uhde (page 376) the background predominates over the figure, which can hardly be said to consist of connected volumes. It is broken up into a number of small planes that tend to merge with the picture surface. Only the faceted structure of the head, which decidedly suggests the head of a portrait, still asserts itself against the non-figural surroundings. The background is formed not of "cubes," but of overlapping planes, which serve as the new structural units. The same evolution is observable in the painting showing the church of Sacré-Cœur in Paris and the surrounding roofs and houses: in diametrical contrast to the weighted, block-like structure of *Horta de Ebro* (page 462), the spatially developed parts of the center and the gradually flattening surroundings seem suspended; they are completely integrated into the surface design.

*Daniel-Henry Kahnweiler*
page 241

In the portrait of Kahnweiler dating from 1910 (page 241), the dissolution of the natural object into small fragments and the splitting up of the partial planes are pushed so far that the figure seems to lose its cohesion, and to blend with its surroundings: here the new intellectual order of the picture begins completely to dominate the order inherent in the subject matter. Only individualized fragments of the head and the hands are still legible in this almost non-objective composition. Here, Analytic Cubism has almost gone as far as possible in its attempt to force the spatial values of the optical appearance into the self-sufficient order of the picture. What remains of the natural object are only the general pattern and the dynamism of partial units. All the more amazing and profoundly characteristic of Picasso's own relation to nature is the fact that Kahnweiler had to sit more than twenty times for this portrait!

*The Accordionist*
page 377

*Spanish Still Life*
page 378

Although 1911 and 1912 saw further progress on the path leading to the elimination of the natural object, Picasso never made the final step toward non-objective or abstract painting, not even with his baffling *Accordionist* of 1911 (page 377), which is a typical example of so-called "hermetic" Cubism. In relation to such works the question of the subject matter designated by the title becomes nearly meaningless. Accordingly the still life, with its less obtrusive subject matter, moves to the foremost place as regards pictorial themes. Side by side with this development, the expression becomes depersonalized, so that it is sometimes difficult to distinguish between the paintings of Braque and Picasso, who were closely associated at that time. Color continues to be kept in neutral, subdued tones. Picasso still clung to only *one* subjective factor, which is connected with the shading of the facets and plane particles—namely, his personal, dispersive brush stroke. But here too a change was in the offing, which must be discussed in the context of his new general conception of the picture.

(p. 153) *Card Player* 1913/14
(p. 155) *Vive la France* 1914

*Reclining Woman* (1915)

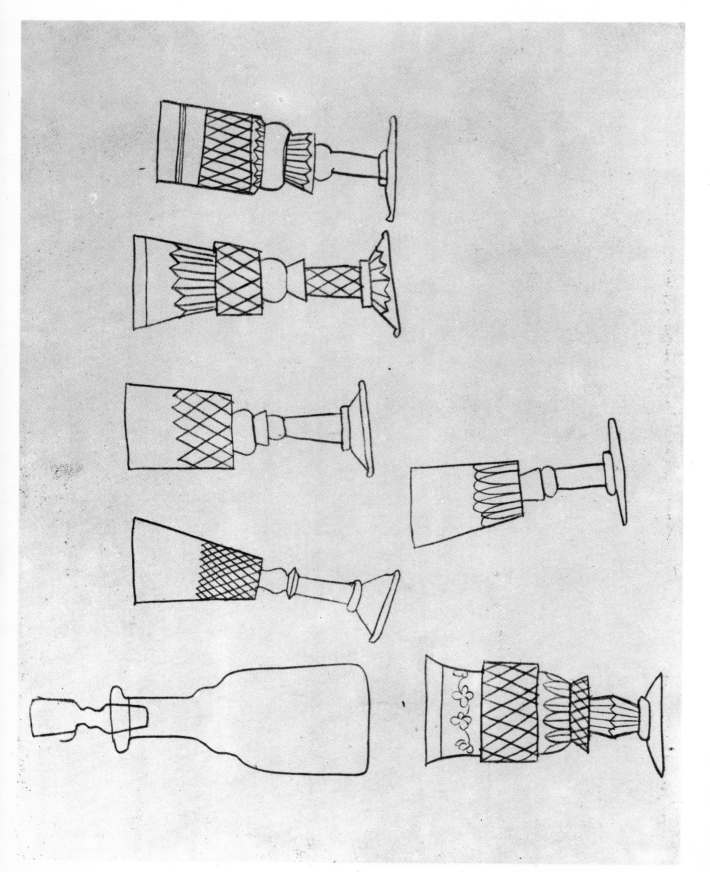

*Decanter and Glasses (1914)*

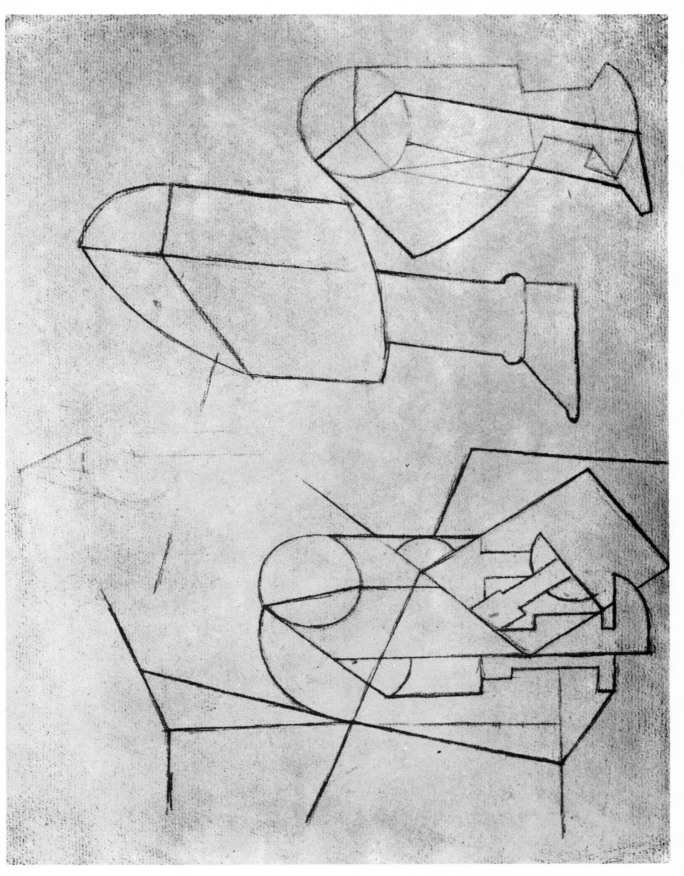

*Studies of Glasses* (1914/15)

159

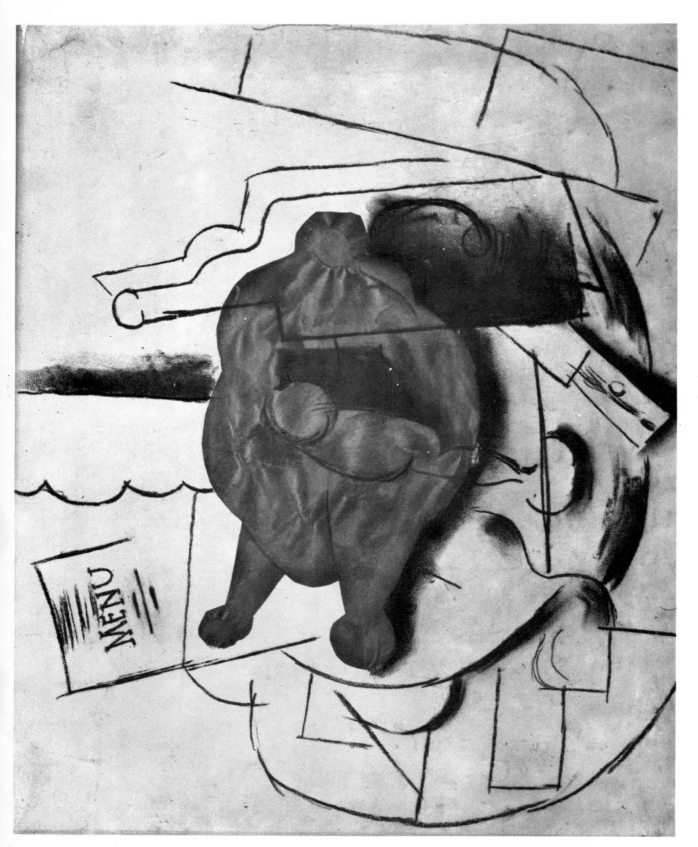

*The Roast Goose (1913)*

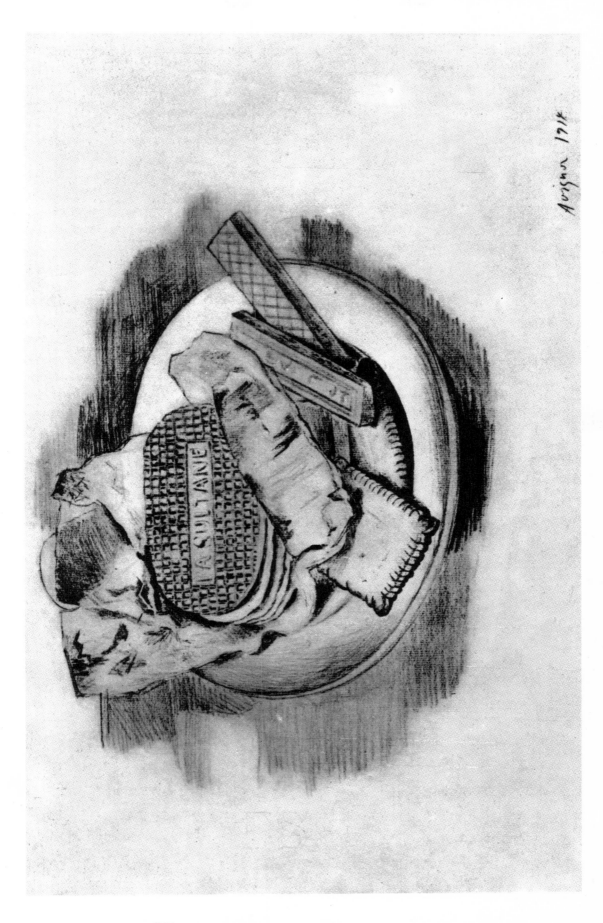

*Plate with Wafers* (1914)

*Violin* (1915)

*Violin* (1915)

*Woman in an Armchair* (1916)

*Still Life with Bottle and Guitar* (1924)

### Evolution of Cubism

According to Kahnweiler, "Picasso left behind what he himself had created, and transformed Cubism, which began as a school of severe discipline, into a doctrine of freedom." This puts it rather well: today the concept of Cubism is far broader than its original meaning based on the cubic formal structure of the works of 1908 and 1909. Analytic Cubism, which breaks up natural objects, was followed by Synthetic Cubism, the second great phase of the movement, which aims at re-assembling the fragmented objects in the picture in accordance with the artist's formal intentions.

Note 11

This fundamentally new approach was first clearly formulated by Juan Gris, who in 1910 began to paint in a style very similar to Picasso's and Braque's. In 1921 he discussed the principles of his aesthetic system and briefly reviewed his experiences, defining the new creative process as a "synthesis," and describing it as a path leading from abstraction to reality, from the general to the particular—the reverse of that followed by Cézanne and Analytic Cubism. "Cézanne transformed a bottle into a cylinder," Juan Gris declared, "but I start from the cylinder to create an individual object of a specific type: from a cylinder I make a bottle. For Cézanne, architecture is the goal; for me, it is the starting point." The new objective is to "re-humanize" the abstract, to transmute spots of color into real objects. In conclusion Juan Gris likened the new "synthetic" way of painting to metric poetry, and the older way of painting, which starts with the object, to prose: "This new painting is to the other as poetry is to prose."

Note 12

The comparison is exact. Impressionist painters liked naturalistic and psychological novels; the Cubist and lyric poet Picasso scorned them. Synthetic Cubism affirms and emphasizes the creative potential of pure form. The historical impact of Cubism, whose influence cannot be gauged even today, began to be felt only when it entered the second phase of its development, even though this second phase is inconceivable without the first, and even though both are the work of the same artists. The change of direction took place—if a date must be given—around 1912; but the first signs can of course be discovered earlier.

For many years it was to be the aim of Cubist painting to combine color and form elements into objects which recalled only this or that aspect of the accustomed natural things, but which were just as individual as natural objects because they were born of individual creative imagination. It was thus important to get the beholder to discover associative clues within the picture that would enable him to link the new kind of "object" with what was already familiar to him. To guide the beholder's eye, the Cubists first resorted to rather clumsy devices —the so-called *détails réels*, realistic details which were intended to serve as signposts in the necessary re-translation from the language of abstraction into that of reality. The device was invented by Braque in the spring of 1910, when he painted into a still life (now in the museum at Basel) a realistic nail, with its exact shadow, as a bit of *trompe-l'œil*. Only later were these auxiliary devices, often supplemented by captions emphasizing the "realistic details," applied systematically and with greater refinement.

*The Roast Goose* page 160

As late as 1913, in his *The Roast Goose* (page 160), Picasso used the *trompe-l'œil* in a very obvious manner: the characteristically detailed roast, cut out of colored paper, is pasted on the drawing. The technique of *papiers collés*, or *collage*, was particularly favored from the early days of Synthetic Cubism, because it is more suited to the two-dimensional character of the picture surface than illusionistically painted details. While the eye is attracted by the roast pasted in at the center, the charcoal drawing is developed around it in overlapping planes, some of which are shadowed along the edge, thus seeming to rise from the surface like a relief. The roast, too, casts a shadow, which ties it more closely with its abstract surroundings and makes them more real to the beholder, who now interprets the oval forms as a plate, and the outer contour as a table. The two-layered bottle at the right and the little glass at the center, which partly cover the roast, produce the effect of overlapping in space. In the foreground we can also recognize a knife; and the sheet of paper with the inscription MENU—a *détail réel*—at the upper left enhances the illusion. Such a use of written or printed characters, mostly referring to the subject of the picture, can be found in Braque's works as early as the summer of 1910; it is a symptom of the final break with the four-hundred-year-old tradition of spatial illusion in European painting, and also a symptom of the kinship between modern painting and the non-illusionistic medieval painting which frequently included lettering in two-dimensional designs. During the second decade of this century Picasso, too, frequently resorted to this device; in addition to the usual mastheads from *Le Journal* and bottle labels, we find the inscription MA JOLIE, taken from a sentimental French folk song, and in one instance, some Russian characters.

*Violin, Bottle, and Glass*
Cl. Cat. 65
*Woman in an Armchair*
page 380
*Still Life: Ma Jolie*
Cl. Cat. 64

Because the illusionistic effect of traditional painting requires a homogeneous surface, it had been impossible for many centuries for painters to attach to the surface of the picture elements made of materials other than paint, such as the gold leaf and other ornaments often used by medieval artists. In resorting to the technique of *collage*, the Cubists did not seek to enrich their paintings with costly materials; indeed, they favored worthless materials, such as pieces of old newspapers, rags, etc., as though to emphasize the purity of their aims through the use of the most unpretentious materials. By incorporating into the picture such fragments of reality which operate as catalysts,

 (p. 167) *Still Life in Landscape* 1915

they encouraged the beholder to interpret the painted parts, too, as real objects; the fragments of reality thus are the standard by which the painter judges how far he has succeeded. This is the case if the real and painted elements of the surface are perceived as homogeneous integral parts of the intended object, and if the picture surface is rich enough to assimilate the alien body effortlessly. Moreover the *collages* serve to enhance the attraction of the flat composition mainly through their diverse structures and patterns. For the painter's objective attitude toward his own work has now gone so far that he renounces the individual character of brushwork as such, and uses every possible means to give the surface an impersonal character: among other things, he roughens the surface by adding sand or sawdust to his paint, or imitates wood grain, marble veins, and similar patterns (page 153). Such imitation is legitimate in so far as the illusion in this case is created by two-dimensional means.

Usually, in the still lifes of the year 1913 the object is drastically simplified. Most of the geometric elements are linked together to form musical instruments whose shapes too are essentially geometric. All the more complicated and subtle are the color combinations and patterns of the surface whose delicate relief effects appeal to our sense of touch. At that time Picasso often aimed at such sensual effects. We can see this in a pencil drawing, *Plate with Wafers* (page 161), which at first seems naturalistic, but whose beauty, on closer inspection, lies in the sensitive differentiation between the various "wafer" patterns, in the brilliant surface of the plate, and in the soft texture of the paper against the rough one of the table. Moreover the perspective arrangement of the objects results in a surface pattern that comes close to contemporary Cubist compositions.

When Picasso applied the devices just described to human figures, the results were at first no less baffling to the untrained observer than the portraits done in the style of "hermetic" Cubism. Probably the best-known example is the *Student with a Pipe*, formerly of the Gertrude Stein collection (page 379), whose face consists of an angular surface and of separate, curved "cheeks" into which the ears have been inscribed according to the principles of the *"plans superposés."* The back of the head with long, wavy hair under the brown paper cap is similarly defined. The slightly receding plane of the face with two small circles standing for the eyes, lines indicating the mouth and mustache, and an elongated red-dotted nose, seems turned in relation to the lines of the frontal shoulders and neck; the pipe cutting across the blue-gray shadow at the left heightens the perspective illusion. The spatial layers, the alternation of rectilinear and curvilinear forms, and, above all, the extreme contrast between abstract surfaces and realistic details add up to a fascinating effect. Even more richly differentiated is the important painting *Woman in an Armchair* (page 380) representing a woman in a chemise seated in an armchair. The pencil drawing of a reclining woman in foreshortened view, reproduced on page 157, belongs to the same group of works. In this drawing the touch of mockery that characterized the *Student with a Pipe*—we are almost tempted to speak anachronistically of a Surrealist effect—is based on the contrast (which is achieved by perspective means) between the large naturalistic soles of the feet and the geometrically simplified body.

In a number of still life compositions dating from 1914 (page 155) the texture is enriched by a loose and decorative Pointillist technique. These Pointillist works with their subtly graded colors, in which delicate green and red tones predominate, have been compared to eighteenth-century Rococo works, and they count among Picasso's most refined coloristic inventions. In the *Woman Seated before a Fireplace* of 1914 (Georges Salles collection, Paris) and in the *Man with a Pipe* of 1916, in the Art Institute, Chicago, these ornamental principles are applied in the treatment of human figures. Whereas here small patterns serve as the ornamental vehicle, in a later Cubist period in the 1920s the arabesque and structure, particularly of still life objects, were to assume a decidedly Baroque character (page 164).

Consistent with the general tendency of that period is the emergence of works of a new type, the so-called *objets*, or constructions. They actually belong to the domain of sculpture, but they are so closely linked with the problems of Picasso's painting that they must be mentioned here. These *objets* serve no practical purpose, nor are they representations of functional objects; they are artifacts constructed for their own sake, from fragments, though sometimes they suggest real objects, such as musical instruments. Once again the artist strives to achieve his purpose by using materials as worthless as possible—scrap from a carpenter's shop or even from a dustbin. Crudely finished bits of wood are pieced together, seemingly playfully, and the resulting construction is comparable on a higher level of reality to what Juan Gris described as Synthetic Cubist painting, or to a model for such painting. For the function of the Cubist object was in a way like that of the manikin or lay figure of Old Masters.

Many of Picasso's drawings are actually related to such constructions. The *Violin* (page 162), for example, is drawn in such a way that it suggests the perspective rendering of a violin constructed from wood fragments. We see the cross sections of individual parts; the greatest emphasis is on the clarification of the rich spatial relations, just as in the case of a wooden manikin. Picasso himself confirms that in painting his guitars he was motivated not by an interest in musical instruments as such, but solely by an artistic aim: he says that they began to mean something to him only after he had painted them. In a sheet belonging to the same series of drawings (page 162) the three-dimensional model has been entirely forgotten; all the elements—they evoke a musical instrument—are flattened into the plane. If the previous drawing makes us think of a cabinetmaker, this one suggests a bookbinder. Instead of the three-dimensional details, we now find numerous graphic details distributed over the various planes—bass viol strings, handwritten characters, sound holes, and finally the glass cup on the little table; the straight lines often end in the void, conforming to the law of overlapping planes. Tone values indicated by different hatchings suggest a richly differentiated surface. As a composition in a frame, the alternative method of this second drawing seems more closely knit, and even very refined despite the sketch-like treatment, so that we are again reminded of Juan Gris's reference to the "poetic" quality of this kind of painting. Finally, it is clear that the construction shown here is in some way anthropomorphic, not only because the artist conceives of the bass viol as an instrument whose proportions are derived from the human figure,

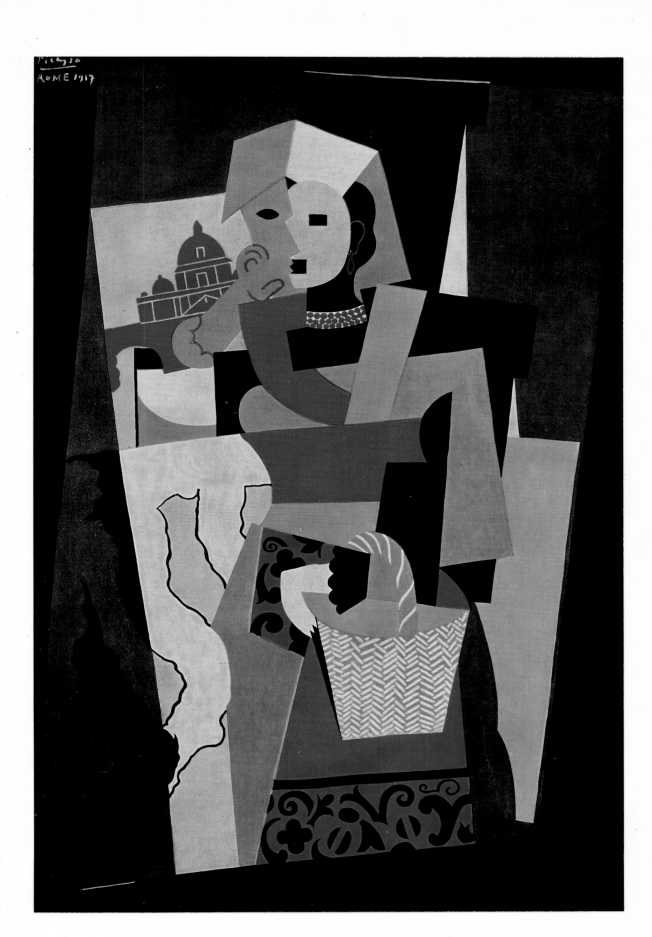

but also because in arranging the various elements he was at least unconsciously motivated by the vision of an agile human body. We even possess closely related drawings in which similar abstractions are interpreted as marionette-like figurines—an important confirmation of the Mediterranean quality of Picasso's art.

The reader has surely noticed that in the drawing just discussed the table is not shown from a single point of view: whereas the legs are seen from the side, the tabletop, in terms of perspective, is seen from above. We can see the same peculiarity in the table of a little gouache of 1920 (page 383) and in many other works. This is one of the most important devices of Cubism, which does not feel bound by the appearance of objects, but which unfolds its image of things in a sequence of separate conceptual steps. For instance, to show the mouth of a glass the artist adds a circle to the rectilinear outline (page 159). Cesare Brandi wittily compared the motion of the eye around the object, which generates these multiple views, to the revolution of the sun around the earth in the Ptolemaic system. Picasso consistently uses the device also in representing human forms, for instance when he juxtaposes the frontal and profile views of a head (page 221). This splitting up of the description of an object is paralleled by the independence of the linear structure from the color structure, a discovery that later became common property. Line and color, although inseparable in the actual appearance of objects, are not inseparable in the imagination. Hence contours are no longer obligatory: lines and patches of color need not correspond, and the tension between them serves to enrich the structure.

*Table with Guitar* page 383

*Studies of Glasses* page 159

Cl. Cat. 84, 100, 116

Let us return now to *Table with Guitar* (page 383). The musical instrument it shows has been subjected to the law of multiple views, i.e., this object which is three-dimensional in nature has been broken up, and the fragments have been put together in a new way, in accordance with the laws governing the surface, and with a view to the composition as a whole. The head of the guitar is shaped like a triangle—Picasso often uses such an "abridgment" for the human head (page 75). The stripes of the bridge and of the strings are echoed in the stripe pattern of the table. Larger, overlapping, variously colored planes serve as a foil and frame for the objects on the table. Nowhere do the parts behave in accordance with the laws of perspective, and yet an amazing effect of depth is achieved, for the diagonal borders of the large planes are interpreted as foreshortened lines in conformity with our visual habits. This is one of the methods used by Cubism to bring about the desired integration of the object only in the beholder's imagination.

*Sleeping Nude* page 75
*Head* Cl. Cat. 69

The human form is subjected to a similar treatment in the *Woman in an Armchair* of 1916 (page 163) and the *Italian Woman* of 1917 (page 171). The seated figure is composed of plane segments; their textures differ in density and shading, and they are arranged in such a way that they seem to overlap. Yet the total effect is emphatically one of solid space. How is it brought about? The foreshortened lines of the chair, with its curved armrests, induce the beholder to translate the structure of the figure into the same spatial language: in analogy to the chair, he interprets the dividing lines between the white planes, let alone those between the shaded ones, as the outlines of the human figure. The round contours of the arms, in conjunction with the dark rectangular

*Woman in an Armchair* page 163
*Italian Woman* page 171

*Still Life with Casserole*
page 80

planes inscribed into them, suggest solidity, as was the case with the *Casserole* (page 80). Moreover the shading produces the illusion of spatial relief, as can best be seen in the head. This head is the result of four different overlapping views, each of them appearing as a flat, differently shaded segment. The white "profile" is pushed forward by the black view which, in turn, does not sink into the background because it is placed on top of the white frontal view. This white frontal view is in its turn supported by the fourth, striped plane; thus the head presses toward the beholder in several layers. The additional fact that these are alternately rectangular and round forms strengthens the impression of movement in depth; as though to confirm this, one eye is round and the other rectangular. Since there is no base line, the head is the spot from which the whole composition, with its marvelous symmetry of forms and shading, is suspended. Finally, the row of tacks on the right side of the chair plays an important part because of the density of the stripes which creates the effect of a plane within its purely linear surroundings. Picasso discovered many structural laws of the type illustrated by this relatively simple example.

*Woman in an Armchair*
Cl. Cat. 81
*Bather* Cl. Cat. 83
*Three Musicians*
page 179

Similar structural relations account for the fascination of the *Three Musicians*, now in Philadelphia (page 179), which Picasso painted in Fontainebleau in the summer of 1921, and which, with another version now in New York, marks the climax and, for the time being, the conclusion of strict Synthetic Cubism. In this poetic painting an effect of solid space is produced exclusively by flat and ornamental graphic elements. Three masked figures—a Harlequin with a violin, a Pierrot with a clarinet, and a monk with an accordion—are shown seated at a table, playing their instruments. Their shapes, costumes, and gestures are shown in detail without the use of structural linear contours, which still appear in the numerous preliminary sketches of 1920. Even the teeth of the clarinetist and the mustache of the accordionist are represented as small closed planes. By 1921 Cubism was no longer the only style in which Picasso liked to express himself, but the Cubist devices had lost nothing of their effectiveness. Picasso used them even decades later, as can be seen from various examples discussed in our introductory chapters.

*Masks* Cl. Cat. 82

### Classical Interlude

The outbreak of World War I had separated Picasso from his Cubist friends. He stayed in Paris but his work was affected by the general unfavorable conditions. Cubism seemed on the way to becoming a dogma. "Montmartre and Montparnasse were under dictatorial rule," writes Jean Cocteau. "Cubism was going through its austere period. Objects that could be placed on a café table and Spanish guitars were the only distractions permitted."

Note 14

Cocteau is to be credited with having persuaded Picasso, in 1917, to accompany him to Rome, to design the scenery and costumes for Diaghilev's ballet production *Parade*. This work, as well as his association with dancers, the Italian milieu, and the ancient sites—he visited, among other places, Pompeii—had a refreshing effect on the painter. Picasso's failure to distinguish himself as a stage designer is plausibly accounted for by Cocteau: the settings he designed were too dynamic, too prominent, and even the costumes by themselves appeared to be full of movement. Nevertheless, he subsequently designed scenery and costumes for Diaghilev's productions of *Le tricorne*, *Pulcinella*, and *Cuadro flamenco*. He went to London in 1919 on the occasion of the performance of *Le tricorne* (the other ballets were shown in Paris); his designs for this ballet and for *Cuadro flamenco* were very Spanish and colorful. Picasso here adapted himself to the specific requirements of the theater, and was deliberately more ingratiating than in his other kinds of work. His designs for *Pulcinella*, produced in 1920, familiarized him with the world of the Neapolitan *commedia dell'arte* and brought him into temporary association with the composer Igor Stravinsky whom he had met in Rome. From Diaghilev's Russian dancers he also chose his wife, Olga Koklova; his friends, the poets Cocteau, Apollinaire, and Max Jacob served as witnesses at the wedding ceremony. Also, during those years he reaped a rich and unexpected harvest in the field in which he was most at home.

The famous names just mentioned are also titles of a number of his most outstanding portrait drawings, mostly done in pencil. The series begins in 1915, when he portrayed the art dealer Vollard in three-quarter view, seated on a chair, his legs crossed in a typical model's

*Igor Stravinsky* page 183

pose. The drawing is meticulously realistic: no little wrinkle of the clothes or the necktie, no hair of the mustache, is missing. This portrait is a far cry from that of the art dealer Kahnweiler, painted ten years earlier.

Above all, Picasso shows himself willing to enter into the psychology of his subjects—in short, to take his task of portraitist seriously. There is no doubt that he was inspired by Ingres who, to quote Jean Cassou, "was the last portraitist able to cope with the faces of his contemporaries and to treat them with *noblesse.*" Like the painters of the generation after Ingres, Picasso generally displayed such sympathy only toward men of importance and personal acquaintances. But there is a deeply moving human quality in his portraits of intimate friends, as in the 1915 drawing of Max Jacob (page 182). As for the technique, no more need be said than that it attains the quality of Ingres—an amazing accomplishment on the part of an artist who but a single year earlier, in 1914, had illustrated the same Max Jacob's *Le siège de Jérusalem* with extreme Cubistic etchings (page 19). Picasso's psychological understanding is particularly visible in posthumous portraits done from photographs and other data. Among these are the large drawing of Renoir, done in 1919, the year of his death, showing him half-paralyzed in an armchair, and with a marvelously animated facial expression; the drawing of Mallarmé he did many years later (page 247); and the lithograph portrait of the Spanish Baroque poet Luis de Góngora, whose style has been said to be related to Picasso's. Around 1920, parallel to his Ingres-like portraits with their delicate shaded detail, Picasso created a linear type based on the contour (page 183), exemplified in his portraits of Stravinsky, with their hairline precision. It is the same linear style that Picasso has used for decades in treating mythological subjects, or, again, in the portrait of Balzac, of 1952 (page 67).

Even before his Italian trip, Picasso, after years of purely Cubist work, once again took up the representation of the human form, at first in portraits. This has occasionally been interpreted as a sign of weakness, a result of his isolation during the war years. It would be more correct, however, to speak of a period of relaxation following a period of tension, for one of Picasso's essential characteristics since that time has been his use of both the Cubist and the "classic" style, often in the treatment of identical subjects. It must be noted, however, that his works executed in the "classic" style are often intended as a slighter echo of the original version; the very fact that most of them are small drawings may prove this. Even though his Cubist paintings during the first war years occasionally contained elements reminiscent of human forms, indicated for instance by titles such as "The Harlequin," the individual forms in these paintings scarcely suggested the lines of the human body. Yet it would have been strange if an artist as responsive as Picasso to the human figure had entirely lost interest in it. His intimate contacts with the world of the dance seem to have reawakened his delight in the natural grace of man, and the ancient masterpieces he saw in Italy may have helped to give a classic turn to his treatments of the human figure. John Flaxman and his artistic heirs had developed a suitable technique in their strict, linear art, and some of Picasso's own pre-Cubist drawings had already pointed in that direction.

*Study for the Curtain of the Ballet "Le tricorne"* (1919)

*Max Jacob* (1915)

*Igor Stravinsky* (1920)

*Neapolitan Woman* (1919)

184

*The Sigh* (1923)

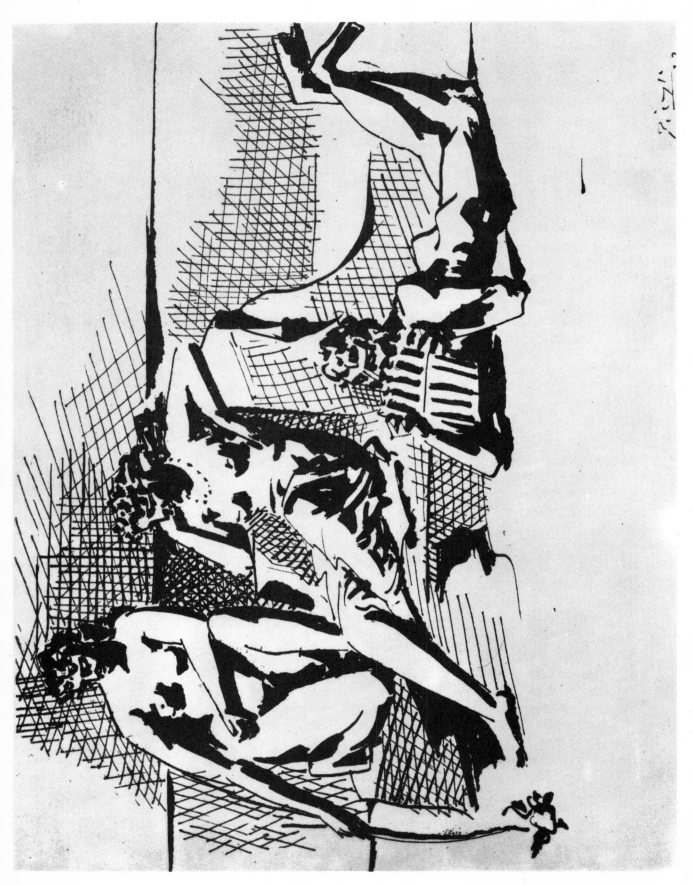

*Two Nudes and Youth Playing the Pipes of Pan* (1923)

The *Neapolitan Woman* (page 184)—through his work for *Pulcinella* Picasso had come close to the milieu depicted here—is anything but a study from a model. It is a firmly constructed, lyrical work in the terms of Synthetic Cubism; only the subject matter and the devices are different. The seated figure is well-balanced and self-contained; compositionally it is reminiscent of the high, narrow Cubist pictures. Elements that are complete in themselves, such as the right arm or the fish, are part of the picture surface; the left arm and the basket with its rough texture appear as overlapping planes. Also the feet turned sidewise and the folds around the knee, which are shaped like mathematical curves, are adapted to the flat character of the picture, without the slightest regard for anatomy. The more three-dimensional quality of the upper part of the figure corresponds to the foreshortened bench. A certain incompatibility between the ornamental beauty of the lines and the tendency to fullness of volume is determined by a new stylistic purpose, which will be discussed below. While an expressive tendency reminiscent of the Blue Period, except for the heavy forms, asserts itself in the fingers of the right hand, the expression of the head, with its regular outlines, has been neutralized to the point of immobility.

*Neapolitan Woman* page 184 and Cl. Cat. 80

Although it is composed exactly like a Cubist still life, the well-known water color *Siesta* of 1919, which shows two sleeping peasants, reveals a tremendous preoccupation with volume—probably encouraged by Renoir's late works. In 1920, this preoccupation creates figures which are literally colossi, concurrently with the most delicate line drawings. At that time Picasso fashioned a race of giantesses with powerful limbs, strongly modeled by light, ponderously inactive in resting or standing positions, without sensual charm in their nudity, and set against severe folds of drapery. They are painted statues, such as had been anticipated in some figures of 1906, although without the Baroque quality. In these works Picasso translates into the language of plastic form what Juan Gris meant when he said that he started from the cylinder to create an individual of a special type. Picasso assembles his titanic women from abstract volumes. That is why their faces, influenced by Hellenistic models, lack expressive life. Their forms are like those of Adam not yet animated by the divine breath—sullen, unwieldy masses. On the other hand, the forms themselves, colossal and rounded almost to the point of bursting, contain a Baroque expressive element, which frequently appears with equal vigor in later works.

Cl. Cat. 101–108, 255, 256 *Seated Nude* page 387

*Head of a Man* page 386

After 1922 the exaggerated massiveness gradually subsides, the swellings recede, the ponderous Baroque forms occasionally yield to a graceful, idyllic infatuation with Rococo forms, with pairs of lovers and cupids. Here, the plastic effect is often produced by sharp lights and darks, as in the monumental canvas *Pipes of Pan*, painted in 1923, and particularly in the magnificent drawings of figure compositions of that year. When they are done with the pen only, the deep shadows are produced by hatchings which are at times systematic, at times scribbled, but which, as in sculptors' drawings, follow the form.

The sheet showing Pan with a flute and two nymphs playing with a crab (page 186) obviously echoes Poussin in its heavy splotches of shadow, in its arrangement of the figures, and in its bucolic mood. On the other hand, the forms of the slender women with their thin joints

*The Pipes of Pan* Cl. Cat. 110 *Reclining Nude and Young Man with Pipes of Pan* Cl. Cat. 86 *Two Nudes and Youth Playing the Pipes of Pan* page 186

are more like the Neo-Classic ideal of the eighteenth century. But what is most remarkable in the drawing is the manner in which the figures are integrated with their surroundings, which might be described in naturalistic terms as a beach. The figures are completely surrounded by networks of lines of varying density, which combine with the white patches of the limbs and the large splotches of shadows into a surface design; that surface design exists independently of the three-dimensional composition of the figures. Its counterpart can be found in certain "flat" still lifes of the same time which have the same sort of network effect. We can see that the postures of the nymphs and the positions of their limbs are adapted to the flat character of the whole, and that the exaggeratedly angular forms of the man and the striped pattern of his pipes and his fingers are even more adapted to the over-all system. Thanks to the crab motif, the white of the sheet becomes the perspective foreground. This is a completely successful magic trick. The artist has once again reserved the final metamorphosis for the beholder's imagination.

The emotional coldness of the giantesses of 1920 and 1921 often yields in the works of 1923 to a warm tenderness, as in the *Young Girl and Little Boy* (page 390) or in the more frequently reproduced *Lovers* in Chicago, showing a couple before a window. The bright and luminous colors of the theatrical costumes betray the influence of Pompeian color. The delicate tones of the Basel Museum's seated *Harlequin*, of the same year, go so far as to take us back to the "Circus Period" of 1905. The peculiarly sentimental mood of this picture also characterizes the classic line drawings executed in 1925, when Picasso went to Monte Carlo to attend ballet performances there. Unlike the pencil drawings of 1919, these are done with ink, and for that reason have an even harder, almost glassy quality. For the most part they show groups of male figures dancing. Usually one of the figures whose legs are parallel to the picture plane serves as a point of reference in space for determining the spatial positions of the others. The indolence of their motions matches well the dreamy, absorbed expressions of the faces, and stands in striking contrast to the solidity of the figures which are muscular and soft at the same time. Here the artist yields to the fluent harmony of the long lines without deviating from correct perspective foreshortening in the traditional sense. By indicating the vanishing lines he himself challenges us to verify his perspective—and find it correct! In other drawings—both earlier and later—he has no such ambition: the harmonious interweaving of the white spaces among the black threads of the drawing is predominant, and anatomy is sacrificed to the expressive mobility of the limbs. This technique culminates in the etchings for Ovid's *Metamorphoses* published in 1931, in which the purity of the lines, the sparing use of shading, and the balance of the composition come close to perfection (pages 35, 37). In the etchings for Aristophanes' *Lysistrata* (1934), restrained treatment of subject matter and purely linear balance of the sheet are dropped in favor of greater decorative richness. In the 1940s, at Antibes, Picasso once again achieved sublime lightness in his linear style (page 60).

(p. 189) *Mother and Child* ca. 1922
(p. 191) *Paul Sketching* 1923

### Picasso and Surrealism

After 1927 Picasso's works contain features that may be termed Surrealist. Even though slight tendencies in this direction occasionally are to be found before 1927, they are not yet explored consistently. While it can be shown that the gradual progress toward Cubism in his paintings obeys an inner necessity, Surrealism was an influence from the outside. Picasso took from it only those elements which could enrich his own art; he used it just as he had used the art of the past or of non-European cultures. Moreover he was influenced less by individual Surrealist painters or their works than by the new vistas they opened, as well as by his association with the leading poets of the movement: for Guillaume Apollinaire, the champion of Cubism, before his untimely death also gave Surrealism its name. Picasso was closely connected with the Surrealist poet Paul Eluard, after the mid-thirties. From about that time he himself wrote Surrealist poems which he planned to publish with Vollard in 1939, accompanied with his own marginal drawings. On the other hand it cannot be denied that leading Surrealist painters, among them his younger compatriot Joan Miró and the German Max Ernst, influenced him to some extent. Picasso even took part in Surrealist exhibitions. But although André Breton, author of the Surrealist manifestoes of 1924 and 1930, includes him in the movement, Picasso is no more a Surrealist than Paul Klee, whose works also contain some Surrealist elements. But although Picasso's contact with Surrealism is only peripheral, a brief discussion of its nature and aims may be useful at this point.

Like Cubism, Surrealism is based on the breaking up of the natural object. As early as World War I, Dadaism, the Swiss-born progenitor of Surrealism, had uprooted objects from their familiar contexts and broken them up in an arbitrary manner. The Surrealists collected these naturalistic fragments of objects and reassembled them in unusual, indeed paradoxical and perverse, patterns. They combined parts of the human body with pieces of furniture or factory chimneys, flowers with railroad signals or clinical appliances, thus achieving baffling effects. They often used the technique of *collage*, but not as the Cubists had

*Reclining Woman*
page 157

Note 16

193

done. To them it was not the shapes but the recognizability of the fragments which was important.

Surrealism finds its theoretical justification in its preoccupation with
the unconscious: it starts from the fact that in our dreams we associate
things that can never be associated by logical standards. The Surrealist
painter explores this unknown world, and his aim is to record the
fantasy and symbolism of the unconscious. Therefore he must, at least
in theory, renounce conscious, volitional artistic creation. To eliminate
the conscious, personal factor he resorts to such methods as automatic
writing, and becomes a medium, a discoverer of revelations made
manifest through him, thus more or less surrendering to chance. In
actual practice, such complete self-alienation can scarcely be achieved,
but in theory Surrealism differs sharply from Cubism, which proceeds
consciously and deliberately. What is reported about Picasso's attempts
to make automatic drawings in a dark room is worth mentioning in this
context. At the first trial he declared that he knew that he was drawing
the head of a woman; at the second trial he declared that he did not
know it, but he drew the same head facing in the opposite direction. As
Cesare Brandi puts it, "his unconscious repeated his conscious performance." No wonder that the Cubist Picasso never subscribed to the principles of Surrealism, even though he made use of some of its discoveries.
What he appropriated primarily was the Surrealist "metamorphosis."

The need to unify the heterogeneous components of Surrealist painting led to the Surrealist "metamorphosis." This offered the opportunity
for the linking together of those fragments. In these metamorphoses
technological forms are born from natural growths, and man-made
objects suddenly develop monstrous organic excrescences: anything can
change into anything, as in fairy tales. The artist enjoys complete freedom and joyfully unleashes his creative energies as though he had
wrested the secret of life from nature and were now in a position to
direct biological growth according to the whims of his imagination.

*Bather* page 392

Picasso's series of *Bathers* (page 392), drawn at Cannes in 1927, shows
us specimens of such monsters: we get the impression that various parts
of the human body have been stimulated by injections to produce grotesque excrescences. As far back as the early twenties Picasso had
manifested a tendency toward such exaggerations in some paintings of
nudes on beaches. For instance a thigh or a foot was tremendously
oversized in relation to the figure as a whole, or to its tiny head; but
then such disproportions were the result of exaggerated perspective
foreshortenings. Cesare Brandi has established that the well-known

*Three Dancers* page 203

*Three Dancers* of 1925 (page 203) contains Surrealist elements, but there
they still play a subordinate part. Not so in the *Bathers* of 1927. Here
the human figure serves merely as the starting point; although certain
segments can be identified as the head, the arms, the legs, and the
breasts, these elements are arranged with Cubist freedom and linked

*Metamorphose* page 434

together in a metamorphic pattern, so that they seem to grow out of
each other. The result is something like an amoebic formation or some
fantastic plant. Aesthetically, at least, we cannot help but admire the
vitality and robustness of these females.

*On the Beach* page 211

In another series of small beach scenes with figures in striped bathing
suits, playing ball, painted at Dinard a year later (page 211), Picasso
again disregards the natural proportions of the human body. Here the

194

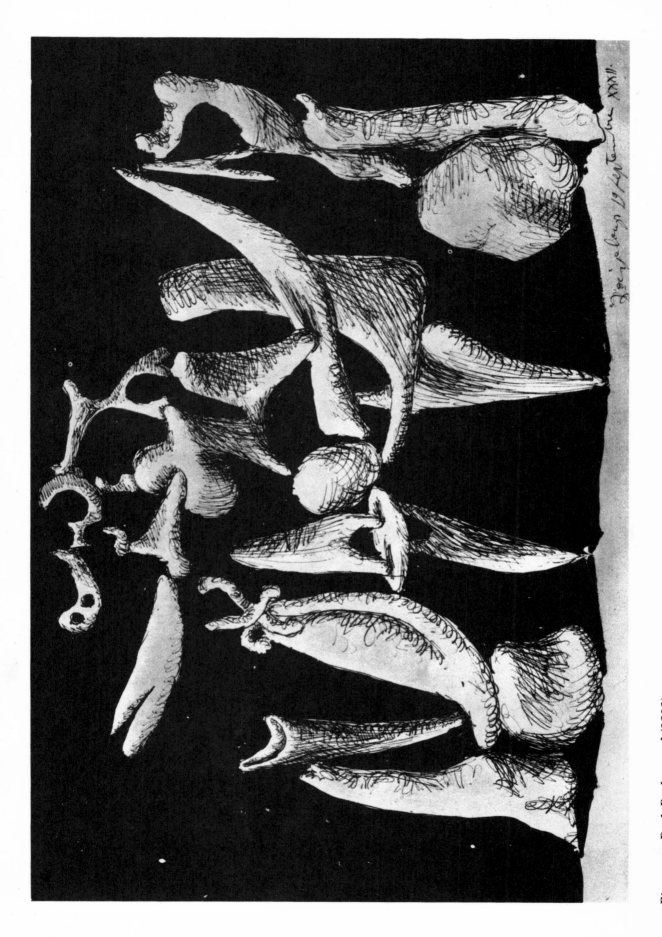

*Figures on Dark Background* (1932)

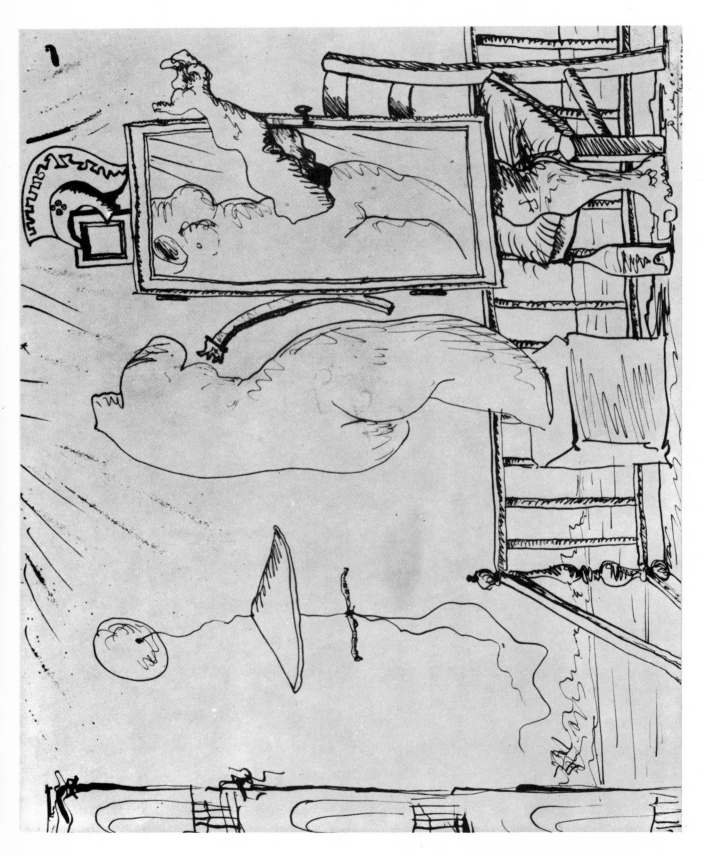

*Torso* (1933)

*On the Beach* (1933)

*The Fall of Phaëton* (1930)

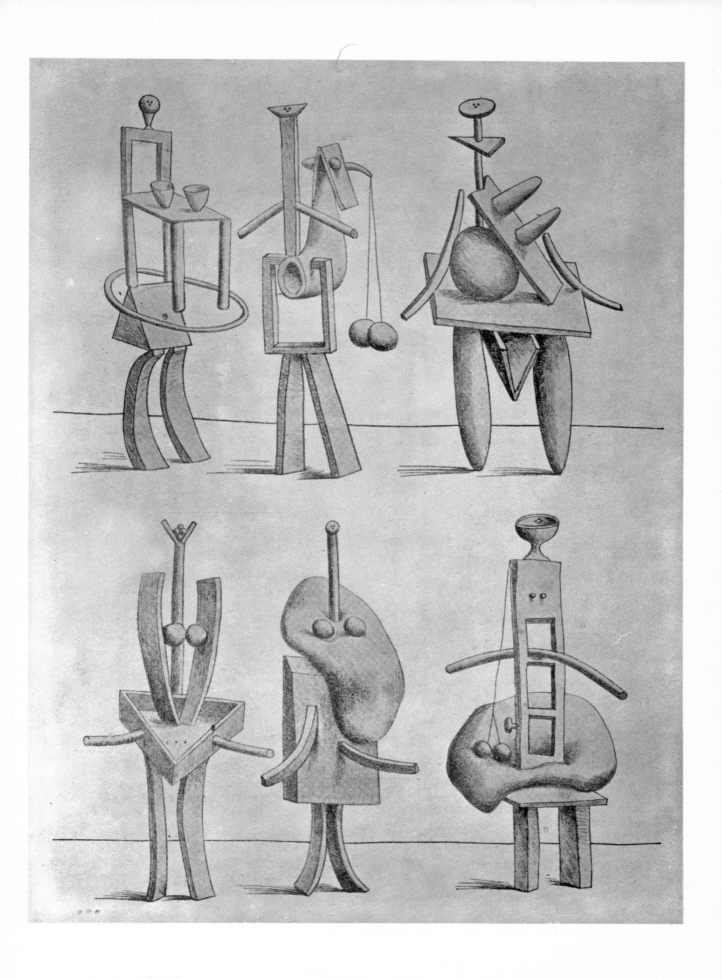

*An Anatomy* (1933)

*Surrealist Still Life* (1934)

treatment is two-dimensional and the interest is focused on the lively gestures of oversized arms eager to catch the ball. Maurice Gieure has given us a particularly detailed analysis of these works of the Dinard period, of their erotic subjects and psychological background. In the *Seated Bather* of 1929 (page 393) and related works, some of which partly date from a much later time (page 483), fantastic pseudo-natural growths are combined with machine-like structures—a conception which might be paralleled with the modern tendency to use organic forms for technological designs (streamlining). The seated bather's "human" posture and gestures are all the more striking in view of the technological articulations of the form. Moreover, in order fully to understand this figure one must keep in mind the aspirations of modern sculpture. All these attempts to give plausibility to imaginary organic-technological phenomena of growth were fruitful preliminary steps to subsequent artistic solutions.

*Seated Bather* page 393

*Seated Nude* Cl. Cat. 264

Surrealist in inspiration is also the idea of "monuments"—painted or sculptured representations of "unnatural" growth or striking combinations of fragments of diverse origins. During his visit to Dinard and Cannes Picasso made a number of drawings which he conceived as designs for monuments to be set up along the Croisette, the seaside promenade at Cannes (page 395). They consist of vertical, crudely modeled organic fragments pieced together in such a way that they arouse in the beholder associations of living creatures. A composition of this kind is also the aquatint drawing of 1932 (page 195), one of a series of Surrealist variations based on the Isenheim *Crucifixion*, of Matthias Grünewald. It is constructed of undefined forms reminiscent of bone fragments, and the resultant form—chiefly because of its upright posture—suggests vague similarities to organisms.

*Figures on Dark Background* page 195 Note 17

The method used here is related to a specific Surrealist technique invented by Max Ernst in 1925, and based on the fact that the creative imagination is stimulated by amorphous or irregularly shaped objects, such as clouds, rocks, fragments of walls, and tree barks, which the unconscious interprets as figures. This technique was named *frottage* because Max Ernst actually made contact rubbings on paper with his pencil when first drawing such irregular structures. In order to exclude conscious creation as far as possible, Ernst freely admitted chance into the realm of art—a method since exploited by many other painters. Looking at Picasso's drawing, we recall that the same hallucinatory imagination is at work when people discover human shapes in the mandrake root. Little gnome-like figures appear in related drawings of that year, beings such as occasionally haunted Picasso's early works. This drawing, however, is striking chiefly for the way in which its elements are fitted together. The artist's share here is far more active than it is in the Surrealist *frottage*. And this is characteristic of Picasso.

The Surrealist influence is most strongly apparent in 1933, when Picasso sketched a series of drawings called *An Anatomy* (page 199), showing a series of little figures put together of organic and non-organic components, reminiscent of the "little men" that children occasionally piece together out of dried fruit and matchsticks. The machine-like elements in these figures can be traced back to the Cubist *objet* period as when, in a drawing of 1912 (page 18), Picasso unconsciously gave human proportions to a construction devoid of organic elements. This

*An Anatomy* page 199

*Construction* page 18

was long before Max Ernst had begun to give human traits to technological appliances. Animating these shapes in anthropomorphic fashion is as characteristic of Picasso as his active and conscious steering of the imagination.

He does not record dreams, but constructs images, even when his manner is as Surrealist as in some pen drawings of July 1933 (page 196), where he brings together objectively unrelated elements that are usually associated only in dreams. We see a porch bordered by a railing, whose spatial relation to the house at the left and the distant landscape is not defined. On it are assembled a torso of Venus, a window casement on a broken chair, isolated human limbs (in plaster), an ancient helmet, and an ordinary bottle. In addition to the contrasts of texture—stone, glass, plaster, wood, metal—the chief stress is laid on the different degrees of reality. The stone and plaster reproduce natural human forms; Venus reappears in the glass as a reflected image, cut by the massive sturdy arm; the helmet has the unreal quality of the past; the chair is a wreck; only the bottle is fully "real," although all the other objects are also shown in their true spatial extension. They do not add up to a still life, but behave anthropomorphically: we get the impression that the Venus, although she has no head, contemplates herself in the mirror, and that the plaster arm, as an element of the vertical structure which begins with the foot at the bottom and ends with the helmet on top, is upraised in a gesture full of pathos. Also the peculiar floating figure at the left seems to be endowed with life. It recedes somewhat in perspective (because of its proximity to the house), and its obvious lightness as against the earthy heaviness of the other objects in the picture introduces an additional contrast. Furthermore we may observe an opposition of forms in the organic round, and artificial angular, elements. In a related water color of the same year (page 197) similar elements add up to a fundamentally different effect: the anthropomorphism of the "Surrealist" Picasso gives enough common character to the heterogeneous objects to let us imagine a beach populated with insect-like human beings.

The clearly delineated, stylized heads of women, dated 1929 (page 327), are paintings that can be interpreted as sketches for a gigantic monument. The differences of scale—the cosmic one of the sky and of the round earth surface which supports the monument, that of the men walking on the monument, and that of the head—are hardly compatible. For although the "woman's head" and the "monument" are here identical in intention, they do not seem compatible because the detailed, flat treatment of the head and the cubic treatment of the monument are not at all identical from the point of view of form.

Even this example shows that in Picasso the Surrealist surprise element is based on form rather than subject matter. In the large pen drawing of 1934 (page 200) he follows a path entirely his own. To be sure, we still find naturalistic fragments of objects, such as the hollow plaster arm hung on the wooden wall and the spear to its left, as well as supranatural growths, such as the grotesque creature with two legs and one arm, which is somehow related to the bull's head drawn on a sheet on the wall. But what is crucial for the composition is the graphic elements, particularly on the right side, and the flat arrangement of the variously articulated parts, interlocked in accordance with Cubist rules.

(p. 203) *Three Dancers* 1925

The figure forms in this drawing—two overlapping human profiles intersected by a little table with a vase (one of the profiles is linked with a helmet), and a third, horizontal profile—are doubtless Surrealist features that enrich the composition. Nevertheless, the artistic law governing the strong and compact forms in this drawing and their life in space and on the surface is Picasso's own, and it is a law that bears the unmistakable stamp of Cubism.

## Symbolic Themes

As we have shown, Picasso made considerable use of Surrealist devices such as linking heterogeneous elements and levels of reality, or the process of formal metamorphosis; but in doing so he was guided by conscious artistic objectives to a greater extent than the Surrealist painters. This does not mean that the unconscious does not influence his art. His works, like those of other artists, unquestionably contain dream-like and "archaic" elements (as the term is used in depth psychology), and symbols that spring from the collective unconscious.

Symbolic themes preoccupied and sometimes even obsessed Picasso in the 1930s when he came to grips with Surrealism. The period in question culminates with a kind of crystallization of the themes in *Guernica*, the masterpiece of our century. A discussion of Picasso's unconscious symbolism necessarily touches on various psychoanalytic and even psychiatric interpretations of his works. These have been unsuccessful because they did not pay sufficient attention to the specifically artistic content of these works. Hence it is not surprising that

Note 18

Picasso reacted rather violently to C. G. Jung's characterization of him, on the occasion of the Zurich exhibition of 1932, as a "schizophrenic." On the other hand Picasso himself pointed to a more fruitful approach when he declared in 1935 that a photographic record of the transformations of his pictures might be useful: "Possibly one might discover the

Note 19

path followed by the brain in materializing a dream." Only by following the symbolic themes in a number of related works which "the painter paints to unload himself of feelings and visions," can we hope to discover their meanings at least in rough outline. Accordingly our discussion will begin with the early works.

We have two pen drawings enriched with colored chalk, dating from 1901, in which the two main protagonists of Picasso's symbolic works, the bull and the horse, are rendered in a relatively objective manner: the bull, which is light in color, is shown in repose, without indication of sex; the horse is dark, and is built like the elegant saddle horses that Liebermann was fond of painting, and may reflect Picasso's fashionable preoccupations in Barcelona at that time. Characteristically, it is a mare—as is usually the case in the later works. During the same year

(p. 207) *Seated Woman* 1927

Picasso treated the tragedy of these animals in several paintings of bullfights; particularly the fate of the picador's bleeding horse, gored by the bull, is depicted with obvious sympathy.

*Bullfight* page 115

These two motifs—the bullfight and the symbolic treatment of the bull and the horse—were later combined. In 1917 Picasso made a large number of drawings, in most of which the raging bull and the horse lying helpless on the ground are a self-contained group, isolated from the bullfight as a whole. The massiveness of the attacking bull is here opposed to the weakness of the horse with its outstretched legs; and the color contrast between the black bull and the light horse, and the different sex of the two animals, underscores this opposition. In chalk drawings of the same period the bleeding horse vainly tries to rise, its bowels hanging from its abdomen, its neck outstretched in agony (page 236). The theme of the dying horse, particularly of its head, had often been treated by Picasso before he treated it monumentally in *Guernica:* we find the heads of dying horses in some of the etchings for Balzac's *Unknown Masterpiece* of 1931, where they are shown with bulls (page 394). In the etchings of the spring of 1933, known under the collective title *L'atelier du sculpteur*, the horse and the bull are again sometimes united Surrealistically, on the same sheet.

*Dying Horse* page 236

*Seated Nude Surrounded by Sketches of Animals and Men* page 394

We may say without exaggeration that Picasso has been obsessed by the subject of bullfights from his earliest years. The various aspects of the bullfight are deeply engraved in his memory. As a young man he often earned the price of his admission to the Plaza by making bullfight drawings which he sold on the eve of the contest; later, like another Goya, he represented the various phases of the bullfight in striking drawings (page 345), etchings (page 396), or ceramic plates (page 451). And this, despite the fact that he has not returned to Spain for many years. One is almost tempted to say that this theme was favored by his absence from Spain; it appears for instance in 1919 in the sketches he made in London for the ballet *Le Tricorne*.

*The Picador* page 396
*Bull and Horse* page 345

*Study for the Curtain of the Ballet "Le Tricorne"* page 181

The significance of the bull and the horse is not confined to the parts they play in the bloody drama of the bullfight. This is evident in the pencil drawings of March 1921, in which the relationship between the two animals is portrayed as relatively gentle and peaceful, and even more evident in the etching *Bull and Horse* of 1927 (page 394), in which they are represented as playful domestic animals: nothing here reminds us of the dreadful seriousness of the moment. However, the contrast between the unwieldy, aggressive, brutal, and savage bull, and the graceful, sensitive, and gentle horse, i.e., the sexual characteristics of the male and the female, are decisively stressed. These sheets do not embody a life and death struggle, but a playful contest between the sexes, in which the animals assume specific roles. But this pleasant, erotic symbolism is not all. It is supplemented by and suffused with the symbolization of further, more extensive realms of life.

*Bull and Horse* page 394

We see this, for instance, when we compare the "peaceful" scene of the etching with the brutal attack represented in the brush drawing of May 26, 1935 (page 397). While the overtone of sexuality is clearly present also in the later sheet, the sharpening of the contrast suggests a new interpretation: the bull has now become the embodiment of untamed nature, of evil. The concentrated strength in the fore part of the body, expressed particularly in the tremendous tension of the line

*The Beast* page 397

of the neck, and the gigantic swishing tail invest the bull with a destructive fury, to which the delicate horse, characterized as weak even by the technical treatment of its forms, can only oppose the innocent purity of its trembling fear. The motif once again includes bullfight details: the raging bull with the deadly sword thrust into his neck and *banderillas* in his back, and the boards of the ring enclosure are indicated by horizontal strokes. Moreover it is worth noting that while the event has become more demonic, the bull has become humanized through the emphasis laid on the upper body and the detailed treatment of the facial features. Finally, the connection between the battle scene and the bearded profile head at the right edge, which is contrasted to the main action by its lofty repose, is not unessential, and by no means accidental.

A month earlier, in a mock attempt to liberate himself from his obsession with the bull, Picasso had made a pen drawing of a hippopotamus-like monster, in which characteristics similar to those of the bull in the above-mentioned drawing are exaggeratedly stressed. Picasso's Spanish bent for the monstrous and the demonic is manifested not only in the national symbol of the bull, but also in other animal forms, above all in the lithograph of the uncannily phosphorescent *Toad* of 1949 (page 424).

Comparable to the bearded profile head of 1935 is the equally larger-than-life, motionless head of a female spectator of a bullfight in the etching of September 8, 1934 (page 396), which, like the later drawings, belongs to a group of works produced by Picasso during those two years at Boisgeloup, in Normandy. Here the whole bullfight has become demonic; even the building and the public are drawn into the apocalyptic vortex, so that the little heads of the crowd appear simultaneously everywhere in the chaos of the struggle, even between the teeth of the diabolical bull. The true adversary of the bull seems to be not so much the picador as the horse that carries him and rushes forward although it is severely wounded. This time even the head of the horse does not express gentleness and suffering; instead, it is convulsively distorted. But the most noteworthy symbolic figure is a female matador whom the bull has tossed over his back and whose upper body is formed Surrealistically of nude breasts and an over-long neck and head. We find the origin of this figure in drawings of 1923, which show a picador lying across the back of the raging bull, his glance turned upward. In a painting of September 1933 and an etching of June 20, 1934, the figure has become a woman, and the dying horse is now also flung across the back of the bull.

The female matador reappears in the large etching *Minotauromachy*, which sums up this whole group of works: the drawings mentioned above will have prepared us for the discussion of this etching. But let us first consider a few more representations of the Minotaur, which prelude the appearance of the monster in the large etching.

As early as 1933 the Minotaur is treated in various ways in a series of etchings. About a year later, also at Boisgeloup, Picasso made a brush drawing in vertical format (page 398) which shows the Minotaur holding in his arms a girl sacrificed to him. The bull-headed monster is now so humanized that essentially only the head and position of the shoulders are animal. This is the result of a transformation that can be followed step by step, and whose genesis in Picasso corresponds to the collective

(p. 211) *On the Beach* 1928

origin of such hybrid figures of mythology. Picasso was not primarily inspired by the old myth, but the transformations suggested to him by his unconscious finally coincided with the mythological image of the Minotaur.

The downward-curving figure of the girl in our drawing is closely related to the female matador of the 1934 bullfight etching, as well as to a group of very decorative, stylized, richly curved nudes of 1932 who are characterized by a flat treatment and lively colors. Each of these canvases shows a nude painted in cool tones slumbering on a sofa against an ornamental background combined with flowers and other objects, as, for instance, a luminous red pillow. Such an ensemble, and the ingratiating round contours, with the head thrown back, give these pictures a particularly joyful, even sensual character; at the same time the expression of the sleeping figures suggests that they are having nightmares. Before these nudes we cannot help being reminded of the nightmarish visions of John Henry Füssli; both are born of dreams. In several later drawings, these hedonistic nudes of Picasso are transported to a realm of terror; they are surrendered to the Minotaur, who rapes the helpless girls in scenes containing details that are clearly reminiscent of the destruction of the horse by the bull.

*Dream* page 221

An important formal link between the nudes and these drawings is a small oil painted as early as 1932, in which the same type of woman appears, leaning on a bearded man. Since, in addition, the Minotaur appears in several vivid drawings of 1936 as the outright enemy and destroyer of the horse, the equation "woman—horse," as it was anticipated decades earlier in the illustrations for the *Unknown Masterpiece* (page 315), finds a new confirmation in connection with the Minotaur theme.

*The Rescue* Cl. Cat. 136

*Minotaur and Maiden* page 53

*Woman and Horse* page 315

All the dream symbols discussed so far—the bull, the horse, the woman, hybrids, and spectators—as well as some new ones, appear together in the *Minotauromachy* of 1935, a large etching measuring $19^{1}/_{2}$ by $27^{1}/_{4}$ inches (page 401), the most important symbolic work of Picasso prior to *Guernica*. We shall use it here to explore the possibilities of a coherent interpretation, with the reservation imposed by Picasso himself, in a statement he made that same year: "How can anyone enter into my dreams, my instincts, my desires, my thoughts, which have taken a long time to mature and to emerge into daylight? Above all, who can discover from them what I was really after—perhaps against my will?"

*Minotauromachy* page 401

Note 21

We shall begin with listing the elements of the picture. The scene is laid outdoors, on a beach—a sailboat can be distinguished in the distance. At the left a closed space is formed by a tower-like building and an abutting wall. At the center we find the familiar dying horse with its bowels hanging from its belly; across its back lies the female matador, her eyes closed, her breasts bared, her sword raised in a gesture of self-protection. At the right we see the Minotaur, with the human body, gigantic bull's head, small tail, and claw-like toes that appeared in the 1934 caricature of the monster. He extends his colossal right arm above the central group in the direction of a burning candle held by a little girl standing at the left; in her other hand she holds a bouquet. Behind the girl, a man in a loincloth climbs a ladder; his oversized bearded head is shown in profile, and his gaze is directed to the main action. In a window niche in the tower two women watch a pair of doves on the sill.

While the figure of the Minotaur and the presence of the sea in the picture undoubtedly refer to the ancient myth and its Cretan origin (moreover Picasso may have been particularly interested in Crete, as the birthplace of El Greco), the other elements of the composition cannot be traced to any antecedent whatsoever. What can they tell us about Picasso's artistic imagination and its unconscious motivations? Freudian analysts who are chiefly concerned with the latter interpret the bull, the horse, the matador, and the two doves as symbols of sexual events, and the contemplative figures of the little girl who watches these events with astonishment, and of the bearded man who is running away from them to a higher world, as disguises of the painter himself. More generally, psychoanalysts account for many elements in Picasso's art, and even for the changes of style, by postulating childhood trauma. Even granting that there is an intimate connection between artistic activity and sexual behavior, such an interpretation leaves the actual phenomenon of art out of account. Picasso's symbols—like those of Chagall—may derive from archaic and sexual elements, but having been transferred to the domain of art, they are subject to different laws. "A work of art is more than the motives which called it into being," as one Freudian interpreter says correctly in an otherwise abortive study of Picasso's works.

Note 22

Jungian psychology casts considerable light on the contents of the etching, but inevitably hits wide of the mark when it attempts to combine the dream elements into a logical system, which can be explained in rational terms. The interpretation given by Curt G. Seckel, which we sum up here, deserves consideration though it suffers from the same drawback. According to Seckel, the *Minotauromachy* symbolizes the Jungian "journey to Hades," and its action is an encounter between the luminous daylight world and the dark underworld. The same symbolism can be found in the Spanish bullfight. The Minotaur embodies the irrational violence of the unconscious depths. The horse and the matador are symbols of the world of justice and reason; they embody the female principle and are thus interchangeable. The little girl with the light and the flowers is an image of what is best and purest in man—his creative soul. Guiltless and invulnerable, she knows nothing of "the self-conscious seduction by the pure idea, nor of the fascination of the powers of darkness"; she is a symbol of "man restored to his wholeness." The burning candle in her hand stands for the highest Eros, whose shining light pierces the darkness; the Minotaur's colossal hand tries vainly to ward off this light. "The creative act of the eternal marriage between light and darkness is brought to life in its full complexity in this picture."

Couched in such general terms, this interpretation sounds convincing enough. We may paraphrase it for our own purposes as follows:

Picasso represents the defeat of vulnerable, highly organized forces by the overwhelming forces of barbarism. He pictures the former in female symbols, and the latter in the male symbol of the bull-headed monster which draws its strength from the untamed depths of sexuality. Thus Picasso is testifying to his high respect both for the female principle and the virile forces of his own nature. The *Guernica* will show

*Guernica* pages 233/34

(p. 215) *Paul as Pierrot* 1929
(p. 217) *Still Life on a Table* 1931

that these symbols may also stand for much more comprehensive human experiences. The little girl's serene confidence unquestionably embodies a supreme value that mankind has retained in the desperate crisis of our age. The women with the doves and the man on the ladder reflect on the action without intervening in it. The man, as contrasted with the child, is insecure; his immobile head, loosely joined to the body, indicates a high capacity for intellectual knowledge.

Such an interpretation does not imply that the *Minotauromachy* was composed in a spirit of cold calculation, which would be incompatible with the artistic unity of the work. At the same time, however, we must keep in mind that the artist who uses symbols which originate in the unconscious elaborates them by processes which are in part rational, and that their original contents undergo profound changes before they are revealed in the work of art.

In addition to contributing to our insight into the creative process, the *Minotauromachy*, like the works of the Blue and the Rose Periods, clearly refutes the thesis, frequently advanced, that Picasso and his art are "soulless." The inwardness of the child, the dreaminess of the matador, the meditativeness of the spectators, the horror in the face of the horse, and even the dark fury of the Minotaur are deeply felt expressions of the psyche.

Between 1935 and 1937 Picasso went through a long fallow period (he had experienced a similar one in 1927), during which he composed some of his Surrealist poems. *The Dream and Lie of Franco*, etched in January 1937, is also half-literary in character: the plates are accompanied by a satirical poem, and the arrangement of the little scenes is like that of an American comic strip. The occasion for this work was the Spanish Civil War, which broke out in the summer of 1936. Picasso, who until then had shown no interest in politics, now became a resolute champion of the Loyalists; he even accepted the directorship of the Prado (in this case a directorship in name only), and sold several paintings for the benefit of Republican Spain. He produced this series of etchings to serve as propaganda against the Franco government. They cover two plates done in aquatint. Each plate is divided into nine scenes; only five scenes of the second plate belong to the Franco cycle.

The symbols of the bull and of the horse appear here in conjunction with a Surrealist figure which stands for Franco and, with changing emblems, occurs in several variations. We are particularly interested, in anticipation of our discussion of *Guernica*, in the relation of this figure to the horse and to the bull. The very first scene shows a belligerent Franco astride a horse whose bowels hang from its belly in the manner familiar to us. In the eighth scene too he is shown torturing the winged horse and driving a lance through its body. In the tenth scene, the winged horse, body torn open, is dying at Franco's feet (page 400). In the twelfth, a white horse, obviously dead, lies on the ground; under it we see the bearded head of the man on the ladder in the *Minotauromachy*. It is worth noting that this twelfth scene is in obvious parallel to the eleventh, which shows a landscape with a dead woman: in other words, here too horse and woman are equated. The bull appears for the first time in the fifth scene, as a dangerous adversary of Franco, who succumbs to it in the last two scenes. In the very last one, whose arrangement is strikingly reminiscent of the etching of 1927 (page 394),

*Dream and Lie of Franco, II* page 400

219

Franco surprisingly assumes the shape of a horse, though he retains his characteristic head. Now it is he who dies as horses die in the bullfight arena. In all the other scenes the horse is pictured as a creature tormented by Franco, while the bull is always unmistakably his superior in strength. We shall have to take these facts into account in the interpretation of *Guernica*, to which the last four scenes of the second plate of the Franco series are closely related.

(p. 221) *Dream* 1932
(p. 223) *Farmer's Wife on Stepladder* 1933

# Guernica

Next to the *Demoiselles d'Avignon*, Picasso's most important work historically is *Guernica* (now in the Museum of Modern Art, New York), named after the Basque town destroyed by an air raid on April 26, 1937. The very title of this canvas, chosen by the painter himself, as well as its large size (11 feet 6 inches by 25 feet 8 inches) and the circumstances of its first public showing (about which more later) emphasize its special character. Juan Larrea, who devoted an extensive monograph to it, justly praises it as "the most famous painting of our time. No other picture portrays and defines our age so completely." We shall make no attempt here to substantiate this judgment which, considering our closeness to the work, cannot pretend to be more than an anticipation or intuition. We shall confine ourselves to defining the place *Guernica* occupies in Picasso's development; ir doing so we shall also gain some insight into its exceptional artistic importance. We begin with a brief description of the painting, which will serve as the basis for a discussion of its genesis and an interpretation of its contents.

*Guernica* pages 233/34

The canvas shows a shallow space like that of a stage. Its left half, illumined by a large lamp, suggests an interior; the burning house with several openings in the right half produces the illusion of an outdoor scene. The central figure, which belongs to both halves of the picture, represents a horse, pierced by a spear, collapsing on its knees. In front of the horse we see a dead warrior, clutching the hilt of a broken sword in his right hand, near which a small shoot rises from the dark ground; his head and left arm occupy the extreme lower left of the canvas. A half-clothed female figure, gazing upward, seems to crawl from the right toward the horse. Above her a screaming woman leans from the window. Her enormous profile is turned toward the center; the outstretched arm with the lamp, and the hand and the breasts in the window are hers. At the extreme right, in front of the crumbling wall of the burning house, and partly covered by wreckage, there is a third woman, surrounded by flames, with a fearfully deformed head and reaching arms. To the left of the horse, the largest figure is a bull in an aggressive attitude. Its head is turned sidewise, and its tail is upraised; its body seems curiously to merge with a table that recedes diagonally to the right. Above the table is the outline of a bird with stretched neck and open beak. In front of the bull there is a woman with a senseless child in her arms; her face with its open-mouthed grimace is turned heavenward.

The flat composition follows a strict triangular design. The lamp in the woman's hand is the apex of this equilateral triangle whose right side is formed by the woman approaching the horse, and the left by the hind part of the horse and the dead warrior on the ground. The woman with the lifeless or sleeping child, the bull, the bird, and the large lamp, as well as the house with the leaning woman and the burning woman, are outside the triangle, to its left and to its right. The predominant formal means are the flat elements of Synthetic Cubism of the 1920s, which are used in a particularly characteristic manner in the treatment of the horse. While the bull's head, and to some extent the human heads, are shown in the multiple views of Cubism, the oversized limbs of the figures at the lower ends of the canvas are reminiscent of the elephantine forms of the period between 1920 and 1923; and while the Expressionistic human faces mark the continuation of a graphic development begun a short time earlier, the horse's head is treated Cubistically and with relative realism. Nevertheless, this work which represents formally a synthesis of various periods is unified in its total effect, not least thanks to the sober, "abstract" coloring—black, gray, and white— which is in keeping with the tragic events portrayed here and with the Spanish spirit of Picasso. The painting is not, however, devoid of delicate coloristic effects, since there is a subtle contrast between the diluted yellowish tonality of the natural canvas and the sometimes blue-gray mixture of black and white pigments, on the one hand, and the white-gray-black scale of the background, on the other hand. For instance, the warm effects seen in the bulb and the rays around the large almond-shaped white lamp and in the hair of the screaming woman are set off against her bluish flesh tones; and curiously enough, the flames around the burning woman at the right are also in cold tones.

As for the genesis of the composition: if we set aside its emotional, intellectual, and artistic antecedents, we must distinguish two main stages—the preliminary studies, and the revisions made on the canvas itself. Picasso had been commissioned to paint a representative work for the Spanish Pavilion of the Paris World's Fair as early as January 1937; he had not yet begun it when the news of the bombing of Guernica gave him the idea for the painting. On May 1, that is, a few days after the air raid, he prepared the first preliminary pencil sketches on blue paper (page 235). The drawing reproduced here is the earliest of about seventy known studies connected with *Guernica*. It contains the most important motifs of the final version—the dying horse at the center, the bull at the left, the bird above his back, the tower-like house at the right, and the woman with the outstretched arm in the window. Moreover, one or two human figures lying on the ground and a kneeling figure to the right of the tower are summarily indicated. On the same

*Composition Study for "Guernica"* page 235

(p. 227) *Woman in an Armchair* 1937

day there also reappears the dying horse of the drawings dated two decades earlier (page 236), and on the following day the upraised head of the horse receives a clearly defined and deeply moving form in several drawings and a study in oils (page 402).

*Dying Horse* page 236

*Head of a Horse* page 402

At the same time Picasso progressively clarifies the formal structure of the composition, although he is still primarily concerned with the choice of motifs to be portrayed. The woman holding the light approximates her final state; the fallen warrior lying under the horse and clutching his weapon is drawn more distinctly, and in one of the studies a small winged horse is seen emerging from the wound of the larger animal. A horizontal study directly preceding the work on the canvas (page 404) already shows the picture space framed by architectural forms, as well as the triangular pattern of the composition and the distribution of tones. At the center of this study there is a wheel, presumably of symbolic significance, and on the ground there are the heads of several victims; one of these heads, like the head in the twelfth scene of the Franco series (page 400), is within the outline of the horse.

*Composition Study for "Guernica"* page 404

*Dream and Lie of Franco, II* page 400

After May 8, Picasso worked intensively on the kneeling woman with the child to the right of the horse. Then, as the work progressed she was split up into two separate figures—a woman who occupies the same place as the woman in the finished picture (but without the child), and a woman with a child to the left of the bull. A woman with a child on a ladder appears only tentatively in drawings of May 9 and May 10; she is later replaced by the burning woman before the house.

The painting itself underwent radical changes in May and June. We can follow them with the help of eight photographs taken by Dora Maar. A comparative study of these, which cannot be undertaken here in detail, gives us interesting glimpses of Picasso's method of working.

*Guernica I* page 405

Particularly revealing is the first state of the drawing on the canvas (page 405), because it shows a number of auxiliary compositional lines entirely independent of the motifs. These lines helped Picasso to orient himself on the enormous surface and to determine the place and dimensions of each figure, and they have partly been preserved in the final state as lines separating the "color" planes. The central axis, probably one of the first lines, if not the first, that the painter drew on the empty canvas, indicated the altitude of the compositional triangle, the apex of which is formed by the light held by one of the women. The right side of his triangle, too, is indicated as an abstract line and the triangular patterns next to the burning woman on the right are developed from earlier representational forms. Here, the bird is at the right, lying on his back on the ground. Otherwise the right half of the canvas is substantially the same as we see it in the final version, except for the changes mentioned in connection with the preliminary studies. But the left half went through several mutations: least changed is the woman with the child at the extreme left, most changed is the bull, who originally extended from the center of the picture to its left border. The hind part of its body was to some extent covered by the horse, and by the enormous upraised arm of the dying warrior on the ground.

In the second state, this arm is treated symbolically, with the raised fist holding laurel branches in an aura of light. Subsequently this arm is entirely eliminated, and all that remains of the aura is the large eye-

229

shaped light source, inside which a bulb was later inserted as a "pupil."

*Guernica IV* page 407

In the fourth state (page 407), a crucial regrouping has taken place. While in the previous states the horse's head was bent down and enclosed by the contours of its body, now Picasso has decided to paint it as it appears in the study of May 2, i. e., to disentangle it from the chaotic mass of the body parts, and to secure for it a dominant effect by placing it under the large lamp against a dark background. This compelled him to swing the body of the bull a full 180 degrees to the left, and to represent it foreshortened. As though anticipating this change, he had, already in the third state, placed a crescent in the empty space

*Guernica III* page 406

of the upper left corner; the form of the crescent now appears in the bull's tail. The gap between the bull's head and the horse's head was filled by the curious "table" that lies in half shadow; above it was placed the bird, which in the first state had been lying on the ground at the right. The white strip cutting across it was part of the bull's back in the previous states. Finally, the dead warrior holding the broken sword (the other human figures lying on the ground which were shown in the preliminary studies have now been eliminated) has completely changed his position in the course of the progressive stages. Only the fist with the hilt of the sword and the little plant growing above it have remained in the same place. All these formal changes refute the assertion made by Raynal in his most recent book about Picasso: "*Guernica* no longer displays a reflective search for form; here Picasso completely surrenders to his emotion."

In interpreting the contents of *Guernica* we must proceed on two levels at the same time. Some of the motifs and episodes can be accounted for realistically as showing the consequences of the bombing of defenseless people and animals: such motifs, for instance, are the woman with the child and the woman falling into the flames. Other elements seem to be allegorical or at least susceptible to several interpretations; for instance, the large lamp above the horse's head is characterized as an earthly source of light, but at the same time the saw-tooth rays endow it with a metaphysical meaning. Just as in the case of the *Minotauromachy*, it would be erroneous to try to interpret *Guernica* point by point, as though it were a rebus. In conversations

Note 23

with an American painter in 1944 and 1945 Picasso explicitly denied that his works, including *Guernica*, were *conscious* symbolic allusions to specific persons or political events. Only after a long discussion did he concede the possibility of *unconscious* political references.

With this in mind, let us try to elucidate, as far as possible, the meaning of the picture. We shall begin with the central figure, the horse. We cannot agree with Larrea, to whom this horse symbolizes the death of Spanish Fascism, and thus Picasso's wishful thinking. Such an interpretation is contradicted by the fact that the horse in *Guernica* certainly has the sympathy of both the painter and the beholder. As we have seen, this has always been the case in Picasso's works, including *The Dream and Lie of Franco* etched in 1937. It is true that in the last scene of the series Picasso portrays the end of "Franco" as the death

*Dream and Lie of Franco, II* page 400

of the horse gored by the bull; but this "horse" is not a real horse, as is proved by its Surrealist head, which is not the head of a horse. The expression of mortal anguish in the *Guernica* horse must under no circumstances be confused with the repulsive features of that fantastic head. Accordingly, the relation of the horse to the fallen warrior is not one of hostility; this warrior is, rather, represented as a closely related fellow sufferer, like the female matador in *Minotauromachy*. That he has fallen for the cause of justice is attested by the broken sword, which, for instance in a drawing of May 9, 1936, serves to destroy the Minotaur, who is conceived as the embodiment of evil. Likewise, the woman holding the lamp over the dying horse is not hostile to it. On the contrary, she gazes at its agony with horror and compassion; and the woman below her seems to be stumbling in the direction of the horse in order to come to its aid. All this suggests that the horse is meant as the symbol of innocent suffering, with no specific political or national connotations.

Note 24

By way of exception, the bull in *Guernica* is not represented as the adversary of the horse: the horse even turns toward the bull as though seeking help. In this respect, *Guernica* differs, for instance, from a masterful ink drawing of 1934. The woman in this drawing is the precursor of the woman holding the lamp in *Guernica*, but whereas the figure in the drawing seems to shrink back in horror, the woman in *Guernica* is actively interested in the events. She shares with the bull the circumstance that neither is personally affected by the catastrophe. Consequently we may interpret her as a spiritual symbol, a universal Mother perhaps, or, as Brandi suggests, as personifying "civilization" or "history." This time the bull too is a sacred symbol, not a representative of "darkness and brutality," as Picasso himself characterized the bull in his still life with a bull's head, of 1938. Thus we may agree with Larrea that the bull symbolizes the continuity of the Spanish nation, and hence is shown protecting the lamenting mother, whose child Larrea, no doubt correctly, regards as alive. The bird to the right of the bull may also be a symbol of hope, particularly because it seems to be the successor to the little winged horse emerging from the wound of the larger horse in an earlier drawing.

*Head of a Bull*
Cl. Cat. 146

All in all, *Guernica* is a fearful indictment of violence whose *ultima ratio* is destruction. By formally combining complex symbols with a portrayal of the terrible effects of impersonal modern warfare, Picasso achieves a convincing objectivity of statement, which may claim universal validity. He has not portrayed an individual battlefield, but has painted the horrors of technological warfare. We must not, however, overlook the motifs pointing to a higher world in this supposedly nihilistic picture. Destruction rains from the sky, but all the victims of the disaster raise their eyes toward heaven, even though they may do so in malediction rather than in hope. There is an unmistakable transcendental upward movement, indicated by the large lamp at the top of the picture, directly above the most atrocious scene. This triumphant light does not signify the victory of violence over innocence, but, quite otherwise—the victory of compassion over cruelty. Compassion is one of the strongest motivations of Picasso the artist: this can be seen in many of his early bullfight scenes. In *Guernica*, compassion expressed in the divine features of the woman holding the light dominates the portrayal of cruelty, just as the light coming from above dominates the darkness. In support of this interpretation we may quote the opinion of Edvard

Note 25

"*Documents*" page 505

Note 26

*Weeping Woman*
page 237
*Figures* page 31

*Weeping Woman*
page 399

*Cat and Bird* Cl. Cat. 148
*Nude Dressing Her Hair*
page 251

Munch, certainly a competent critic, who in 1937 was strongly impressed by the picture (and especially by its restrained color): "This painting is not cruel at all—imagine how Goya would have done it—and yet it represents war. It's good that pictures running with blood are no longer painted."

In June 1937, as soon as it was completed, the painting was moved to the Spanish Pavilion at the Paris World's Fair and exhibited in a vast hall, with a large mural by Joan Miró and a mercury fountain by the American, Alexander Calder. Without doubt Picasso had intended this work as a protest against modern warfare, and used it for political purposes. Since then he has eloquently championed the view that the artist, like any other man, must participate in the life of society and help to shape it by his art. His statement made in 1937, "My whole life as an artist has been nothing more than a continuous struggle against reaction and the death of art," expresses not so much a political as an artistic, more accurately, an artistic-political credo. The attempt to combine art with politics confronted Picasso, as it did many other great artists of our century, with a difficult problem, and occasionally exposed him to conflicts. Larrea tells us that late in 1937 "certain Spanish politico-social authorities" demanded that *Guernica* be removed from the pavilion, "as an anti-social and ridiculous picture, wholly inadequate for the wholesome mentality of the proletariat." This step was finally prevented by propagandistic considerations of Picasso's international fame. The public condemnation of Picasso's portrait of Stalin on the occasion of the Russian dictator's death in March 1953 provides us with another example of the misunderstanding of his art on the part of political authorities.

Even after completing *Guernica*, Picasso treated some of its motifs in a number of smaller drawings and lithographs. Among these studies is a series showing the head of a weeping woman done in the fall of 1937 (page 237), in which physiognomic forms combined with elementary schematic lines, ending in heavy dots to indicate tears, produce a violent Expressionistic effect. The last of this series is a little masterpiece, the head of the *Weeping Woman* of the Penrose Collection in London (page 399) Here physiognomic elements, lines, and colors achieve a perfect synthesis. Picasso's lyrical force is overwhelmingly revealed in this picture which expresses profound emotion in severely disciplined form. The woman's eyes are obviously intended as a metaphor of polished diamonds; we are reminded of Braque's remark that if a poet is permitted to liken the ascending movement of a bird to a dagger, a painter should be permitted to portray a dagger as a bird.

We find some of the broader implications of *Guernica* treated in a number of other works. One of these, of 1937, is the painting *Birdcage*. The desperate longing of the captive creature represented here symbolizes the sufferings of man as a prisoner of fate. The cruelty of the laws governing nature is expressed in the *Cat and Bird* of 1939. Another work related in spirit to *Guernica* is the *Nude Dressing Her Hair* (page 251) dated Royan, March 6, 1940. (The motif is further elaborated in a sketchy drawing of June 19, 1940.) In this woman, whose demonic ugliness is stressed by her essentially graceful action, the deformations characteristic of the *Guernica* figures have become almost physically

*Guernica* (1937)

*Composition Study for "Guernica"* (1937)

*Dying Horse* (1917)

*Dying Horse* (1937)

*Weeping Woman* (1937)

*Portrait of a Girl* (1944)

238

oppressive. The effect is not ridiculous but grandiose, like that of a Sphinx—the Sphinx of World War II. Finally, we are reminded of *Guernica* by the *Charnel House* of 1944–48, which is painted in the same subdued colors as the older work, and which is intended as a moving, realistic rather than allegorical, requiem for the silent victims of a degenerate brutality.

*The Charnel House*
Cl. Cat. 184

## Portraits and Landscapes

During World War I Picasso, as a Spanish citizen, was exempt from service in the French army; he also preserved his personal independence during the occupation of France in World War II. He continued to work in Paris in the face of difficulties and dangers, displaying a truly Archimedean intrepidity. His perseverance did not fail to impress friend and foe alike, and he fully deserved the special gallery he was granted in the Salon de la Libération, the Autumn Salon of 1944, where he exhibited nearly eighty paintings. Picasso achieved this triumph not because he had been politically active, but because for years he had deliberately fortified his status as an artist. His weapon in this struggle was, as he himself declared, a more disciplined art: "Very likely for the poet it is a time to write sonnets," he said, referring to that period.

Throughout the war years he continued to develop his formal ideas. But at the same time he became more dependent upon those aspects of nature and art with which he was familiar, thus gaining a firmer hold on reality. Just as he had turned to Buffon's *Histoire naturelle* during a personal crisis in 1936, during World War II he showed a greater interest than usual in portraits and landscapes. Thus his predilection for the motif of the small tomato plant on the window sill (page 257), which he painted a number of times in August 1944, just before the Liberation of Paris, suggests a sympathy with the unfailing life-forces of growing nature. This sympathy represents a reaction against the gloomy misgivings he had recorded in the expressive still life compositions of the preceding years, such as the large *Still Life with Bull's Skull* of 1942 with its sonorous violet tones, or the *Still Life with Blood Sausage* of 1941, which shows a serving table in the restaurant Le Savoyard, and which is pervaded by somber grays (page 411). Raynal says of these pictures that in them Picasso's palette "has put on mourning."

During the Liberation of Paris, Picasso painted a number of naturalistic portraits, among them the water color of a young girl (page 238). In this context we shall briefly discuss his fundamental conception of the portrait, and we shall try to show that Picasso's art rests primarily

*"Documents"* page 505

Note 27

*Tomato Plant and Decanter* page 257
*Still Life with Tomato Plant* Cl. Cat. 182

*Still Life with Bull's Skull* Cl. Cat. 161
*Still Life with Blood Sausage* page 411

*Portrait of a Girl* page 238

240

(p. 241) *Daniel-Henry Kahnweiler* 1910

on his experience of individual form, even where he seems to have lost contact with it.

Picasso has painted portraits in all his periods. Though he sometimes conceives his task in a very broad sense, his intention is always to render an individual encounter. He once told Jedlicka that the effect of his portrait drawings is based not on external similarities, but on the recording of a specific mood. Whether such a mood is expressed through "circles, ovals, curves, dots, or geometric figures drawn on paper," the composition is valid, he says, as a portrait of a given person who has determined a given mood in the painter. Individualized traits are always present in Picasso's portraits even though at times the beholder can scarcely recognize them. They are present for instance in the *Portrait of Mrs. H. P.* (page 253), of 1952, in which the figure is shown with a fantastically wild abundance of hair. If we consider the various portraits of Sabartés, dating from very different periods (page 364, 408, 481), we find that in all of them Sabartés' personal characteristics are unmistakably rendered, despite enormous stylistic differences. We recognize him even in the portrait of October 22, 1939, where he is shown wearing a ruff, despite the curious Surrealist distortions. Even though Sabartés' glasses are not on his nose, they are there, nevertheless.

*Portrait of Mrs. H. P.*
page 253
*The Glass of Beer
(Jaime Sabartés)*
page 364
*Portrait of Sabartés*
Cl. Cat. 247
*Jaime Sabartés* page 408

Sabartés gives us a charming account of his visit to Antibes in 1946, when Picasso, in a playful mood, sketched his friend as a satyr with horns, flute, and the inevitable spectacles. In this instance as in many others Picasso, who is not always talkative, used his art as a means of communication—and we must keep in mind that even his verbal communications often convey meanings that cannot be expressed in rational terms. His relationship with his subject is always a personal one: he has never painted anything to which he had no emotional response. He once told Kahnweiler that he had found it "monstrous" that a woman painter had represented a pipe although she was not a smoker. In addition to individualized traits, Picasso conveys imponderable personal characteristics. For instance, his portrait of Madame Nush Eluard of 1938 (page 409) expresses feminine charm, even though the face is distorted and shown in multiple views. This portrait seems no less a likeness than the naturalistic one of 1941.

Note 28

Note 29

*Nush Eluard* page 409

During the war the painter Dora Maar was his favorite model. The numerous portraits of her show common individual traits, although some are far removed from naturalistic likeness. Her vigorously sculptured, expressive head (page 410), with its characteristically asymmetric face, attracted him both as a painter and as a man. For like all great portraitists, Picasso—he has said so himself—is concerned not with a physical or intellectual likeness, but with an emotional image—the "feel" of the subject. He spent several weeks painting Dora Maar in 1941; during that time her mother was dying, and knowing this certainly helps us to understand her expression in the portrait. Its coloring—the green-and-red-striped silk dress is shown against a blue background—characterizes a peculiar twilight state of the soul.

*Dora Maar* page 410

The fact that Picasso's artistic interests are determined by his natural, personal interests is again proven by his portraits of Françoise Gilot, whose full, symmetrical face appears in a great number of portraits and mythological figures dating from the post-war years (page 57).

*Head of a Girl* page 57

Because Picasso is essentially Mediterranean by nature, he is less interested in landscapes than in figures. The occasions on which he did paint landscapes and his way of painting them are all the more significant. While he has treated landscape motifs in all his periods, he has done so, for the most part, intermittently and without any specific objective. He became much more interested in such motifs during the last war: being confined to Paris, he felt an urge to re-create the city in the period of its greatest distress. For this reason it seems legitimate to begin our discussion of Picasso's landscapes with a group of views of Paris executed between 1943 and 1945. More than three decades earlier Picasso had painted small oval views of the Ile de la Cité in the abstract style of "hermetic" Cubism. The later pictures too are relatively small, usually horizontal, rectangular views of the Seine (Picasso's apartment at 1 Boulevard Henri IV, like his studio in the Rue des Grands-Augustins, was situated near the river). The only vertical canvas in this group, a view of Notre-Dame seen through an arch of the Pont Saint-Michel, gives us a characteristic glimpse of his method: he freely combines several natural views into a new spatial organism.

Note 30

It has been shown by means of photographs that a view of Notre-Dame such as Picasso gives us does not actually exist, and that his composition combines at least three different views. For instance, if one stands on the far side of the Pont Saint-Michel it is impossible to see Notre-Dame through an arch; and the next bridge, the Pont Notre-Dame, can be seen only if one is under the arch of the Pont Saint-Michel. The synthesis of the different views enhances rather than diminishes the individual characteristics of the object, even though the architectural motifs are extremely simplified. The Pont Saint-Michel with the wreath in the spandrel and the stone balustrade is as clearly recognizable as is the cathedral with its three western portals surmounted by pointed arches, its royal gallery, the large rose window and the arcades above it, the truncated towers, the flèche, and the flying buttresses of the south side.

Landscape page 391

Picasso used this method, in which the foreground serves as a frame for the distant view, in other landscapes, thus obtaining a compact composition. Back in 1924, in Juan-les-Pins, he had painted a seascape with the hills of the Corniche d'Or in the background, seen through a round opening between architectural and garden motifs: the effect is as though one looked through a porthole. While the parts of the picture that form the frame are entirely flat and decorative, the view of the hills produces an effect of depth. Here Picasso was certainly influenced by his experiences as a stage designer. Similarly, in the canvas *The Studio Window*, dated July 3, 1943 (page 413), the background is compressed by a vaulted structure like the arch in the view of the Seine just mentioned. Sidney Janis compared the picture with a photograph of the same view, which shows that in reality neither the wall nor the water pipe bends toward the right, as they do in the painting. The radiator with the curved pipe in front has acquired a kind of organic life, suggesting a monster lurking before the window which is conceived as a kind of cavern. The vertical part of the pipe leads to the rectilinear abstract forms of the wall and of the window whose ledges frame the background—a motif for which Max Beckmann had a particular predilection. But in Beckmann the out-of-doors appears as an overpower-

The Studio Window
page 413

(p. 245) *Maïa with Sailor Doll* 1938
(p. 251) *Nude Dressing Her Hair* 1940
(p. 253) *Portrait of Mrs. H. P.* 1952

*Portrait of Mallarmé, with inscription imitating the autograph of Edgar Allan Poe (1945)*

*Knight and Page-Boy* (1951)

*The Toilette* (1943)

*Two Nudes* (1946)

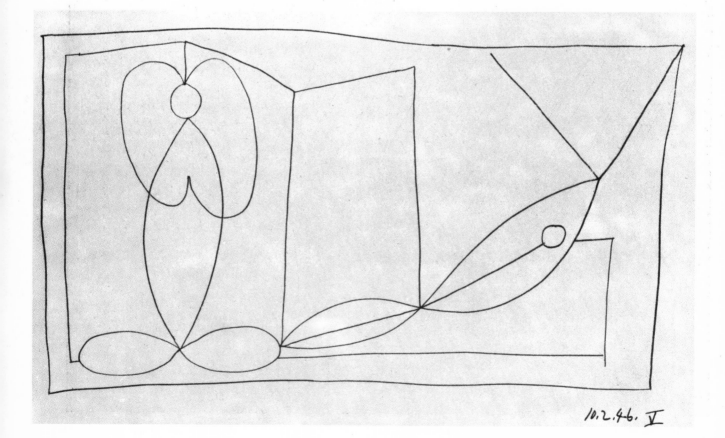

10.2.46. V

*Two Nudes* (1946)

250

ing, limitless world which besieges and oppresses man, whereas Picasso subjects the world of the rooftops to a stereometric order, which makes it seem less threatening than the familiar objects close by, such as the radiator. By faceting the roof forms, the experienced Cubist controls all the threatening, unruly elements, just as he had done a generation earlier. He used the same devices in his views of the Ile de la Cité of 1945, capturing the varied spatial effects of a historic city quarter in a system of rigidly controlled forms.

An oil canvas of February 1945 (page 259), which is articulated into abstract light and dark planes, again shows Notre-Dame, this time not through an arch, but as part of a broad panorama. Here too the organization of the forms recalls the faceted structures of early Cubism, with this notable difference: the variously colored planes are not arranged so as to produce the effect of solid volumes, but are systemically geared together through long radial lines. The prominent geometric order of the picture now results in the subordination and deformation of the natural motifs. Not only bridges and houses, but also parts of the cathedral are arbitrarily distorted, and they merge with the forms of the church of Sacré-Cœur which is actually at a considerable distance. We are reminded here of the oil study of Sacré-Cœur surrounded by the roofs of Montmartre that Picasso painted in 1909, when Cubism was still in an early phase. Even in that early period he did not render a segment of reality, but—in line with his method of that time, which differs greatly from his method of 1945—inexorably subjected his scene to the compositional laws of his style at that time.

*View of Paris, with Notre-Dame page 259*

In a variation on the theme of the Cité, dated March 1, 1945 (page 415), abstraction is considerably developed. The actual elements of the scene—the portals, the rose window, the flèche of Notre-Dame—are so completely dissolved in the design that only an expert can decipher them. The plane of the picture is covered with a web of vigorous radial lines which suggest a steel scaffolding centered on the circle atop the flèche. Picasso's method of articulating the picture surface by radial planes is perhaps best clarified by a comparison with the related and yet entirely different method used by Lyonel Feininger in his city views. Feininger too divides the plane by radial lines, but he invests the spatial layers and their complicated optical refractions with a disembodied transparency, beside which Picasso's scaffolding seems robust and material. Compared with Feininger's spiritualized reflection of the external world, Picasso's picture is a rigidly organized, independent, new creation, in which the original experience appears merely as *le souvenir d'un souvenir.*

*View of Paris, with Notre-Dame page 415*

Picasso correctly pointed out that there is no formal difference between such city views and his nudes or still life compositions. He said there was no good reason why "people should notice a nose drawn horizontally across a face, while a similarly distorted view of a bridge does not shock them" (conversation with Kahnweiler, September 9, 1944). Certain still life compositions showing a basket of fruit and a spice jar, dating from 1942 and 1943 (page 415), actually offer striking stylistic parallels to the views of the Cité. And just as Picasso distorts and dislocates faces in representations of human figures, he also distorts and displaces the cathedral and the bridges in a view of

Note 31

Note 32

*Still Life with Basket of Fruit page 415*
*Still Life with Spikes of Flowers Cl. Cat. 168*

Notre-Dame dated April 14, 1945 (page 414). We know that the lavender coloring of this picture is the result of a visit he had recently made to a friend's lilac garden which filled him so completely with the sensation of this color that he imposed it on the alien motif of the Cité. This is characteristic of the way Picasso's art originates in personal experiences.

In a painting dated June 25, 1943, the so-called *Le Vert-Galant*, another Paris motif is treated—a little park at the western tip of the Cité near the Pont Neuf (page 414). Here the painter deliberately aims at a picturesque and decorative effect. Once again he bends the trees to form a kind of peephole through which the eye is led to the bridge with the statue of Henry IV (whose nickname, *Le Galant*, had been transferred to the park). The Cubist substance, as it still appears in the triangular facets at the bottom, is here subordinated to the flat decorative treatment of the powerful tree trunks, and particularly, of the ornamental oval forms of the foliage. Here too it is possible to name earlier works as genetic foundations of the later synthesis. The flat, decorative design can be traced back to landscapes painted in Juan-les-Pins in 1920, whose *collage*-like surface structure represents a variant of Synthetic Cubism (page 384). A characteristic detail is provided by the almond-shaped sun with its jagged corona, a motif strikingly similar to the central light in *Guernica* (page 233/34). As for the spatial treatment, the tree forms and the peculiar crowns of spiky leaves in *Le Vert-Galant*, which are reminiscent of Van Gogh, can be compared to the pastel landscape of Fontainebleau, of 1921 (page 385). The feeling for simple, monumental form and the sculptural modeling of this pastel readily disclose its relationship to the gigantic women of the same period (page 189).

The style of *Le Vert-Galant* with its rounded treetops and Cubist triangular planes reappears in 1946, in the almost playfully ornamental gouache landscapes of Ménerbes (Vaucluse), which are closer to the "*collage*" than to the "radial-plane" type (page 420). At times these compositions remind us of Paul Klee, the magician who conjured up unreal landscapes for spiritual promenades; but beside his subtle, northern-oriental fantasy, Picasso's art seems popular, robust, indeed, almost naturalistic! Even in 1951, at Vallauris, Picasso's landscapes were for the most part small and decorative. The main motif is usually a narrow, many-storied villa surrounded by lemon and orange trees, whose fruits glow in the dark greenery; the spatial structure is influenced by the *Café* painted at Royan in August 1940 (page 416).

But at the same time Vallauris saw the emergence of an entirely different landscape style. It was at Vallauris that Picasso discovered the beauty of southern winter scenes, and captured this previously unexplored beauty in, for example, the relatively large oil dated December 22, 1950 (page 425). It does not show a magically unreal snow scene, but portrays nature at its most forlorn and desolate: nature devoid of all sensual adornment, all luminous colors, even of the festive blue of the sky. More than any other, this picture of solitude, *soledad*, reveals Picasso's Spanish soul. The leafless olive trees expressively stretch their bare branches toward the gray sky, as though in extreme despair; their ugly contorted forms are arranged beside each other in harsh light grays and dark browns. The same withered quality appears in the brown palm tree which, in the middle distance, looms against the

(p. 257) *Tomato Plant and Decanter* 1944
(p. 259) *View of Paris, with Notre-Dame* 1945

impenetrable sky. Brown, too, is the soil in the foreground, which gives the effect of a huge, gaping wound, while the gray reappears in the dead surfaces broken only by an occasional window of the horizon. Only in the scarcely protruding roof of the house at the right is there a bit of glowing red. But the furrowed planes of the middle ground extend their mournful, passive green over the entire width of the picture. The murky, dull harmony of gray, brown, and green reflects the tormented desolation of wintry nature, whose cry to the overcast sky is very much like that of the human figures in *Guernica*. If we analyze the formal elements of this strikingly expressive landscape, we discover here too instructive preliminary stages. For instance, the anthropomorphic gestures of the tree branches derive formally from Cubist abstractions, as a glance at the tree forms in the owl pictures of January 1947 shows (page 90). Picasso had made similar Cubist studies of tree trunks as early as 1944, and these in turn are based on vivid drawings made two decades earlier. In his copy of Poussin (page 417), which also dates from 1944, and which will be discussed in the next chapter, the trees in the old master's painting are reinterpreted in the same way.

*Studies of Owls* page 90

Note 33

## Antibes

*Night Fishing at Antibes* page 263

The ancient shores of the French Riviera have always held great attraction for Picasso. After his first visit to Juan-les-Pins in 1920, he often returned there to spend the season, combining recreation with work. The summer before the outbreak of World War II he stayed at Antibes, where in August he painted a remarkable visionary life-size canvas, *Night Fishing at Antibes* (page 263). Sabartés, who was with him in those anxious days, has described the unusual method Picasso adopted for this painting. He began by covering three walls of his studio with canvas, and trimmed it down to size only after he had painted it.

The monumental composition shows two girls standing on a stone jetty at the right; one of them is holding a bicycle and eating an ice cream cone. To the left of these girls, who are painted in somewhat smaller scale, two fishermen in a boat are spearing fish by the light of a lantern. The fantastic charm of this nocturne is based on the felicitous combination of the effects of light with nocturnal colors, ranging from black, through blue, various ghostly greens, and a murky brown, to a dark violet. This violet, which is used for the view of the town and Castle of Antibes in the upper left-hand corner of the picture, here strikes for the first time, on the eve of the war, a coloristic note that will recur many times in the oppressive years to come. The pale flesh color of the human figures glows between the warm radiance of the lamps and the cool brightness of the fish. The coloring clearly reveals the Spaniard; the magic light suggests the inspiration of El Greco; the singleness of mood is compelling; figures and landscape are in perfect harmony. Among Picasso's few nocturnes one, dating from 1951, represents his garden at Vallauris; it too combines artifical illumination and starlight.

In the summer of 1946, Picasso went from Ménerbes to La Garoupe, where he stayed at a friend's villa. On September 8, during one of his visits to the beach of Golfe Juan, he met Dor de la Souchère, director of the museum of Antibes. This proved to be a historic meeting. De la Souchère expressed a desire to have something of Picasso's in his museum, and the artist, in a pleasant mood, immediately agreed. The result was one of the happiest, most productive, and ingratiating

(p. 263) *Night Fishing at Antibes* 193?

phases of his artistic career. The fortunate coincidence that De la Souchère happened to have a large supply of fiberboard on hand, which suited perfectly the large compositions Picasso was planning then, led to the creating of a unique Picasso museum which is already a legend and has become a goal for devotees of modern art. Picasso soon decided to move into the museum, giving up the comforts of the villa. A studio with everything he needed for his work was set up for him in a large hall on the second story. The considerate director even went on a trip so that Picasso could familiarize himself, undisturbed, with his new abode. Everything about it was indeed unusual. For the so-called Musée Grimaldi is situated in the old Castle of Antibes, whose little acropolis has been settled since prehistoric times. Later a Roman castle stood there; then the place was occupied by bishops; in 1386 it became the property of the Genoese family Grimaldi. They sold it to King Henry IV, and for a long time it served as the residence for royal governors.

Old things and houses have always fascinated Picasso (incidentally, the building in the Rue des Grands-Augustins in Paris, in which he has maintained a studio since 1937, is a seventeenth-century palace). Gertrude Stein was certainly right when she said that Picasso, who always ventures in new directions, finds inner peace in old things; his "classicism" may be similarly accounted for. The venerable museum at Antibes with its sunny terrace and cool inner court, situated on an elevation overlooking the coast, offers an exciting mixture of the past and the present. Its collections of ancient stone monuments on the ground floor have been placed under the same roof (occasionally even in the same room) with Picasso's works, most of which are on the upper floor. The museum thus presents us with a tangible proof of the vitality of Mediterranean art and of its mysterious continuity: for the ultimate, the hair-roots of Picasso's art reach down into the same deep strata which nourished the art of Antiquity.

Note 34

Picasso's *Guernica* anticipated the horrors of World War II; *La joie de vivre*, the main work of his Antibes period, testifies to his inner liberation from the oppressive gloom of the war years. In *Guernica*, women symbolized the agony of war victims; after the hostilities, women symbolize the joy of living. In a literal and figurative sense, women are the central motif of Picasso's works of 1946, which may be described in their aggregate as a glorification of woman.

*La joie de vivre* pages 267/68

This new attitude toward the world of the senses, and toward woman as its highest embodiment, was not sudden; its beginnings are discernible in works executed during the war. A large pencil drawing of December 1943 (page 249), which portrays a woman in an armchair attended by a maid, is completely under the spell of fairy-tale loveliness and fancy. The sword lying on the floor in the foreground is the only object reminiscent of the symbolic sheets of the 1930s; its owner, however, is no longer a female matador, but a truly feminine princess. Similar marvelous nude figures can be found among the works of June 1944: continuing the classical drawings of the 1920s, they glorify the soft, full, fluid lines of the feminine form (page 331). Finally, there are the eighteen different states of a lithograph showing a seated and a reclining nude, executed in December 1945 and January 1946 (page 250). The main motifs of this work reappear later in boldly abstract pencil

*The Toilette* page 249

*Girl with Necklace* page 331

*Two Nudes* page 250

drawings. In one of these, dated February 10, 1946, the legs of the woman sitting in front of the screen, the double curve of her hair and breasts, as well as the arms of the reclining figure, are only indicated by lines that seem to be made of thin, flexible wire; but with such calligraphic grace that they are an eloquent expression of femininity.

While the works leading up to *Guernica* are interrelated thematically, those announcing *La joie de vivre* reflect predominantly formal concerns. Thus, a new form of graphic abstraction is embodied in eight charming variations on a nude, dated January 13, 1946. The technique used here is a combination of cutouts and lithography (page 61). The little figures acquire a vegetable, indeed a flower-like, quality; and in a painting finished on May 5, 1946 (page 412), Picasso seems to have aimed deliberately at the metaphor woman-flower, so consistently are the parts of the woman's body arranged asymmetrically as stem, blossom, leaves, and fruits. The forms are so intricately constructed that one is tempted to compare them to wire flowers. And yet this is not a toy-like miniature, but a picture of considerable dimensions!

As Antaeus' strength was restored by contact with the earth, Picasso's imagination was repeatedly refreshed by contact with nature. At the age of fifty-six Picasso found in Françoise a fountain of youth. But in his variations on a nude dated Paris, June 22, 1946 (page 273), he is by no means dependent on his model. With obvious sensuous pleasure and delight in the elegance of the contours, the painter varies the proportions of waist and buttocks, and playfully produces incredible contrasts. He gives us the feeling that he drew these graceful figures so effortlessly that he could have gone on endlessly creating further variations. A few days later he explored another, abstract, aspect of the same theme by representing the woman standing with her arms joined above her head in purely geometric linear structures, mostly in terms of intersecting triangles (page 273). The following day, June 29, working directly from nature, he tested this abstract system in the two-color lithograph of two pigeons (page 501). The outlines of the birds, particularly the triangles indicating wings and tails, do not coincide in the violet-red and the gold-yellow plates; the motif and the direction of the lines diverge strongly. But when the plates are printed one on top of the other, a vibrant, restless animation is achieved, which the beholder experiences as movement. A similar effect is produced by the nude figure of June 28, which throbs feverishly in comparison with the five nudes of the drawing of June 22.

During this very fruitful June in Paris, Picasso painted his first large mythological canvas, *The Rape of Europa* (page 422). After a very abstract preliminary version, he did the subject in highly simplified, monumental forms of almost ponderous plasticity. Only after renewed contact with his Mediterranean roots during the coming months at Antibes was Picasso to bring such subjects fully to life. Still, these Parisian studies prepared the way in both format and technique for the creations at Antibes.

Not only the importance of the female body in these Antibes works, but also their bucolic and Bacchic themes can be traced back to the war years. To begin with, we have a watercolor and gouache version of Poussin's *Bacchanale* in the Louvre (page 417). The fact that Picasso painted it during the battle of Paris (August 24–29, 1944) is of truly

266

symbolic significance. On the one hand, this great work of the past provided the same sense of security as the close dependence on nature in his other works of that time; on the other hand, his choice of precisely this picture for copying heralds a turn to relaxation and exuberance after his obsessive imagery of the war years; once again life wins out over death. In his free copy of the Triumph of Pan, Picasso remains faithful, on the whole, to the individual figures and motifs of the model; but he has translated the original forms and colors into his own idiom. Surrealistically distorted and classical forms are charmingly, sometimes humorously combined. One of the figures at the center of this picture, the maenad in the billowing, violet drapery who beats the tambourine, clearly anticipates *La joie de vivre*.

Toward the end of August 1946, Picasso worked on a three-figure composition, which in a sense synthesizes the Bacchanale motifs and earlier formal experiments recorded in various sketches, such as the drawing of June 28 (page 274) and the *Two Pigeons* (page 501). Each of the sheets done in August shows the maenad with the tambourine at the center, and a flute-playing faun to the right; the figure at the left varies, frequently being a faun performing a handstand. *La joie de vivre*, a large canvas measuring 47 1/4 by 98 1/2 inches, which Picasso began after moving to the museum of Antibes, is a direct continuation of these sketches. The importance of this work—and this is true of all the Antibes works—lies in the fact that these mythological themes are not intended as some kind of classical revival, but are Picasso's intuitions, through which the Mediterranean spirit speaks to our own age. Or, to use psychological terms, Picasso's art succeeds in transforming archetypes of the collective unconscious into visible and understandable symbols. An exuberant wealth of forms emerges in Antibes and comes to life in the pictures: fauns, nymphs, and centaurs vie with each other in playing boisterous games with young goats.

*Two Pigeons* page 501
*The Dance on the Beach* page 274
*La joie de vivre* pages 267/68

Cl. Cat. 193. 198. 200. 204

The timeless mythological world which now definitively supplants the grandiose allegories of terror—a world of peace and beauty succeeding the world of war and ugliness—requires a monumental scale such as that required by the historical *Guernica*. Picasso made no special preliminary studies for *La joie de vivre*, as he had for *Guernica*: this time he developed his idea almost entirely on the canvas itself, and the successive states were photographed by Michel Sima. Here—just as in the sketches executed in August—two large male figures flank the dancing maenad: the faun playing a flute has remained, but the other faun has become a centaur, who also plays a musical instrument. Between them now there are two young, leaping goats, and the scene has been transferred to the edge of the sea, on which a sailboat drifts by.

As we know, Picasso has always been fascinated by the theme of the dance: dancers appear as early as 1905 in his etchings of Salome and in various circus scenes; in 1917 Picasso was closely associated with the Diaghilev dancers, one of whom he married in 1918, and through his work as stage designer he remained associated with them during the years that followed. Groups of dancers, treated cubistically or classically, appear time and again in the twenties, as in the *Three Dancers*, of 1925 (page 203), where an ecstatic dancing nude also dominates the design. After a visit to a circus in 1933, three acrobatic dancers once again struck Picasso's imagination: they bear a sisterly likeness to

*Three Women Dancing* Cl. Cat. 109
*Three Dancers* page 203

Note 35

the figures on the beach of the year before (page 39). This trio is related to the three figures in *On the Beach* (page 211) painted at Dinard in 1928, whose landscape background of few strong colors—the yellow of the sand, the deep blue of the sea, the light sky, and the dark rocks ——anticipates the scenery of *La joie de vivre*. Thus, like *Guernica*, the great Antibes painting crystallizes a number of motifs that can be traced back to earlier periods; and like *Guernica* it is an authentic artistic revelation.

To illustrate the changes revealed in the successive stages of this painting, we shall now consider different states of the maenad (page 61). This figure, as it appears in the initial state, is strikingly similar to the abstractions of the lithograph of January 13 and to the "wire-flower" woman of the painting of May 5, 1946 (page 412). Later it becomes more naturalistic, its color is enriched, and its movement differentiated through the addition of feet. (The figure of the goat is similarly changed and becomes more lifelike and more expressive.) In the end the figure, originally robed, has become a nude; all that remains of her garment is a kind of veil indicated by the fluttering ends on top. This nude was unmistakably influenced by the full-breasted women with exaggerated, narrow waists sketched in June (page 273); but the buttocks are shown in a different view, in the Cubist manner. The forms of the arm and of the tambourine, which were originally round, are angular in the final version. The reason for this change becomes apparent once we examine the changes in the other figures and in the composition as a whole.

Sima published six different states of the flute-playing faun (pages 418 and 419), where the initial geometric form was supplanted by an intermediate, more naturalistic one and finally by a very different, definitive form. The scenery has undergone a similar transformation. The dark foothill that originally formed the background on the right (page 419) has been eliminated except for the horizon indicated by the boat, so that the outstretched upper body of the faun is set off against the light-blue sky. In the final state the curiously slender figure of this faun is echoed in the graceful little tree at the right.

The lower body of the centaur at the left, initially very block-like, has become organic, filled with latent movement, and like the body of the maenad is shown in several views. The centaur has not gone through the same transformations as the other figures; only his upper body with its long neck and little head has been readjusted with an eye to the changes in the faun.

The original scenery showed a mountain range silhouetted at the right. Later the landscape parts were largely eliminated, and in the final version the bodies of the figures are placed, frieze-like, between the earth and the horizon. This "horizon" is not conceived abstractly, but yields to the spatial impulses that emanate from the figures. There is no sharp line of demarcation between the two zones, and the upper bodies of the three main figures are distinct, and clearly interrelated, against the background of the sky. Now we can see why the originally round arms of the maenad have been replaced by angular ones in the final version: the change was necessary because after the elimination of the mountain range, angular forms appeared only in the sailboat.

The plant at the lower left which is unsubstantial in the definitive state has also undergone a complete transformation for the sake of the maenad. It was originally sketched as a cactus, made up of full-bodied oval shapes, but its importance was reduced to secure a dominant effect for the central nude figure. (Incidentally, the maenad is not at the geometric center of the picture, but a little to the left of it; the balance has been subtly restored by the insertion of the goat at the right.)

The non-naturalistic coloring, especially of the figures, follows a severe canon of relatively few tones, in keeping with the monumental character of the picture. Predominant are the delft blue of the sea and sky, which also appears in the upper bodies of the flute-players and in the nude, and the complementary yellow of the sand and, particularly, the large sail. Next to these colors the eye is chiefly attracted by the chocolate brown of the maenad's hair and veil, which also appears in conjunction with olive green in the bodies of the figures at the right, and by the red of the centaur's forelegs. The surface is for the most part shiny; the color arrangement brings into relief the triangular structure of the composition, which is similar to that of *Guernica*. The *Guernica* pages 233/34 sides of the triangle are reinforced by black planes.

"Antibes" stands for more than a specific style or period. It is the symbol of a frame of mind, of a new approach to ancient imaginary themes. The prophetic nightmares of the pre-war years have given way to mythological daydreams, in which the imagination is populated with antique beings in the glimmering southern light. Although the twentieth-century painter's mythology—his centaurs, nymphs, and satyrs—are not generated by an instinctive conception of the world, but by an intellectual act, he draws on the same unconscious layers of the soul as the ancients who conjured up these magic figures. Picasso's large and small works produced in the fall of 1946, which seem like a garland of flowers around *La joie de vivre*, embody his longing for and faith in a simple, earthy life. Nothing in these works reminds us of man's predicament in a technological age; everything in them is eloquent of happiness: men, women, and animals are shown enjoying themselves and each other, united in a divine enthusiasm which includes all instincts and passions. Any of these works could legitimately be entitled "Joy of Living."

The triptych reproduced on page 275 consists of three panels, each *Triptych* page 275 the same size as *La joie de vivre* (page 267). It shows a flute-playing satyr, a leaping young goat, and a centaur with a trident on his shoulders, drawn with the brush in bold, monumental outline on a white ground, where we can still discern vestiges of older studies. The rhythmic flow of the faun's playing, the young goat's graceful capers, and the centaur's overflowing vitality are expressed with great simplicity and clarity. With the same powerful and fully controlled sweeps of the brush Picasso later drew figures in white oil paint on the glass panes of the large showcases between two rooms of the Antibes museum. The same motifs recur, warmer, more idyllic, and more tender, in small-sized pencil drawings. One of these shows a faun peacefully playing his flute while his beloved and a slender young goat listen to him intently. Another drawing, more animated, joyful, and rapturous, shows a family *Family of Centaurs with Doves* page 60 of centaurs trying to catch doves (page 60).

In the representations of these godlike creatures music and games acquire an almost sacred quality. Paganism, which has been confined to museums, has come to life again, so simple in its pristine freshness that it even has a popular appeal. As Picasso himself said, "This time at least I knew that I was working for the people." In 1947 he executed an etching representing the birth of the last centaur at Piraeus (page 63). The naïve story of this centaur, whose mother died while giving birth to him, and whose aggrieved father descended to the underworld, is told here concisely in the language of pictures.

The same group of bucolic motifs includes what is perhaps Picasso's profoundest and noblest representation of an animal—the four-foot-high painting of a goat in repose against a white background. The figure is actually a line drawing; only the fore-part of the body is done in gray paint (page 476). The forms and the spirit of this animal are rendered so lovingly that they seem to reveal to us a secret of nature; in this respect, this goat is superior even to the magnificent aquatint illustrations for Buffon's *Histoire naturelle* (page 310). The work which concludes the Antibes period is the colossal mythological painting *Ulysses*, which was done in 1947. This tall canvas composed of three panels, each measuring $98\,1/2$ by $47\,1/4$ inches, shows Ulysses' ship tossed on the waves; demonic figures lurk behind the sail, and the wild magnificence of the sea is rendered in blue and green tones.

The reawakened, sensuous orientation of Picasso finally produced a considerable number of still lifes, some of them of great delicacy, at Antibes. Here, too, the monumental note is present; it appears most convincingly in the *Still Life with Knife*, measuring $37\,1/2$ by 69 inches, and painted in vigorous colors on grained wood (page 421). The Cubist spatial structure of this painting resembles the later of the two *Reclining Nudes* (page 76), which is also painted on grained wood. The melon at the center, on a table of dull yellow, is also central as regards coloring, with its triad of green, orange, and black. The surrounding planes are black and gray against a violet and brown background. The glass beside the melon, and a couple of small lemons above it, enrich the composition by a luminous blue and a yellow green.

Still larger, but more delicate in its effect because of the light, ethereal treatment, is a still life showing a fish with a pitcher, bottle, and fruit. The graceful oriental, apparently metallic, pitcher (Picasso represented it in several works) is, in its flexibility and decorativeness, particularly characteristic of this period. The coloring, without strong accents, is nuanced in beige-rose, blue-gray, and greenish tones. Its flatness, transparency, and cheerful effect are in marked contrast to the *Still Life with Blood Sausage* (page 411), which Picasso painted during the war in the somber black-gray-white scale of *Guernica*. The sinister quality of the objects—the slippery coils of sausage, the menacing point of the knife—and the somber mood of the gloomy atmosphere refer, according to Picasso himself, to Philip II. And his comparison of the forks and knives protruding from the drawer, with poor souls in purgatory, is a valuable aid to our understanding of the picture. Here, expressionistic forces originating in dark regions were at work—and it was only at the Côte d'Azur that the last shadow of these forces was dispelled.

The small still life compositions Picasso painted at Antibes are free from all such obsessions, and their colors are as cheerful as they are sophisticated. Most of the pictures are of horizontal format and show

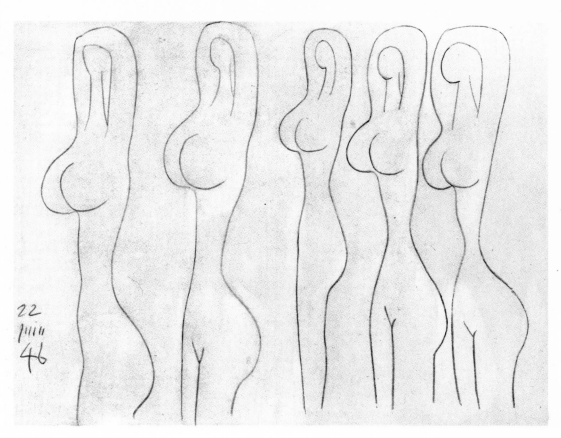

*Nudes in Profile* (1946)

*Maenad* (1946)

273

*The Dance on the Beach* (1946)

*The Dance on the Beach* (1946)

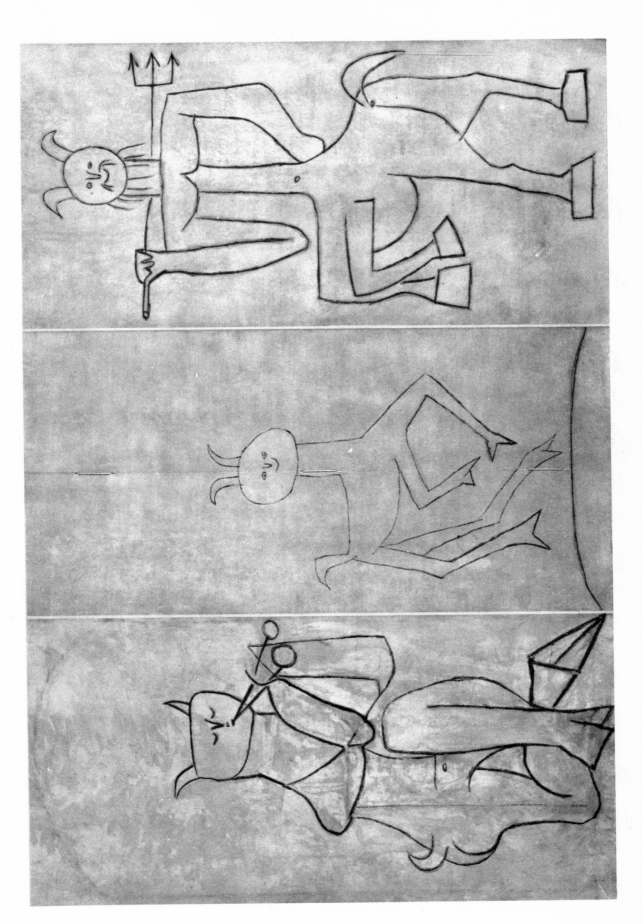

*Triptych* (1946)

*Musical Faun* (1948)

silvery blue fishes with green lemons, or iridescent cuttlefish. The luster of the enamel-like paint occasionally reminds us of ceramic glazes. Of outstanding coloristic beauty is the tall, narrow *Still Life with Vase and Three Sea Urchins*. Here the brown and orange sea urchins are set off against the white and gray tablecloth. Branches with violet and blue leaves, and one salmon-pink flower rise from a dark-green vase which serves as a transition to the sea urchins. The light background is alternately blue-gray and pale yellow. The surface of this picture directly simulates the fluidity of a glaze.

## Vallauris: Ceramics

One of the notable characteristics of the small still life canvases Picasso painted at Antibes is the technical treatment of the surface. Aside from artistic considerations, the specific features of this treatment may have been determined by an attempt to secure greater solidity and, by the same token, greater durability of the colors. These little canvases which seem covered with a glaze are only a step away from the use of clay tiles. Picasso took that step. One still life in the museum at Antibes is painted on nine large tiles framed in wood; the muted shades of color (yellow, brown, green, black, and white) against the light brown background are divided within the tiles by incised contours, and the glazed, not entirely smooth, surface lends this ceramic painting greater animation. But this work has remained isolated; for Picasso was not so interested in the durability of colors and the special enhancement they received through the ceramic technique, as in a new method of combining painting with the third dimension. He did not want to produce ceramic paintings, but to decorate ceramics with paintings which possess an additional dimension and, by the same token, a higher degree of reality than the usual, flat picture surface. There was still

*"Documents"* page 505

another attraction, namely, that ceramics are, theoretically, objects of practical use. On the memorable day of November 2, 1945, during a visit to Mourlot's workshop in Paris, Picasso had conceived a passion for lithography, the artistic and technical possibilities of which he extended by the most original methods. Similarly, after discovering ceramics, he devoted himself to it with undiminished enthusiasm. Picasso has never been interested in complicated techniques for their own sake, but only for the sake of their artistic possibilities. He discovered ceramics just as he had discovered lithography, almost accidentally. We know how this happened from an account by the Ramiés, manufacturers of earthenware.

In the summer of 1946, before moving to Antibes, Picasso visited the Madoura pottery at Vallauris, a ceramics center just behind Golfe Juan on the French Riviera. At that time Picasso amused himself by modeling a few little clay figures. On returning there a year later he became enthusiastic, and was soon "at home" in the workshop, operating the potter's wheel, firing the clay, and painting it. The companionable atmosphere of the workshop was a welcome change from the solitude of the studio. Picasso mastered the rudiments of the craft, and worked with various materials, from ordinary terracotta to soft-paste porcelain, glazed and unglazed. He had many new technical ideas and improvised continually, but without ever observing the rules: no potter at Vallauris could have employed him as an apprentice. Even though the Madoura workshop was distinguished by its technical versatility, Picasso invented entirely new methods, particularly (as one might have expected) of coloring the ware. He used finishes of all kinds, from the simplest clays to silver *(cristaux d'argent)*, often combining the most contradictory elements for the sake of certain coloristic effects. He was just as inventive in the employment of opaque colors and glazes. He used metal oxides and clays, but few enamel paints; on the other hand, he rediscovered a kind of half-enamel paint through which he could get very rich effects.

Picasso's experiments with ceramic techniques cast a revealing light on his general approach to art. Here, as always, he followed seemingly accidental impulses, regarding "the malice of things" not as a hostile force, but as a welcome stimulus. The treacherous intricacies of the firing process, for instance, were only a challenge to a fighter like Picasso: he drew new inspiration from every failure. For accident plays a far greater and more inevitable part in ceramics, which deals with colors that look quite different after the firing, than it does in the graphic arts. Picasso's productivity was increased by the continual excitement: one afternoon he painted twenty pieces so different in expression that they actually seem to reflect a whole gamut of emotions.

Painting is dominant in the oval plates (12 5/8 by 15 inches) and the round plates (7 1/2 or 8 5/8 inches in diameter), which Picasso produced by the hundreds. In one year (ending in the fall of 1948) he manufactured six hundred oval plates, whose proportions offer the more favorable compositional opportunities. His total production reaches into the thousands, and nowhere do we notice a weakening of his inventiveness. Some plates may be less successful than others, but the same is true of his paintings—it would be unnatural were it otherwise. On these plates we find almost all the motifs Picasso treated in paintings and drawings during the last decades—primarily bullfight scenes and mythological figures, most of them in series of variations often containing ingenious new ideas.

The first experiments (page 441) directly continue the sketching technique of his brush drawings and the corresponding lithographs: for instance, a large sheet of February 2, 1947 (page 477), shows a centaur and a bacchante whose blacks and whites create a very "coloristic" effect owing to the broad brush stroke technique. Such a technique is particularly suitable for ceramic ware, whose absorbent base does not favor precise outlines. The comparison of the lithograph with a ceramic plate (page 281) showing a faun holding a shepherd's stock and accompanied by a goat scarcely requires comment. For all their crudeness, the figures, painted boldly with the brush and without corrections, are extremely expressive. Characteristically enough they are not confined to the flat bottom of the vessel, but extend to the curved part and to the border, thus participating in the third dimension of the object itself.

*Decorated Ceramics*
page 441
*Centaur and Bacchante*
Cl. Cat. 204

*Decorated Plate
(Faun and Goat)*
page 281

The same is true of the colored picture space surrounding the figures which are kept in a dark tone of grayish-white tinged with red. Seemingly formless patches of color in warm tones against the azure-blue ground produce a kind of airy landscape around the figures; the ground plane is accented by emphatic spots of cinnabar red.

Some of the round plates are decorated with scenes whose treatment is even more "painterly," and whose stylistic origin in drawings and lithographs is even more discernible. The decoration of the flat vessels is generally in the figure style inspired by the Mycenaean cameos, which is used in idyllic scenes, combats of centaurs, and, particularly, in bull-fight scenes. This highly individualistic language of forms, tending sometimes to realism, sometimes to abstract signs, appears everywhere, from the technically simplest *grecqueries* (Picasso's term for them) in black on red, to the bullfight scenes which are the most highly differentiated as regards technique and color. Just as these paintings were completed in a few moments, so the emphasis in these scenes is on the spontaneous action conveyed through the comma-shaped, discontinuous flecks of the brush (page 449). In this way the painter achieves both austere silhouette effects in black and white, and illusionistic effects in rich colors. In one of the most precious plates in the museum at Antibes—of a bull and picador in violet-blue against a sea-green background which has a purple-red border edged in black—Picasso has added depth by incising the contours.

By using these and related methods, Picasso created numerous plastic and spatial variations in, particularly, two large series of ceramics. In the series of plates whose inner surfaces are decorated, the faces —frequently of fauns—were often crudely cut into the soft clay, leaving ridges at the borders. Pupils and nostrils were pierced in similar fashion, or the features were modeled separately and then attached. Other effects were obtained by the smooth or rough treatment of the medium, and by the contrasts produced by combining relief-like elements and painted decoration.

Even more varied are the plates decorated with still life compositions. Here, with an inexhaustible richness of motifs, Picasso covers the whole span, ranging from graceful ornamentation to a plastic realism which recalls the method of the sixteenth-century Palissy ceramics, for which casts from nature were used. Marine animals, sausages, fried eggs, knives, spoons, and forks are modeled more or less in the round (page 449). Between these two extremes countless steps, combinations, and abstractions are possible, and this possibility only increased the fascination of experimenting with different degrees of reality; and the fact that these are utilitarian objects provokes the artist to play with different degrees of reality. Picasso does not even reject perspective illusion; he paints a glass, its shadow, and a lemon so that they seem to be standing on the bottom of the plate (page 448). Such effects are even more striking when Picasso treats a plate as though it were a bullfight arena, and achieves a masterpiece of refined make-believe (page 451).

Picasso himself turned and molded his clay ware before matching the paintings to the molded forms. It is his ability to create such combinations that primarily accounts for his unique success in the field of ceramics. It is no exaggeration to say that except for the unglazed majolicas of the Italian Early Renaissance—the most outstanding of

which can be placed beside antique ceramics—Picasso was the first to realize the unity of painting and pottery that had disappeared with ancient Greece. This higher conceptual unity is absent from all other examples of Western ceramics, usually as a result of the division of labor between the potter and the painter. Picasso competes with the great ceramic art of Antiquity—particularly the Cretan earthenware—and often approximates it in his own work. He knew these older works, but he did not imitate them. He discovered the artistic laws which govern them and proceeded independently, developing logically from his own earlier art.

What is particularly characteristic of Picasso is his tendency to give the shape of the clay vessels a representational meaning through the painting. A vase may be transformed into a female figure (page 443) by identifying the parts of the woman's body with the corresponding parts of the vessel—the neck, the shoulder, the foot; the equation handles—arms is almost as natural. With his owl vases (page 447) he took up an idea that Chinese potters had realized thousands of years ago; once again we see the bird's head, shoulders, belly, and feet identified with the corresponding parts of the vessel. Claws, wings, feathers are indicated in various ways by stylized dots; and beak, eyes, and eyebrows are added in paint as partly ornamental, partly animating accents. It is typical of Picasso that his rediscovery of a valid combination of motifs thousands of years old originates in an incidental and quite subjective experience—that of the little owl at Antibes (see page 89). Theoretically this transformation of the abstract parts of the vessels into natural forms can be accounted for by the tendency to proceed from ideal form to a new autonomous objectivity, which Juan Gris formulated in terms of painting, as the path from the cylinder to the bottle. Starting from the ovoid form of the vessel, Picasso arrives at a bird, and once again the beak of the bird becomes the "beak" of the vessel, and the handle can be interpreted as a wing or tail (page 442). While the structure and contours of the vessel are spirited, harmonious, and functional, the decoration avoids naturalism. In other examples, the form of the vessel suggests less obvious interpretations, and the painting is more suggestive, as in the "transformation" of an ibex in repose (page 442), whose limbs, marked in black on light brown, in conjunction with the turn of the head, produce an impression of utmost animation.

Picasso did not immediately understand the technical requirements of ceramics, as is shown by the numerous small sketches for a *Bull* drawn at Antibes as early as September 13, 1946, where he is not sure whether he wants a vessel with one foot or two feet (page 309). Later he produced a ceramic bull with *two* feet (open at the bottom); the small, asymmetric face with horns is sketchily "assisted" with paint. As compared with the other clay animals, we feel that a bull constructed in such a way does not conform to the technical requirements of the potter's wheel. In other instances, Picasso succeeded in combining several ceramic bodies on *one* foot in a manner that does justice to the medium, and once more proved himself unsurpassable in the art of solving complicated problems of equilibrium.

Except when he deliberately intends to make clay *statuettes*, his objects always retain the character of vessels, even though this functional character is sometimes strongly overshadowed by other elements.

*Woman (Vase)* page 443

*Owl (Vase)* page 447

*Bird (Vase)* page 442

*Ibex (Vase)* page 442

*Studies for a Vase in the Shape of a Bull* page 309 Note 38

For instance, certain pot-bellied flasks with ring handles, obviously influenced by ancient Peruvian models, are decorated as heads of satyrs, whose horns end in inconspicuous spouts—a brilliant blending of representation and function (page 446). The transition from "female" vases to statuettes of women which are inspired by Mediterranean votive figurines is a fluid one. Here the modeling of the form no longer obeys the law of the vase, but that of the figure. The proportions and formal characteristics of the statuettes betray their Antibes origin; some of their details—the S-loop that outlines the breasts—seem due to the ornamental habits the painter contracted in decorating vases.

In our last example, the symmetric design and the closed contour follow the structure of the vase; in other instances, Picasso proceeds more freely. The body of the vase is distorted, and the female forms are obtained by light pressures on the soft clay. The heavy arms are modeled separately and attached, the spout is bent inward and is no longer functional. The black-and-red decoration becomes a "dress," and the "arms" reach up to the painted necklace (page 444). The decorated "gazelles" result from curved clay bricks which had served as supports for the ware in the kiln, and had become extremely hard through repeated firings. Picasso often decorated such narrow bricks with caryatid-like, full, or half-length figures, transforming the simplest things into the most magnificent objects. This is no mere "imitation" of primitive accomplishments; rather, the artist here spontaneously rediscovers the fundamental laws of primitive art. By this renewed contact with the art of the most remote past, Picasso emerges as a rare example of a regression which is at the same time highly creative. And he is capable, too, of the most modern refinements, as can be seen from a group of large vases decorated with back views of female figures. When we examine one of these works (page 445), we find it difficult to decide what was predominant in the artist's imagination: the vase which is slender at the top and flares out at the bottom, or the female figure whose broad hips and slender waist suggest the curves of the vase. This figure, with its incised contours, was originally conceived as a nude. The vessel seemed to be finished, but long afterward Picasso repainted it, covering the nude figure with an ornamental garment as delicate as a veil, which enhances the sensual effect of the forms and integrates them even more completely in the third dimension of the vase.

## Sculpture

Picasso shares with many contemporary painters the urge to work in sculpture. In this he is unquestionably motivated by the desire to achieve a higher degree of reality, which was also the primary reason for his interest in ceramics. Because the sculptor deals with three dimensions, he can react to any object in the environment with an immediacy that is denied to the painter. For instance: a natural object can serve, without any change, as the starting point or component part of a sculptural work. Spontaneity of response and inventiveness are prime characteristics of Picasso's unique talent, but the actual modeling of his sculptures often fails to meet the specific requirements of this art. We would not do justice to his sculptural work were we to judge it by standards that can be properly applied only to a professional sculptor. This, incidentally, is true of the sculptural work of any painter, even Renoir. The charm and uniqueness of such works can be understood only in terms of the pictorial style of their creators. Picasso's early sculptures are particularly close to his paintings in those years, and both can be considered together; in later periods, however, they seem to be more independent. His sculptures rarely reveal the continuity we have repeatedly found in considering his paintings. On the other hand, Picasso has occasionally anticipated and stimulated modern sculptors through his own inventions.

*"Documents"* page 505

The plastic style of the Harlequin busts (page 460) or of the contemporary *Head of a Woman*, of 1905, is obviously related to the style of that year's paintings which represent similar subjects. The delicate, vibrant treatment of the surface of the sculptured head is matched by the soft, fluid modeling of the painted figures, and the sensitive facial features are treated with equal delicacy in both. It is as though one of those painted figures had been translated into bronze. If this bust, with its surface largely dissolved into minute patches of light and shadow, still bears some likeness to Rodin's portrait busts, the small bronze *Head* of 1906 (page 433), with its compact, symmetrical, and heavily rounded forms might suggest an affinity with Maillol. Despite their proximity in time, these heads come from two distinct artistic periods, separated by Picasso's summer at Gosol in 1906: the first head is some-

*Jester* Cl. Cat. 32
*Head of a Woman*
page 432

*Head* page 433

what emotional, the second is related to the earliest abstract work. The small, regular, serene but not overly expressive head with the strong jaws, forceful, angular nose, little eyes, and mass of hair that fits like a cap is influenced by the Iberian bronzes with which Picasso became acquainted at that time. In 1907, the year of the *Demoiselles d'Avignon*, he produced a number of figures in wood, which reflect his interest in African Negro sculpture; and in 1910, after the Horta de Ebro period, he made the well-known *Head of a Woman* (page 462) with the typical Cubist faceting of the details. Here Picasso may have felt a strong need to transpose the architectonic character of Cubist painting to an object that is actually three-dimensional.

*Head of a Woman*
Cl. Cat. 54

In a series of small sculptures of 1914, Picasso pursued another Cubist objective—the simultaneous rendering of multiple views. He made numerous wax models of a glass of absinthe on which rests a spoon with a lump of sugar; these wax models were then cast in bronze and colored. The glass is open on one side, which led Kahnweiler to call this "transparent sculpture." (The Italian Futurist Umberto Boccioni had systematically applied the principles of this kind of sculpture in his *Bottle and Plate*, of 1912.) Picasso's *Glass of Absinthe* with its irregular rim and other "painterly" features has the character of a casual but charming toy. Closely parallel to the *papiers collés* of the years preceding World War I are the "musical instruments" pieced together from rough bits of wood and attached to a base in the manner of a relief (page 382). These are not structures reproducing guitars or mandolins, but vigorously three-dimensional constructions made of assorted fragments; in other words, they are new *objets* along the lines of Synthetic Cubism. At that time Picasso produced many *objets* of this kind, also using other materials, such as paper, zinc, or tin; they were lost during the war when he changed studios frequently.

*Mandolin* page 382
*Violin* Cl. Cat. 70

These works manifest with particular clarity the painter's desire for a degree of reality greater than that attainable in painting. They are a radical rejection of illusionism. Such an attitude makes sense only from the point of view of a painter, not a sculptor. The famous anecdote about the bewildered visitor who heard sounds of hammering coming from the studio of Picasso "the painter" thus gains deeper significance. Even later Picasso, this "king of ragpickers" (Cocteau), continued to dignify worthless trash by refashioning it artistically: in 1932, for example, he combined a butterfly, blades of grass, a dry, lacy leaf, a few matches, and a thumbtack to form a small relief of almost dramatic animation and subtle humor.

Picasso became interested in non-naturalistic outdoor sculpture at a very early date, but he never carried out his ideas on so ambitious a scale as another painter, Max Ernst, in his *Lunar Asparagus*, of about 1936. In 1927, at Cannes, Picasso conceived a series of "monuments"; and in the summer of 1928, at Dinard, he made drawings in which elementary, organic, anthropomorphic forms are pervaded by open space. In a lithograph of 1929, the monumental conception is strengthened by the beach cabin in the background and clearly shows the influence of openwork sculpture—*sculpture à clairevoie*—in which the important thing is not the continuity of the sculptural body, but its communication with the surrounding open space. Again Picasso elaborates his metaphor on the human figure: a curious ring-shaped form connects the "torso" to the "legs," the arms are outspread, the breasts and head are tiny. The whole thing anticipates the figures which, as late as 1950, Henry Moore set up in his garden as imaginary members of a promenade whose structural design, in turn, is defined by the sculptured figures. Significantly "modern" in Picasso's invention is the revival of a primitive sculptural idea—the image of man as a vertical pole thickened at one end to indicate the head. This form is the nucleus of a whole series of Picasso's sculptures dating from 1931, which are carved of wood sticks and cast in bronze. In these works the "stick-like" element of the human body is blended with the drapery into a convincing unity, largely inspired by the wood medium.

The group of drawings made in Cannes which represent bathers (page 392)—whose Surrealist metamorphic character we have already discussed—have their sculptural counterpart in the small bronze female figure (page 434) which Picasso made in Paris in 1928. Metamorphosis—the mutation of forms—offered a singular challenge to three-dimensional creation, and it is no accident that this resulted in one of Picasso's happiest sculptural achievements. Solid masses are contrasted with hollow spaces enclosed by lighter parts. The dualism of positive and negative space, which is characteristic of the most recent sculpture, is enriched by yet another dualism. This second dualism is produced by rendering, in sculpture, the two main views of the figure, and is expressed primarily by the displacement of the breasts which provide a strong accent. The resultant form is something between sculpture in the round and the back-to-back reliefs such as are frequently seen atop medieval choir stalls.

*Seated Bather* page 392

*Metamorphose* page 434

Related to this figure is the bronze *Cock* (page 435), which Picasso made at Boisgeloup in 1932. This sculpture occupied a place of honor in the center of the Picasso gallery at the Salon de la Libération of 1944. It could occupy such a place because in contrast to the relief-like works preceding it, its effect is quite spatial. But it shares with the earlier works the contrast between heavy and light forms and their metamorphosis, which is thematically motivated by the juxtaposition of rump and feathers. It is very instructive to compare this *Cock* with another *Cock*, eighty-three inches high, of wrought iron, which Picasso made two years earlier and intended as an open-air exhibit. The two works reflect fundamentally different conceptions of sculpture. Whereas the bronze *Cock* of 1932 is derived from the natural model and, despite parts that enclose and articulate the negative space, is essentially a positive volume, the wrought-iron *Cock* is a construction that only indirectly suggests the idea of the living animal; it has no volume at all, and is an openwork sculpture in every respect. In addition, the special technique applied here, which Picasso learned from González, produces some surprising effects—the tail feathers, for instance, are shaped like leaves, which results in an extraordinarily bold, imaginative creation.

*Cock* page 435

The head of a woman of 1931 is constructed from even cheaper materials, in part, of scraps from a mechanic's workshop. Here, association with the natural object is achieved by even more roundabout means. What the beholder sees even depends on his position, and he can scarcely grasp the artist's intention if he confines himself to one view. Picasso did not, however, attempt to represent time in the manner of Moholy-Nagy's constructions which must be rotated, or Calder's

*Construction: Head* Cl. Cat. 126

continuous motion mobiles. (An interesting formal analogy to Calder's mobiles is provided by Picasso's abstract pen drawings of 1924, reproduced as woodcuts in Vollard's 1931 edition of Balzac's *Le chef d'œuvre inconnu* (page 31), although these designs, like the sculpture of Picasso discussed before, have definite representational connotations). It is characteristic of the anthropomorphic quality of Picasso's imagination that he does not construct complicated technical apparatus in his three-dimensional sculptural works. In his wire sculptures, made around 1930, he effects rich and compact spatial organization by means of simply arranged elements, and even retains the principle of the figure by alluding to parts of the body ("head," "hands").

The Mediterranean temperament that makes Picasso, the sculptor, prefer the compact and the representional also makes him adhere to the static type of sculpture in which the balance depends upon placing the center of gravity somewhere above the base. The magnificent, larger-than-life *Head of a Woman* of 1931–32, cast in light bronze (page 469), has Classical proportions and sober, clearly modeled forms. Austere, yet rich, like the pediment sculptures of Olympia, this is the noblest example of Picasso's work in the full round. It affirms the static principle despite the strongly diagonal axis which becomes an expressive value. Later—and this reflects his specifically tactile disposition—Picasso showed preference for objects that can be held in the hand ("hand sculptures"); they have no top or bottom in the static sense, and their plastic effect is no longer determined by their position in space. Among these are the small head-like forms modeled in 1943 and cast in bronze, which have no fixed base (page 474). Here Picasso is obviously interested less in the round form of the head than in the cavities of the eyes and mouth which invite continuous exploration by touch. Presumably, these attempts anticipate the skulls that Picasso was to model occasionally during the war years. The most impressive of

these is the oversized bronze skull of 1944 (page 436) which, like some medieval skulls, is not a skeletal structure, but a large closed form with a few deeply shaded cavities. The contrast between the protruding cranium and the hollow parts of the face, which is terminated in a harsh line, is heightened by the smooth, shining surface of the forehead and the rough, partly destroyed surface of the cheeks and jaws. These effects are due to the crumbly nature of the wet plaster with which Picasso prefers to build up his figures.

Picasso's sculptural conceptions are often inspired by the form and material of objects, usually fragmentary, that he finds quite by accident. In 1937, for example, he found an old corroded bone which suggested to him the precise outline of the beak and delicate ruff of a bird; with a few touches—mainly, by drilling an eye—he completed the illusion

(page 440). His hand, equally deft with the most vigorous and most subtle expression, can transform rubbish into a unique artistic object, which no one can look at with indifference, whether it inspires admiration or laughter. Occasionally the banality of the original object used by Picasso destroys the illusion, and thus a particular tension is created between the original object or fragment and the new artistic object. This is the case with the famous *Head of a Bull* (page 473) which Picasso conjured

up from the seat and handle bars of an old bicycle (the handle bars are the horns); similarly, the principal parts of the *Stork*, of 1942, are

          (p. 289) *Night Landscape* 195

fragments of a child's scooter. In 1951 Picasso fashioned the body of his *Crane* (page 439) from a shovel, its head from a faucet, and its feet from metal forks whose tines he splayed apart. During the same period he made the *Monkey* (page 481) for whose body he used a large ball, to which he attached the extremities, which consist in part of mechanical bits-and-pieces; for its head he used a toy automobile—the animal's beady eyes are set in the windshield. In each case the primary aspect of the artist's achievement lies in his ability to discover the sculptural possibilities in everyday objects, to the amazement of every beholder.

He performed a comparable feat of the imagination when he saw an owl in the slightly asymmetrical, compressed oval of a pebble ground smooth by nature, apparently even before he had found, at Antibes, the simplest graphic formula for an owl on paper (page 91). On another occasion, around 1950, Picasso cut pieces of tin plate into a small owl with outspread wings, and into a small wagtail, and attached the sculptures fashioned from these pieces to pieces of ordinary brick. The effect, particularly of the wagtail, is amazing: the charming sculpture blends so beautifully with the air around it that one can almost feel the wind that seems to be playing around the tail feathers of the teetering bird. The most original sculptured rendition of the owl, perhaps the most extraordinary of all representations of that bird, is the painted ceramic of 1950 (page 73). The self-contained general design of the extremely simplified body on short legs—the preliminary drawings still show longer legs—is genuinely sculptural, although the effect of volume is dissolved by the uneven treatment of the surface and, still more, by the chiaroscuro of the coloring.

Picasso for the most part models directly in plaster (not in clay)—a technique used by the great stucco-workers of the seventeenth and eighteenth centuries. From this less pliable material he wrests a great range of effects, whether the sculpture is small or large. In this medium even large sculptures must be modeled rapidly. Picasso finished the over-life-size *Shepherd Carrying a Lamb* in one day, in February 1943, after he had clarified his conception in numerous preliminary drawings which extended over a period of six months. This work was cast in bronze in 1944, and set up in Vallauris. The imprint of the hastily applied, quick-drying plaster is still evident in the bronze—a quality which is the main charm in this kind of sculpture.

The almost life-size *Pregnant Woman* of 1950 (page 478) demonstrates a more moderate naturalism, as regards the formal elements, combined with an almost frightening explicitness, as regards the motifs. The generalized head, as well as the arms and legs, are subordinated to the strongly swollen womb and the large breasts, which are smooth, in contrast to the rest of the body. This woman is related to the figures of the *Massacre in Korea*, which will be discussed in the next chapter. Dating from about the same time is the larger-than-life *Goat*, overflowing with animal vitality, which was first modeled in plaster and then cast in bronze (page 438). Photographs taken during the work show that the armature to which the plaster was applied was made of all sorts of worthless objects—an old basket, a lamp, etc. Picasso had modeled over-life-size, naturalistic cats as early as 1941. However, in this powerful *Goat*, which is also a symbol of fertility, naturalism is exaggerated to stress the element of fecundity, but at the same time stereometrically

*Crane* page 439

*Monkey and Her Young*
Cl. Cat. 240

Note 39

*Owl* page 73

*Shepherd Carrying a Lamb* page 437

*Pregnant Woman*
Cl. Cat. 216

*Massacre in Korea*
page 429
*Goat* page 438

simplified. The shoulder region conceived in almost Cubist fashion, for example, contrasts with the swelling forms of the distended udders, whose smooth treatment is, in turn, a striking contrast to the rough surface of the surrounding parts.

The large, severe head of a goat with its narrow, asymmetrical jaws reappears in a still life sculpture of 1952; the rectangular plane of the floor connects the head with a bottle placed directly opposite it, in whose neck there is a burning candle. (Picasso had actually used such a primitive candlestick in Madrid when he was twenty.) Here, in accordance with the principle of Cubist "transparent sculpture," the bottle is open in the back, and the rays of light from the candle have been given sculptural form. The whole sculpture is painted in black and white stripes, which tends to dematerialize it; and the rays of light are bordered in black! But the most prominent feature of this three-dimensional still life is the tantalizing treatment of space which compels the beholder to look at it from constantly changing points of view—the most recent confirmation of the hypothesis that the painter turns to sculpture in order to capture a dimension which in painting is only an illusion. Yet, along with these sculptured works, Picasso also *painted* still life compositions with goat's skull and candlestick in gray monochrome (page 479), with very expressive chiaroscuro effects. Just as he had done in his youth, he simultaneously attacked the problem in painting and in sculpture.

*Goat's Skull and Candle*
Cl. Cat. 238

*Goat's Skull and Bottle*
Cl. Cat. 223

### Ornament and Image. War and Peace

There is an apparent connection between the owl vases mentioned above (page 283) and the large zincograph *Owl* he made with brush and scraper on March 10, 1948, at Vallauris (the same day on which he made six versions, the same size as the owl, of a music-making faun; page 276). The relationship to the painted vase lies in the similar way the dark drawing spreads on the light ground, and the alternation and connection of linear and spotted elements. But the flat surface of the zinc plate yields a form wholly different from that on the circular, bulging structure of a vase. We can almost feel that the representation in some measure derives from the flattening of a curved surface, thus producing several simultaneous views of the front, side, and rear. The broad brush strokes make detailed modeling unnecessary; yet the numerous convex curves create the illusion of a solid body. The total effect, however, is determined by the decorative filling of the surface: a fluidity achieved by the line-and-spot system. In the same way, using the scraper, he has executed the head—without drawing the beak—by reversing the color relations (white on black).

He applies the same procedure to the human figure in the numerous states of the large lithograph *Woman in an Armchair*, which were followed immediately in January 1949 by several representations of animals. The zinc etching of January 7 of lobsters and fish, measuring 30 by 42 inches, has the quality of a still life and combines the stylistic characteristics just described with naturalistic details. Moreover, as a result of the difference in the coloring of the ground, chiaroscuro effects appear around the white planes with curvilinear borders whose richness anticipates the paintings to be discussed below. Also in the *Toad*, painted a few days later (page 424), this mysterious light appears along with the natural ugliness of the animal. The large wash lithograph of the *Dove*, which was made during these same days, is even more pictorial and naturalistic; the beauty and radiant whiteness of the bird may have been intended to make up for the monster-like appearance of the toad. The close juxtaposition and interrelation of naturalistic and ornamental treatment exemplified here are not accidental: they are an essential part of Picasso's subsequent works.

*The Great Owl* page 311

*Musical Faun* page 276

*Toad* page 424

*Dove* Cl. Cat. 209

Prominent among the paintings of 1950 and 1951 are the portraits of Picasso's small children. The style of the double portrait painted on wood, of January 20, 1950 (page 426), is a direct descendent of the 1949 lithographs. The older child, Claude, sits in a small armchair, while his younger sister, Paloma, is seated in a high chair; the tiles of the floor are decorated with a marigold pattern. The large, light surfaces at the upper left lead us to assume the presence of a window whose handle stands out against the luminous background. The two figures are not clearly disengaged from their surroundings as solid bodies, but are part of a flat decorative system in which no distinction is made between figures and accessory parts, or even vertical and horizontal forms (the floor tiles, for instance, seem vertical). The girl's left hand and the boy's right hand, which hold a toy, are entirely ornamental. Following the method we have mentioned in discussing the *Owl* (page 311), Picasso treated one hand positively (light on dark), and the other negatively (dark on light). The other two hands are more naturalistic and spatial, as is the boy's exaggeratedly foreshortened left foot. There is a suggestion of three-dimensional space in the babyish, twisted feet of the little girl, whose position, in relation to the spectator, is not frontal, but lateral. And one might even speak of perspective with regard to the legs of her high chair. The most naturalistic part of the painting is her broad head which attains an illusion of solidity from, especially, the direction of the light. By contrast, the head of the boy, shown frontally and in two profiles, exemplifies Cubist simultaneity. Thus this picture is further proof that Picasso does not hesitate to combine several contrasting artistic principles in one work: the proud freedom from all dogmas, which was particularly striking in *Guernica*, is here reasserted. But the artistic unity of the work is preserved, thanks largely to color and chiaroscuro effects. The two are inseparable: the limited range of the color, which is confined to white, black, gray, and brown tones, is compensated for by the important contribution of light and shadow to the rhythm of the composition. The seventeenth-century Spanish painter Zurbarán masterfully applied the artistic principle embodied here, and Picasso himself referred to this work as "very Spanish."

In February 1950, one month after completing this double portrait, Picasso made a free copy of a famous Spanish masterpiece, El Greco's *Portrait of a Painter*, now in the museum at Seville. As we know from his version of a Poussin painting (page 417), this was not the first time that Picasso tested his powers by re-creating the work of a great master. Another well-known example of such fruitful contacts with the past is his very free lithographic treatment (in ten different states) of Cranach's *David and Bathsheba* in the Berlin museum, which he executed in the spring of 1949. And shortly before painting the El Greco, he had painted a version of Courbet's *Demoiselles des bords de la Seine* (page 428). In this large canvas the ornamental tendency of these years reaches its highest point. The figures seem largely dissolved into colored line and surface ornament, so that only isolated features—heads, hands, shoes— are recognizable. The other realistic elements are enveloped in a mysterious veil of forms; their significance is systematically denied, as Islamic art had done for a thousand years. The affinity between Andalusian and Moslem art—demonstrable also in Picasso's earlier periods— is seldom disclosed as clearly as it is in this painting. The mysterious

*Pages from a Sketchbook* (1952)

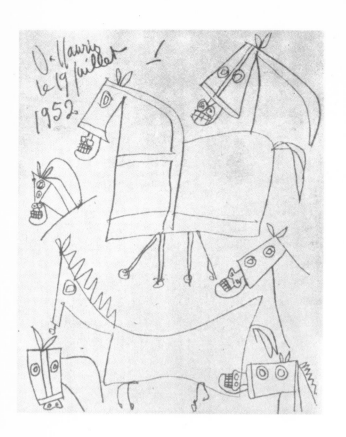

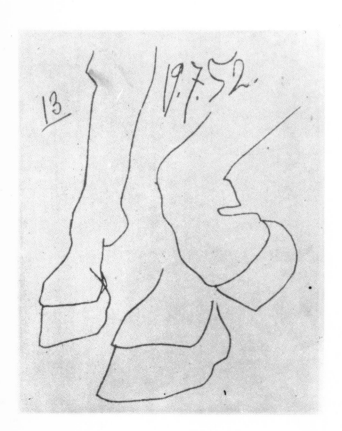

*Pages from a Notebook* (1952)

298

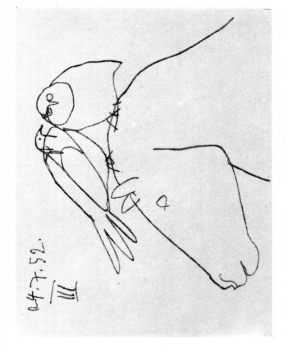

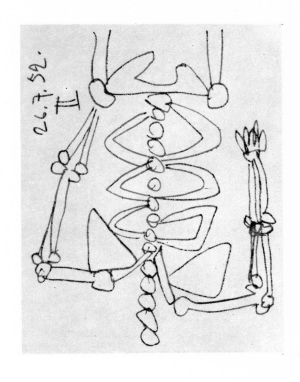

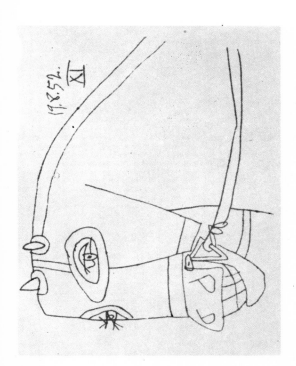

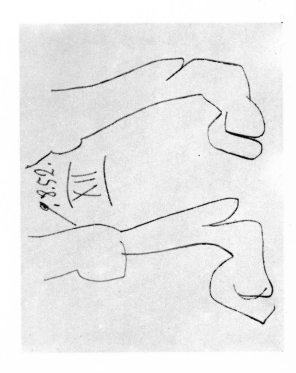

*Pages from a Notebook* (1952)

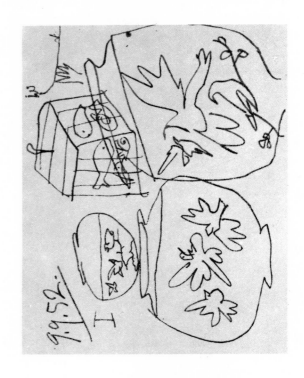

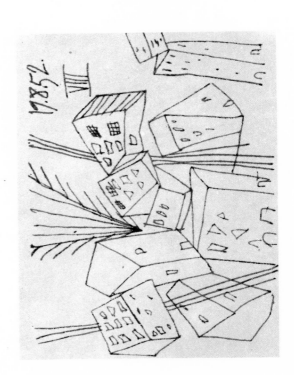

*Pages from a Notebook* (1952)

transformation of nature in *Demoiselles* springs from the same roots as the Spaniard's passion for *peinture écrite* (page 349), an expressive pictorial script without representational content.

*'Peinture écrite'* page 349

El Greco meant very much to Picasso in his youth; in reworking the great Spaniard's portrait, the aging painter proclaims once again that his art originates in his native soil. Even the fact that the painting he chose to copy is in Seville is not without significance, for he likes to recall that he was born in southern Spain, and Kahnweiler's lapidary statement, "Ses sujets sont ses amours" ("His subjects are his loves"), applies here perfectly.

Note 42

A closer comparison of Picasso's Greco (page 423) with the original reveals so many identical details and, at the same time, such arbitrary divergences, that the copy could be described as a kind of portrait of El Greco's work: it is a characteristic Picasso painting, even though the subject portrayed is an El Greco painting. The position of the figure on the picture surface and the distribution of light are largely those of the original; but the decorative organization, which replaces El Greco's spatial conception, introduces geometric elements absent in the original, such as the outline of the easel at the extreme left, or the diagonal in the background, extending from the ruff to the upper right corner. Similarly, the white lines dividing the garment replace El Greco's delicate high lights on the black material.

*Portrait of a Painter after El Greco* page 423

In keeping with these changes, the original three-dimensional form of the ruff with its folds has been transformed into a geometric, fan-shaped pattern which includes the band of rays (originally the painter's brushes); the beard has undergone a similar transformation. Picasso has even translated the sensitive expression of the hands into his own idiom. The form of the hand holding the palette presented no particular difficulty, because its fingers are outstretched; but the raised hand holding the brush had to be entirely reconstructed and related to the form of the cuff.

Picasso has succeeded brilliantly in all this and has preserved the original expression, although he had to dispense with the spatial over-lappings of the fingers. The face is shown both frontally and in profile; the individual features—the little circular chin, the two comma-shaped lips, the bead-shaped nostrils, the little ears attached in a peculiar way —have been treated previously in lithographs. The coloring is related to that of the double portrait of the children, but at the same time it is directly inspired by the subdued tonality of the El Greco painting. The mournful black of the garment and the anemic flesh color are effective also in Picasso's version. The yellow, red, and brown paints on the palette have consistently been translated into Picasso's flat idiom; the light, warm brown of the palette itself is the strongest note of color in Picasso's version. All this confirms the well-known truth that the essential features of a language can best be studied in a translation.

During 1950 the naturalistic tendency in Picasso's painting gains strength. This is evident above all in his handling of perspective. On Christmas Day he painted a large horizontal picture on wood representing his two children, Claude and Paloma (page 307). The floor, with the same marigold pattern as in the painting done earlier in the year (page 426), now seems to recede, as a result of overlappings and foreshortenings. Similar perspective elements appear in the red toy auto-

*Claude and Paloma at Play* page 307
*Claude and Paloma* page 426

mobile in which the boy is seated, and particularly in the figure of Paloma, dressed in blue, who is seen lying on the red carpet next to a toy railroad, her white-stockinged legs raised in the air. Here Picasso actually indulges in exaggerating the perspective effect. Accordingly, the descriptive linear features are more important than the ornamental ones; the multiple views of the boy's face are less obtrusive, and the natural colors of the objects represented predominate, without, however, restricting the painter's freedom.

During the first ten days of January 1951, Picasso painted several single portraits of his children on canvas; we shall consider here the portrait of Paloma dated January 8 (page 427). The organization of planes and the illusion of three-dimensionality are perfectly reconciled in this painting. The right half of the face (as seen by the beholder) still contains a clearly visible profile view, with ear, cheek, and chin; this, however, is subordinated to the unified frontal view of the face. Purely ornamental lines are almost entirely absent. On the other hand, ornamental features have been incorporated into the characterization: they appear in the hands and fingers, in the jagged and wavy borders of the dress, and, finally, in the rhythmically distributed locks of hair. The color contributes a great deal to the stylization: green is dominant in the hair and in numerous contours and shadows of the face; the light blue of the dress and hair ribbon, in addition to the black and the light flesh tone, introduces a fourth color. The asymmetric division of the background into various gray tones harmonizes with and balances the asymmetric arrangement of the arms and of the two sides of the face.

The naturalism of these portraits of children is surpassed in the principal work of 1951, the *Massacre in Korea* (page 429). With this wood panel, Picasso, after an interval of many years, again attacked the problems of painting a historic subject. Its dimensions ($43^{1}/_{4}$ by $82^{3}/_{4}$ inches) are not as monumental as those of *Guernica*, and the smaller size probably influenced the choice of stylistic means and partly accounts for the arrangement as a scene with relatively consistent naturalistic treatment, or, to use negative terms, for the absence of symbols and abstractions that are predominant in *Guernica*. But the two paintings, so different in treatment, are similar in their basic conception and their expressive vehemence. Just as in the older picture, Picasso wants to represent here innocence as the victim of brute force; and the possible intention of blaming one of the warring parties is overshadowed by the universality of the ideas expressed.

The composition is clearly divided into two parts: at the left stands the group of naked women and children at the edge of a mass grave; at the right is a group of heavily armed warriors whose gigantic limbs and hard muscles are reminiscent of prehistoric giants. Their armament (particularly the helmets) suggests medieval knights; in fact, simultaneously with this grandiose portrayal of brute force, Picasso treated the motif of armored soldiers in drawings and lithographs with a humorous touch, conceived as a sort of jocular comment on history. The armored men in the *Massacre in Korea*, where everything is grimly serious, have a robot-like quality: the compactness of the group and the concentrated effect of the weapons directed at the women suggest the impersonal impetus of a war machine. The gigantic foot which, like the barrels of the guns, reaches into the left part of the picture, seems to belong not

*Paloma, the Artist's Daughter* page 427

*Massacre in Korea* page 429

Page-Boys at Play Cl. Cat. 219

*Knight and Page-Boy* page 248

302

to one of the warriors, but to the rigid colossus formed by all of them.

On the left of the composition the women, of different ages, some of them pregnant, are also rendered in an austere formal language, which avoids petty details; their smaller size and the softness of their forms make them strikingly weaker than the men. But unlike the men they have human faces, even though these are very expressively distorted by anguish, suffering, and despair. As feeling individuals they are opposed to the unfeeling mass; flowering, fecund life is contrasted with the technique of destruction. These women cannot be separated from their children, whose reactions to the threat vary according to their age. The teen-age girl modestly covers her breasts; the child at the extreme left, shaken by mortal fear, presses against his horrified mother. The boy at the right does not realize the seriousness of the danger and hopes to escape, while the two little children are unaware of it. One cries and is comforted by his mother, the other is happily engrossed in his own world, playing with a few flowers on the ground. Like the girl with the bouquet in the *Minotauromachy*, he symbolizes the promise of a better future.

*Minotauromachy*
page 401
*War* page 430
*Peace* page 431

Quite different are *War* and *Peace* (pages 430 and 431), the two enormous paintings executed in 1952, which were shown with *Guernica* and *Massacre in Korea* at the great Milan exhibition of 1953, held in the bomb-scarred ballroom of the Palazzo Reale. *War* and *Peace*, like *Massacre in Korea*, were received with surprise, and even disappointment. According to Picasso, the public reacted so unfavorably to his newest historical paintings because it had expected him to treat them in the style of *Guernica*; but, as he observed correctly, the new paintings should not be judged by the same standards. *War* and *Peace*, painted in oil on fiberboard panels measuring 15 feet 6 inches by 34 feet, could not be viewed properly at the Milan exhibition. Picasso had planned them as decorations of the vaulted ceilings of a small chapel at Vallauris. They were installed there in February 1954, and in this dimly lit interior, where the beholder stands in a kind of "dream tunnel" *under* the panels (*War* at the right, and *Peace* at the left), they achieve the desired effect of a magic illusion which cannot be obtained in harsh daylight and by direct confrontation. According to Picasso, the visitors to the chapel would get the best view of these paintings were they to move along the walls with candles in their hands, like sightseers in prehistoric caverns, discovering the figures one by one, and realizing the connections between them only partially. In other words, the aesthetic unity of the paintings should be deliberately overlooked in favor of a space-time experience.

A type of painting that withdraws from daylight can afford to dispense with careful, detailed treatment; indeed, it must assert itself by a certain crudeness of execution. A certain independence of the parts in relation to the whole was in accord with the painter's new conception, which aimed at preserving the spontaneous character of the record of his ideas without burdening it with compositional considerations. This, for instance, is what he says concerning its color: "In modern painting each brush stroke is a precise operation, like a cog in a mechanism. You paint someone's beard; it is red, and this red induces you to readjust everything in the ensemble, to repaint everything around it as though it touched off a chain reaction. I wanted to avoid that; I wanted to paint as one writes, with the swiftness of thought, following the rhythm of the imagination." This creative ideal is even more sharply expressed in the following statement: "If I were born Chinese, I should not be a painter, but a calligrapher. I should write my pictures." This conception also provides us with a key to the special character of the numerous drawings that preceded the execution of *War* and *Peace*.

On April 28, 1952, when Picasso for the first time relieved himself of the ideas besetting him by casually recording them, he still had in mind an entirely different treatment: he obviously intended to contrast war and peace in a single painting. In the earliest compositional sketches (page 297), war is allegorized at the right in the shape of a hybrid creature, half-man and half-owl, hovering in the air with outspread wings, and pouring deadly germs from a cup onto a pyramid of skulls piled up on the ground. The monster is confronted by a man armed with a broad sword, who occupies the center of the composition. A small flowering tree separates the man from the left part of the composition, which shows a female figure reaching up to the tree and a reclining child at the bottom. The style of these pencil drawings avoids all facility, negates all artistic skill, and yet reflects the most consummate mastery in the use of a rich, expressive idiom; in other words, it is entirely in keeping with Picasso's idea of the calligraphic ideal just mentioned. Like a child, but on the basis of a unique artistic experience, he puts down his seemingly primitive signs, and with their help formulates his ideas in a number of variations in the course of one day. It is clear that in doing this he has patterned himself on the non-spatial, "ideational" mode of expression of his little son Claude, and has been inspired by the latter's genuine childishness.

Parallel to the drawings are the more detailed studies of the man-bird (page 297), executed partly in ink, and of the female nude reaching for the branch of the tree; and there appears occasionally a theme that was to preoccupy Picasso the next day, namely, the group of three girls dancing under the tree (pages 65 and 297). In the course of the following days, he elaborated this group into a rich, spatial, and rhythmic motif, creating ever-changing, magnificent interpretations of ecstatic joy. At the same time other ideas are recorded, some of them in connection with the dancing group, some independently. For instance the fruit-picking woman is now shown climbing, while the reclining figure has become a mother giving the breast to her child, whose forms are elaborated by means of the familiar Cubist devices (page 332).

All these thematic studies are continued for several days and are terminated about May 11, judging by the data supplied in the work of Claude Roy. But in the final stage the original tripartite composition has yielded to a bipartite division, in which the warrior with the sword and a dove on his shield is opposed to the hybrid creature that is now represented as a man with a bird's head and wings; the group of the dancing girls is almost crowded out of the picture by the warrior.

On July 19, 1952, Picasso returned to the general theme and enriched it with new elements. He said later that the new conception of *War* had been suggested to him by the somber and wretched hearses that are occasionally seen rattling along the pavements of small towns. On that day he concentrated on the figure of the blanketed horse drawing the chariot (page 298); in its stylization the sketches of an armored knight of the year before once again bore fruit. He gave particular attention to the vicious and stupid physiognomy of the animal. On the following day he represented the man-bird—now equipped with a barbed hook in addition to the cup—and, for the first time, with horns and a screaming open beak (page 298).

On July 24 he made the first independent study for *Peace*, which is in a minor key. Here again the painter thinks first of a conveyance, a barge with a winged horse in it; a dove and an owl—Picasso's favorite birds—are peacefully perched on the horse's head (page 299). Moreover he sketches different variants of a helmeted profile head of Athena, and other studies of female heads, which mark a return of the Arcadian mood in an idyllic scene showing women under a blossoming tree, treated in a decorative, linear style reminiscent of Matisse (page 317). During August the series continues with studies of half-length figures of reclining or standing women, with playfully upraised arms, often executed in an ingratiating, sensuous brush technique; some of these women appear in the same series as the war motifs.

On July 26 the latter are enriched by expressive studies of skeletons (page 299), and in August, Picasso tries to replace the blanketed horse by a camel and a pig, producing quite outstanding expressive studies full of macabre humor (page 300). His ability to render animal physiognomies, to which *Guernica* partly owes its deeply moving effect, is confirmed by the figures of the dray-horses drawing the war chariot, and by the contrasting winged horse of a truly classic nobility (page 298). The collapse of culture in wartime is symbolized (on August 20) by a head of Athena knocked off an archaic statue, and by a disorderly pile of toy-like building blocks (page 300)—motifs which like many others were not used in the paintings. This is also the case of the anthropomorphic armored car of May 5, which expresses in the most emphatic terms the same idea as was expressed by the armored knights and by the group of robots in *Massacre in Korea*.

The execution of the paintings began with the chariot in *War*, and proceeded with the utmost speed, in keeping with Picasso's wish to reduce to a minimum the gap between the idea and the picture. He painted with such haste that reflection could scarcely intervene in the work. The material that has been published contains only one small sketch of the whole composition, made August 30, with the chariot at the right and the warrior at the left (page 300); otherwise the painter followed the impulse of the moment, drawing on the treasure accumulated in the course of many months, and making free use of it. Various sketched motifs, such as the burning book under the horses' hoofs or the reed placed between them and the warrior with spear, thus found their way into the painting. In it the figure personifying unchivalrous, treacherous warfare is a man with a faun-like face who is seen standing in the chariot, and who carries his harvest of skulls in a kind of transparent knapsack. He bends forward, holding in his right hand a sword red with blood; with his left hand he pours repulsive vermin from a cup. Shadowy demons armed with sharp weapons form the grisly accompaniment to the black chariot with its team of horses: like the germs, they are ungraspable enemies. (Picasso experimented with such shadowy silhouettes in drawings of September 4.) The just warrior at the extreme left carries a small pair of scales in addition to his weapon;

the dove on his white shield is drawn over a Medusa's head. In contrast with the many-layered, complex symbolism of *Guernica*, all the allegorical allusions here are very direct and without mystery. Nor is there any mystery in the colors: azure blue serves as the background for the good warrior, mouse gray for the shadows, gray-green for the evil warrior; the cloud behind him is dark brown and the ground under the chariot is blood-red.

The surface of *Peace* is articulated by the background colors. The family group at the right is shown against a green background, the main group at the left partly against a deep marine blue, and partly against the dark brown plane at the upper left corner. The sun, represented as a disc in the three primary colors inside a dark brown plane which is surrounded by a yellow nimbus of rays, is set off against the light background; adjoining it to the right is the contrasting black of the tree with its shining apples. The winged horse at the center and the child guiding it are the end result of the numerous preliminary sketches. The two female nudes are also related to the previously mentioned drawings; even the child in the upper left background, the birds swimming about inside a blue fish bowl, and the little fish inside a lantern-shaped cage had been sketched in advance in September (page 300).

The mythological world of this part of the painting reminds us of the Antibes period, and is formally characterized by a mixture of Cubist and naturalistic elements in approximately equal amounts. Its stylistic affinity with a drawing and a painting of 1944, showing a woman washing her feet (page 312), is positively surprising. The figures are modeled by means of the color, the surrealist and symbolic shorthand indications have disappeared. Nevertheless the figures float on the surface, and the light, carefree mood is stressed by the equilibristic performance, which involves the child mentioned above (with a small owl perched on his head), the boy with the grapes and the fishes, and the woman with the hourglass behind her. The three figures at the right obey a different formal law: the three-dimensionality of the group and the sharp breaks in the hard contours as well as the inclusion of the tree recall some of the drawings of the dancing girls. The mother with the baby at her breast under the vine derives directly from the latter drawings, while the position and the foreshortening of the man who seems to busy himself at a primitive fireplace point back to the 1950 portrait of little Paloma playing on the floor (page 307). The man in front of him, who is engrossed in writing, offers a new, strongly expressive version of the motif of girls drawing, which he had used in the 1930s; his presence here may symbolize the new ideal of painting as a "script." This group of three is distinguished from the figures at the left not only formally, by their light, even flatness, but also by their quiet communion. Characteristically, the mother who is shown devoting herself to her baby at the same time reads a book. The angular, flat style of this part of *Peace* is also that of a vigorously colored painting of 1953, showing a woman wrestling with a large dog.

*Studies for a Vase in the Shape of a Bull* (1946)

309

*Wasp* (1937)

*The Great Owl* (1948)

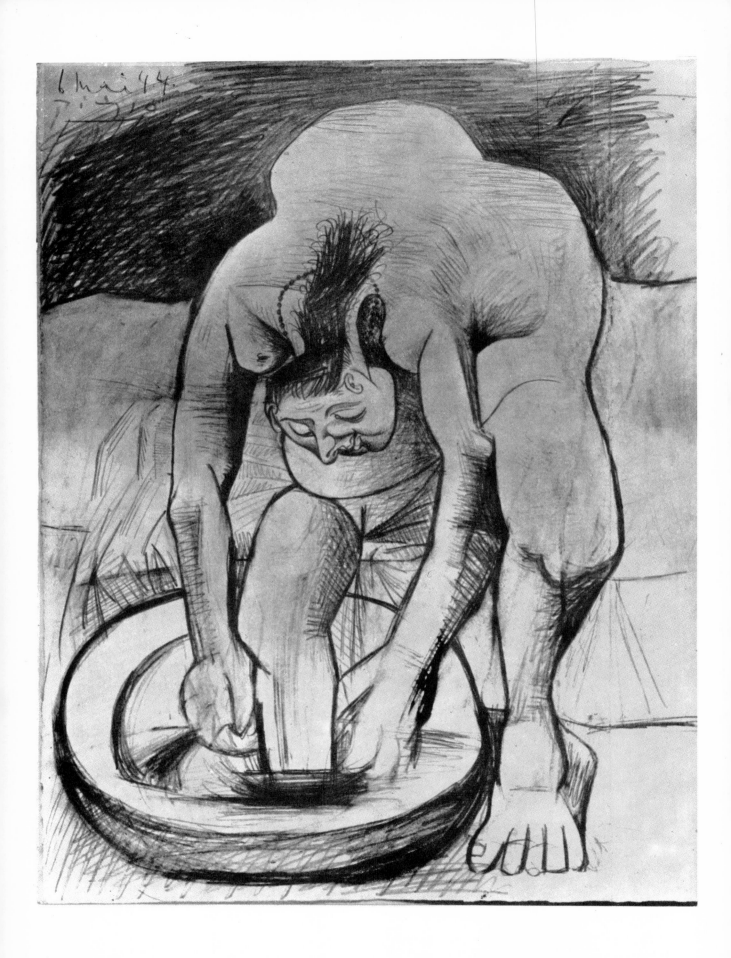

*Woman Washing Her Feet* (1944)

### The Painter and His Model

As a painter of women, Picasso is the greatest of our century; not even Matisse can dispute this title with him. For a while Matisse celebrated woman's natural beauty with an enthusiasm equal to Picasso's —unlike Picasso, he never portrayed her sinister and evil aspects. The female nude has long occupied a central place in Western painting; and Picasso has painted nudes in all his periods. He has treated them in the Cubist, Classicist, Surrealist, and Expressionist styles, but the wealth of formal potentialities he discovered in the female body is only imperfectly suggested by these designations. The lack of understanding which his work as a painter has met is partly due to the indignation he aroused by his unorthodox treatment of the nude, a subject sanctified by the academic tradition. The female figures dating from his abstract period are primarily formal studies, which take the artist's knowledge of the female body for granted but do not reflect his emotional response to his subject. When Picasso remains closer to the model, physiognomic expression becomes possible, and the personal element enters more strongly; then the artist's ideal image of woman emerges, and the content of the scenes he portrays casts light on his general conception of woman and femininity.

Among his early contributions in this field, perhaps the most interesting ones have not come down to us. Sabartés mentions a number of

*Seated Nude* page 374

(below)
*Reclining Woman* 1920

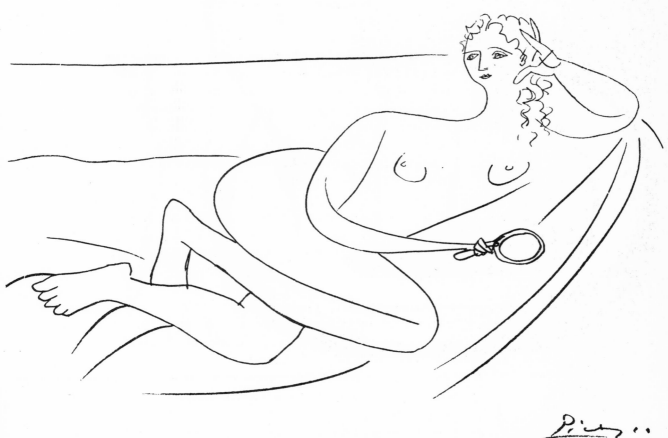

*Nude on a Couch* 1923

graceful pencil drawings done in 1902 and long since lost, of *La bella Chelito*, a dancer and singer who greatly impressed the twenty-year-old painter in Barcelona. He also mentions female nudes roughly drawn with the brush dipped in blue on the walls of the *Zut*, a dilapidated café in Paris which Picasso and his friends frequented in 1904; and more important, a mural in Sabartés' room in Barcelona, representing a half-naked Negro hanging from a tree, with a pair of lovers on the ground beneath him. Even at that early time Picasso combined vigorous sensuality with symbolic meanings in the treatment of sexual love. We have seen how prominent this theme was in the 1930s when Picasso represented the conflict of the sexes in the symbols of the bullfight (page 396) and the Minotaur (page 401). On the other hand, in the Antibes period he glorified woman, and gave us an Arcadian, tender image of happiness in love, this time in the symbolic guise of Classical nature spirits.

A different symbolism appears in the one hundred and eighty sheets of drawings done between November 28, 1953, and February 3, 1954, most of them variations on the theme of the aged painter and his model. Many of the motifs shown here had been treated by Picasso before, but the spirit in which they are presented is entirely new. This graphic commentary on the imponderable relationship between the painter and the reality he experiences is pervaded with humor, irony, and the wisdom of old age. "Never has such stupendous virtuosity been so light-heartedly employed for making fun of art": this, in the words of Michel Leiris, is one aspect of these drawings. But there is also a touch of the tragic in the smiling abstinence of the aging painter. With cheerful resignation he portrays both the eternal beauty of youth and the Platonic devotion of the ugly and even ridiculous painter. This is no longer the Picasso of Antibes and Vallauris, to whom the fullness of life was revealed in a vision of Arcadian happiness, but a lonely man who vainly inquires into the meaning of his endeavors.

Like the serious, symbolic works of the 1930s, these seemingly jocular productions of a lighter muse disclose several layers of meaning. Some are on the surface and legible at first sight; others are deeper, and touch upon crucial questions, particularly that of the relationship between art and life. For to Picasso woman is not merely a favorite subject—she is an essential content of life. Throughout his career Picasso the man has found the complement of his masculine nature in women of a full, genuine femininity; Picasso the painter found in woman the most direct embodiment of nature in all her diversity and magnificence. Woman and nature have always been synonymous to Picasso. In this respect he is like Rembrandt, who is related to him not only as a kindred sexual-psychological type, but also as one of the rare Northern artists in whose works woman occupies a central position. Picasso's interest in Rembrandt's etching technique is certainly not alone responsible for his drawing of 1934, showing the old master and his wife. And it is not accidental that one of the drawings in the series discussed here shows a model of robust physique whose head is adorned with a

*"Documents"* page 506

(below)
*Woman and Horse* 1927

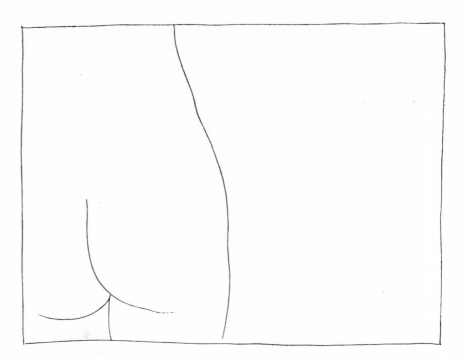

*Nude* 1931

large hat of the kind preferred by Saskia. Finally, Picasso never comes as close to the great draftsman Rembrandt and his chiaroscuros as he does in several sheets, executed in bold washes, treating the theme of the painter and his model.

Some of the very first drawings in our series juxtapose the tall model, with her abundant physical charms, and a male whose poorly proportioned nakedness, lean or fat, is set off against the blossoming forms of the young woman. Later on the contrast becomes more emphatic: the admiring male becomes a misshapen dwarf (page 319) or a stooped old man suggesting a "painter" type (page 322), beside whom the dazzling young beauty with her elastic, flowing lines seems more noble than ever before. It is interesting to note that similarly contrasting couples are to be found in some of Picasso's early works (page 318). The same unbridgeable gulf that separates the unattractive *Amateur* of 1902 from the magnificent female figure beside him is felt by the ugly male of 1954, whose merits are confined to the realm of the mind, as he grovels before the sublime idol he worships. In some of Picasso's works, the element of mystery and fear, as the ultimate expression of the sense of strangeness that man experiences in relation to the other sex, is symbolized in the figure of a sphinx; but nowhere is the same idea presented more magnificently than in a seated nude painted during the war (page 251), which emanates magic awe like a primitive religious idol.

The remote, inaccessible quality of an idol is also hinted at in the drawing of a slender girl of January 4, 1954; the figure is closely surrounded by a number of sharply profiled masculine heads, and bearded heads of the classic type such as often appeared, particularly during the 1930s, in the role of majestic witnesses of symbolic scenes. The tall girl holds a black cat in her hands. This living toy recurs in a number of sheets showing the girl dangling some object on a string and the cat playing with it.

*Nude with Raised Arms* (1952)

317

*The Amateur* (1902)

18.12.53.

*Dwarf and Girl* (1953)

*Girl and Masked Cupid* (1954)

14.1.54. II

*Old Painter and Model* (1954)

*Old Man and Young Girl* (1954)

*Nude and Male Heads* (1954)

*Monkey as Painter* (1954)

The theme of the female playing with the male is most maliciously embodied in a picture dating from 1938, which shows a woman holding in her lap a fettered rooster and the knife with which she is about to slaughter it. A related meaning is gracefully concealed in the portrait of little Maïa with a sailor doll dating from the same year (page 245). In those of the 1953–54 drawings where the cat is replaced by a small baboon, this same element comes to the fore, since the monkey is interchangeable with the ugly male or the painter. Picasso once said at Antibes that people sometimes seem to him crafty little monkeys; and it is not surprising that the monkey is now shown not only mounted on a horse where he takes the place of the dwarfish clown, but also seated before the easel, about to portray the pretty girl. This girl is shown primping before a mirror or proudly displaying her hat—situations repeatedly treated by Picasso as characteristic of feminine vanity. The hat in particular stands for fashion and luxury, pure and simple. That is why the contrast between the painfully distorted face of the *Weeping Woman*, of 1937 (page 399), and her fashionable, brightly colored hat, is so shatteringly effective. For we must not forget that the sufferings of woman and motherhood have often found an interpreter of genius in the painter of *Guernica*.

The figure that occurs most frequently in the drawings is probably that of the aged painter with beard and glasses. He often approaches the quality of caricature as he nearsightedly bends over his canvas or contemplates his model with a matter-of-factness similar to that of the

*Woman Playing with a Cat* Cl. Cat. 277

*Maïa with Sailor Doll* page 245
*Woman and Monkey* Cl. Cat. 230

Note 44

*Monkey as Painter* page 324
*Nude with Hat in the Studio* page 335

*Weeping Woman* page 399

*Old Painter and Model* page 321 (below)
*Painter's Studio* 1927

*Mother and Child* 1951

erotically insensitive Menzel, who claimed that it made no difference to him whether he drew a woman or a crocodile. Sometimes the incongruity is stressed by the lascivious posture of the sleeping model or by the pedantic objectivity with which the painter scrutinizes her beautiful back over the rim of his glasses. Occasionally an ugly old woman wearing thick spectacles is shown attacking the model, while the painter looks on impassively; this scene suggests the desecration of beauty, which reveals itself only to loving eyes, just as a flower responds only to the sun. As though to confirm the painter's erotic indifference, a few sheets show unattractive old women (one wears a humorous classical costume) posing for him: he observes them as persistently as he does the pretty young model.

*Visitors in the Studio*
page 338

Characteristic of the male painter's plight is the further possibility, suggested in several drawings of January 1954, that his place may be taken by an unattractive, elderly woman painter (page 338). Her studio is filled with a throng of critics, a nearsighted race, who pay no attention to the model resting in the background. One such studio scene is combined with a group of ecstatically dancing nudes. Thus this long poem in praise of feminine beauty also treats woman's relation to dance and music—a continually recurring motif in Picasso's work, which finds its climax in *La joie de vivre*.

*La joie de vivre*
pages 267/68

The mask assumes a quite special significance in the relations between the aged painter and his model. With its help the ugly dwarf succeeds in

(p. 327) *Monument: Young Girl* 1929
(p. 329) *Seated Woman* 1947

*Girl with Necklace 1944*

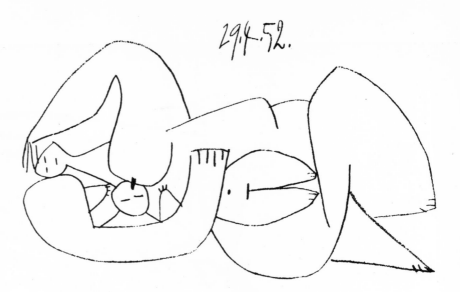

29.4.52.

*Nursing Mother* 1952

*Girl and Masked Cupid*
page 320

*Woman with Monkey
and Clown* page 337

*The Harlequin's Family*
page 133
*The Bath* page 125

*Dance with Banderillas*
page 339

arousing the girl's sympathy; indeed, they are shown hiding from each other behind unshapely masks. So disguised, they engage in carefree games, which do not, however, exclude the erotic element. In a sizable group of drawings (page 320), Eros, represented as a winged *putto*, flits about the charmingly frightened, squirming beauty; but he conceals his face behind a grotesque male mask.

It is only natural that the deceptive world of the saltimbanques and the circus, absent for several decades, should reappear in these drawings. The central figure this time is the clown, whose bearing is as distant as that of the Harlequins of 1905. A solitary figure, he is shown seated facing the nude woman, who may be engaged in putting on a stocking; or we see him gazing upon her enraptured, almost like a worshiper, as she sits enthroned on a chair with an apple in her right hand and accompanied by a monkey (page 337).

While the Pagliacci, who wears his costume like a monastic garb, seems sexless, on another sheet male vigor is embodied in a strong man who lifts the woman high in the air before the clown; the latter, motionless and sad-faced, seems to pay no attention. If we compare this drawing with the Harlequin families of 1905 which it brings to mind, we see that here the woman is no longer treated as man's silent companion. All these drawings rather represent her as victorious over the male and his world. But not only the motifs of this group remind us of the saltimbanques; the tender emotion and the linear character of the early etchings also seem to return in a lithograph such as the *Dance with Banderillas* of 1954. Here the female dancer with her tormenting arrows once again triumphs over the man with the bull's mask, of the kind Spanish children use in their games. A monkey and girl among the spectators repeat motifs of the Rose Period, and the old woman with the headkerchief has left the company of the aged painter to join them. Next to her we see a woman with a tambourine in male costume: she replaces the Harlequin or clown. The disguise and the mask give an unreal touch to this half-mythological and half-theatrical scene, which, however, takes place in a natural setting.

*Nude with Hat in the Studio* (1954)

*The Rehearsal* (1954)

*Woman with Monkey and Clown* (1954)

*Visitors in the Studio* (1954)

A similar mixture of various degrees of reality is displayed in a lithograph entitled *Rehearsal*, showing a pair of nude dancers on a stage before spectators, among them the old woman with the head-kerchief. The faun-like male dancer and the maenad with fluttering hair and mask have the effect of mythological figures making an unexpected appearance in the midst of our disenchanted modern world. Primeval strength and wildness characterize their bodies, in contrast to the passive sensuality of the three female nudes on the right, intended as an image of seductiveness. The portrait-like faces above the defective bodies whose sexual characteristics are emphasized underscore the contrast between ancient nudity and shameless nakedness, which is also expressed in the contrast between the vigorous, strongly shaded outline drawing on the one hand, and the soft modeling and delicate contours on the other. Woman's timeless and time-bound aspects, which in the drawings had still been united, are here clearly separated, and the representative of the eternally feminine asserts her superiority by her place in the composition. To her also belongs the mask, which dominates the design, and which has become the symbol of a way of life for the aging Picasso.

*The Rehearsal* page 336

(below)
*Dance with Banderillas*
1954

The evaluation of Picasso's achievement has gone through distinct stages as his art has grown more complex. Toward the end of the second decade of this century, when he began to paint in his Classical style, admiration for the champion of Cubism (as reflected for instance in Theodor Däubler's laconic statement: "His place in history is secure") was temporarily shaken even among his friends. In 1920, after viewing the works exhibited at Paul Rosenberg's, Raynal voiced his disappointment in these words: "Some of the stars in his eyes have gone out." Nevertheless his faith in the future of Picasso's art and in his inexhaustible powers was so great that he prophesied: "It will be a moving experience to see Picasso's works thirty years hence. I wager that he will still be showing us marvelous things."

At that time Raynal also said: "It is possible that in the end Picasso will make a kind of rule of the human uncertainty into which he has lapsed." This statement anticipated the attitude of Picasso's critics during the following decades. His public became accustomed to his ever-varying periods and styles. It seemed impossible to account for these changes—nor did they depend, as we know from Sabartés, on the painter's changes of residence. Gradually Picasso's mutability itself came to be regarded as an immutable, if mysterious, law of his art. Only since the last war has it been noticed that the forms of his older periods tended to reappear in new syntheses, thus acquiring a new meaning. Yet today the general consensus is that we cannot speak of "development" in Picasso's art, except for short periods such as the "heroic" years of Cubism, from 1907 to 1911.

On the other hand, it has become increasingly clear that works by Picasso from widely separated periods are interrelated, and that his early ideas sometimes reappear later, transmuted and enriched. We have even come to recognize the unusual constancy of his thematic material, as well as his extraordinary persistence in the pursuit of definite artistic goals. "Everything Picasso creates comes from the same center," says Herbert Read, thus summing up the most recent attitude of the critics. He also suggests that "extension" is a better characterization of Picasso's relentless conquering spirit than "development." Picasso's artistic personality can perhaps be described best in terms of the concept of "metamorphosis," which has proved its value as applied to his works.

Such a unified conception of the artist's personality is based on the premise that his work reflects great human qualities—a premise that ought to be self-evident. Picasso's friends often speak of his "heart" (among other things, his "divine simplicity of heart"), and their judgment is confirmed by every unprejudiced person who comes into contact with him. "What you can feel in Picasso is the intensity of his heart, the energy of his passions, his human sincerity" (Claude Roy). The same qualities will be discovered by any sensitive person in the works of this great lyricist. The question whether Picasso is always serious or tries to hoax the public thus becomes meaningless: only to those who do not know Picasso can it occur to suspect his sincerity as a man or as an artist. This is not to say that Picasso in his facetious or ironic moods does not occasionally indulge in the private pleasure of mystifying his

Note 45

fellow men. This trait of his character, however, does not reflect the self-doubt of an insecure mind, but the creative exuberance of a man so sure of himself that he must be granted the right sometimes not to take our era quite seriously. For Picasso has a sense of humor, sometimes bizarre and sardonic, which lurks behind his melancholy gaze and betrays the Spaniard.

The natural steadiness of his character is rooted in his Spanishness, which has decisively stamped the man and his work. His daring pathos, his eternally unsatisfied striving, which Brandi describes as "Faustian," his humor reminiscent of that of Cervantes, Góngora, and Goya, and above all the fantastic image of man he offers us in his works, identify him as a son of Spain. "That is his homeland, the country of men of temperament, the freest men ever produced by the human race" (Cassou). His genius is governed not by norm, but by the spirit of the *capricho*, which endows his personality with a curiously flickering, restless quality.                                                    Note 46

Apollinaire is reported to have said of Picasso that "his spirit is Latin, but his rhythm is Arabic." These two aspects of his Spanish nature also dominate his painting. Because he has the Latin's anthropomorphic sense of form, Picasso never became a non-objective or abstract painter. At the same time his sense of rhythm has enabled him to express his emotions independently of his subject matter. Not one of                                                    Note 47

*Head of a Faun* 1948

341

Picasso's works is the product of his own imagination alone; all of them have been fertilized by something outside himself. That something may be so inconspicuous that those unfamiliar with the *language of things* tend to overlook it; yet, no matter how trivial, it is important enough to stimulate Picasso's creative powers. His love of humble things, his *goût de la pauvreté*, is related to his delight in virtuosity: to make a masterpiece out of rubbish gratifies his ambition. In this, too, he is akin to his friends the poets.

Picasso's incredible virtuosity, whose effect is heightened by the extraordinary rapidity of his responses, accounts for many characteristics of his art. Because his powers are all but unlimited in this respect, he is not interested in perfection. He likes to exploit imperfections artistically, to incorporate them in his compositions, so that he produces what Cocteau calls *un organisme de fautes royales* ("an organism of regal errors"), which is no threat to the work of art. Cocteau is also the author of the amusing metaphor about Picasso being engaged in a race with beauty. "A man who does not run as fast as beauty," he says, "will produce feeble works; a man who runs as fast as beauty will produce trivial works; a man who runs faster than beauty and makes her pant, will force her to catch up with him, and his works will in the end become beautiful. There is nothing more fatal than to run abreast of beauty or to lag behind her. One must keep ahead of her, wear her out, make her ugly, and it is this exhaustion that invests new beauty with the magnificent ugliness of the Medusa's head." Incidentally, Picasso's own definition of genius—"a personality with twopence worth of talent, an error that by chance departs from the ordinary"—sanctions imperfection also in nature.

Just as Picasso's imagination can be kindled by the humblest of things, so it can be aroused by the humblest of experiences. "Nothing pleases him as much as to observe the ordinary spectacle of life." The smallest occasions touch off his creative powers, which aim at "objectifying a stimulus." What he records on the canvas is not an experience of nature or art, but his response to it. This response takes such complete hold of him that the most competent observers describe his state of mind at such moments as a trance. Then the gates of the unconscious open in him, and new visions flood his imagination, enriching his memories of the visible world by other memories, of realms that are invisible. "To draw, you must close your eyes and sing," Picasso says. And the same Picasso who occasionally practiced drawing in the dark often said that painting is a blind man's trade. A chance encounter that he regarded as very significant confirmed him in that view. At Avignon he met a blind artist who painted the Palace of the Popes following the detailed descriptions of his wife who observed it through binoculars. This painter—so Picasso evidently thought—was in a position to keep his emotions free of the compulsion to record visual impressions.

Picasso has always been very emphatic in denying any analogy between artistic creation and scientific experimentation. His best known, though apocryphal, saying, "I do not seek, I find," is directed against the idea that the painter can achieve results by conscious volition. Even when he treats a specific problem in a whole series of works, he fundamentally differs from the scientist conducting a series of tests; for the artist jumps from one solution to another without a fixed plan, and each

Note 48

Note 49

Note 50

Note 51

Note 52

Note 53

"*Documents*" page 503

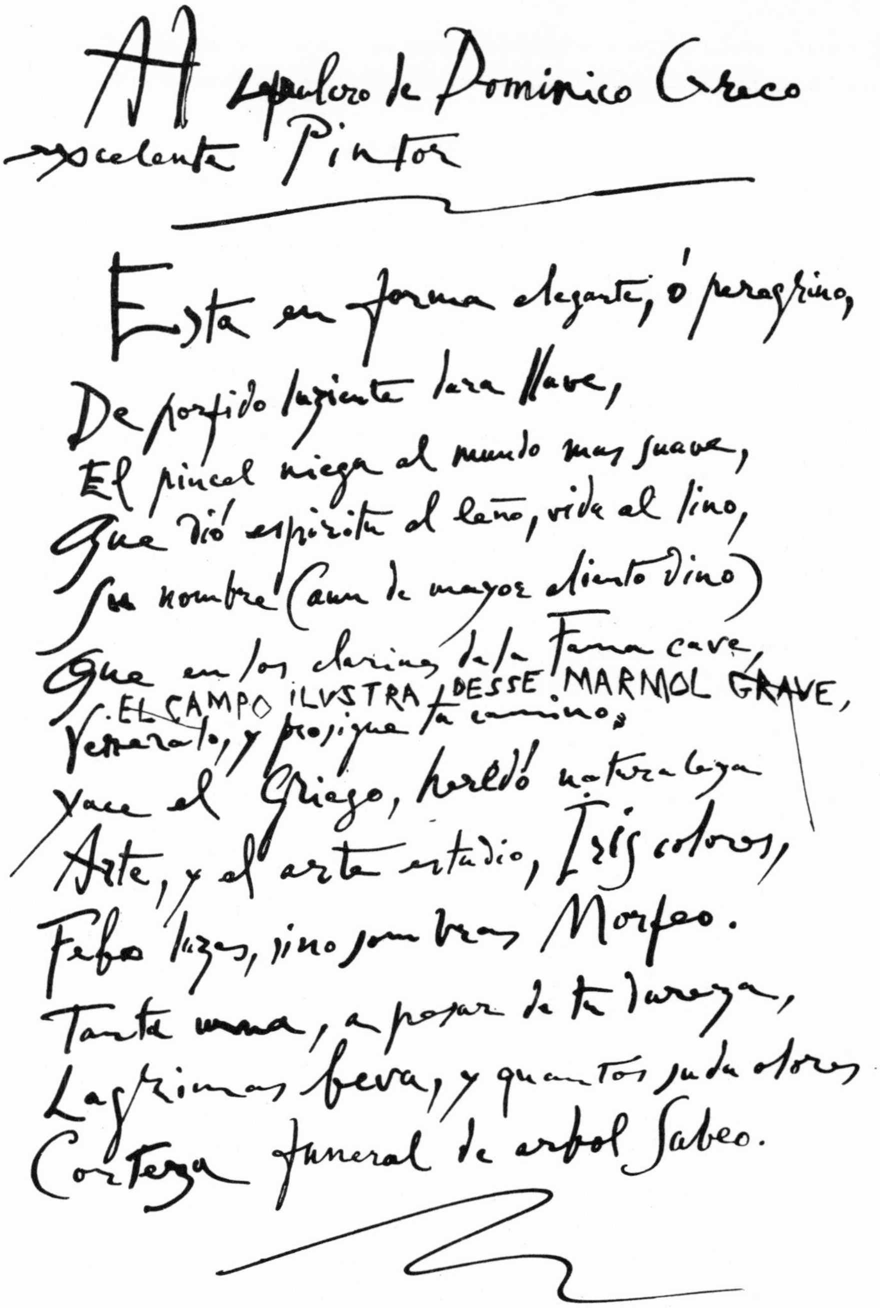

Al sepulcro de Dominico Greco
excelente Pintor

Esta en forma elegante, ó peregrino,
De porfido luziente dura llave,
El pincel niega al mundo mas suave,
Que dió espiritu al leño, vida al lino,
Su nombre (aun de mayor aliento dino)
Que en los clarines de la Fama cave,
.EL CAMPO ILVSTRA DESSE MARMOL GRAVE,
Veneralo, y prosigue tu camino,
Yace el Griego, heredó naturaleza
Arte, y el arte estudio, Iris colores,
Febo luzes, sino sombras Morfeo.
Tanta urna, a pesar de tu dureza,
Lagrimas beva, y quantos suda olores
Corteza funeral de arbol Sabeo.

*"Al sepulcro de Dominico Greco"* 1948

solution is a work of art on its own merits. The artist records his visions; he is, Picasso said, like a thermometer registering the changes of body temperature. And since the process of artistic creation has no fixed direction, it is never completed. Although Picasso often makes preliminary sketches for his larger compositions, his actual work on the canvas is a new process which eventually comes to an end at a certain point but is never "finished." Picasso does not regard any of his paintings as completed in the sense of the works of the old masters, for "to finish a thing is to kill it, to destroy its soul."

Note 54

Note 55

Picasso can at any moment produce a masterpiece without preparation. "A poorly made figure of Picasso results from countless well-made figures, which he erases, corrects, paints over, and which later

*Figural Composition*
1950

serve him only as a starting point. In contrast to all other schools of painting, he seems to end his work with a sketch." This seemingly paradoxical statement by Cocteau reminds us of the part played by imperfection in Picasso's works. Picasso himself expressed the same idea when he said: "What saves me is that every day I do worse." Sabartés adds that the public always accepts Picasso's next-to-last pictures when it is allowed to see his most recent creations.

Since Picasso sometimes fills a canvas in a few hours and does several lithographs in a single day, he often dates his works by the day of execution, not for the purpose of conscientious bookkeeping, but because he regards them as an integral part of his life. Even after his creations

*"Documents"* page 503

344

leave his studio, they do not lead a wholly independent existence; rather their value primarily consists in this, that they are manifestations of his being, that they testify to a specific creative moment. Picasso thinks that so far as he is concerned he might just as well wrap them up and store them away. For the same reason all the paintings he has destroyed were not painted in vain: they have helped him to create new ones. Since nothing is definitive, each creative act is equally significant for the artist. He may, for instance, be satisfied with producing a momentary effect of light, without leaving any permanent trace.

Note 56

Note 57

The human premise of an art entirely rooted in the most personal feelings is a freedom conquered at great cost, a freedom that does not depend on outward success. Picasso the artist, in each of his works, in every single form he has created, asserts his sovereign freedom of decision; Picasso the man, too, is *le bon maître de la liberté* (Paul Eluard). In our age, when popular success carries greater weight than ever before, such freedom implies isolation. Picasso has successfully defended his freedom against all attacks. Sociologically speaking, Picasso, the artist and the man, is the last towering embodiment of individualism, an awe-inspiring example of a romantic "conquest of fate" that is founded upon an immense and unceasing creative activity. But Picasso's intellectual and formal discoveries nevertheless belong to the future rather than to the past, so far as we can judge.

Picasso is never retrospective, he always lives in the present, and he can do this thanks to his almost unlimited capacity for metamorphoses. For Picasso everything is decided here and now, he has renounced all guarantees offered by tradition. Precisely because he is independent of his own and other people's history, he need not be afraid of using whatever good things were produced before him. His regressions are never intellectual, but intuitive, for he has always been convinced that knowledge only confuses the eye and disturbs the immediacy of ex-

*"Documents"* page 503

*Bull and Horse* 1942

perience. It was for this reason that he attached so much importance to his meeting with Henri Rousseau in 1909: the *Douanier*'s art was for him the clearest proof that the Castalian spring of pure inspiration had not dried up even in the twentieth century. We also know from one of his statements that he is not interested in being "understood" by others.

Picasso's influence on the "coming generation" has been as extensive as it has been dangerous; for while many young painters imitate him, only a few understand him. Jean Cocteau aptly comments on this situation: "This Picasso has done a great deal to confuse young painters. He takes it as a dogma that the well-done is overdone, in other words, an inelegance of the spirit. That is why he pretends to recognize the lazy people who do not bother him, and refuses to recognize his adversaries who are thus branded as aesthetes and laggards. For he withdraws all the recognitions he extends. To follow him is to knock one's head against a door. To paint on the door is to be accused of platitude."

In the light of all this it is clear that Picasso cannot pass his discoveries on to disciples, and hence cannot find true successors as a painter. On the other hand, it is impossible in this age of publicity to conceive of an influence more pervasive and more profound than that of his art on his contemporaries. The stimulating power of this art was once aptly described as "the vitamin P." A Spanish friend of Picasso's, at the time of the retrospective exhibition of 1932, called him "the toreador of painting." Nothing could better express the dogged aggressiveness and staying-power of Picasso when he is before the canvas. Such an epithet also suggests that eventually Picasso will gain popular recognition. If Picasso's name, like that of Homer, becomes synonymous with his work, this would prove the capacity of our age for enthusiasm, which, according to Picasso, is what we need most.

Many aspects of Picasso, who now looks back on six decades of the most intense activity, are contradictory, and cannot for the present be explained (he himself would regard any attempt to do so as superfluous).

*"Documents"* page 505

Note 58

Note 59

Note 60

Note 61
(below)
Illustration from *Carmen*, by Mérimée 1949

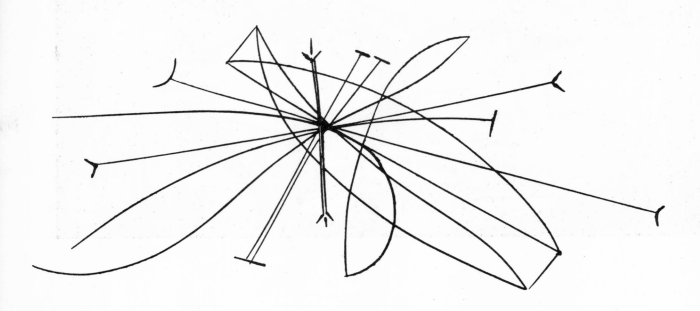

(p. 347) *Women of Algiers* 1955

His oral statements, which have been recorded more or less faithfully, are even more difficult to understand. Picasso's delight in paradox is partly to blame: he must "never be taken literally," says Sabartés, who ought to know. Nevertheless his "declarations" and "letters," some of which at least are apocryphal, reveal quite important things to those familiar with Picasso's mentality. Thus the statements quoted on pages 503–510 seem certainly useful, though more to the initiate than to the tyro. We have made no attempt here to do justice to Picasso as a writer, but the analogies between several of his poems and his paintings are evident even without analysis.

Note 62

*"Documents"* pages 503–510

"*Peinture écrite*" 1941

## Notes and References

1. Maurice Raynal, *Picasso* (Munich, 1921), p. 64.

2. *Ibid.*, p. 32.

3. *La clameur des vierges*, reproduced in Christian Zervos, *Pablo Picasso*, in 7 volumes (Paris and New York, 1932–55), VI, no. 245.

4. D. E. Schneider, "The Paintings of Pablo Picasso. A Psychoanalytic Study," *College Art Journal*, VII (1947–48), pp. 81–95.

5. Jaime Sabartés, *Picasso: An Intimate Portrait*, trans. by Angel Flores (New York, 1948).

6. In the painting *Two Saltimbanques with a Dog*, Collection Wright Ludington, Santa Barbara, California, Zervos, *op. cit.*, I, no. 300.

7. Gertrude Stein, *Autobiography of Alice B. Toklas* (New York, 1934), p. 22.

8. D.-H. Kahnweiler in *Le point*, XLII (1952), p. 24.

9. James Johnson Sweeney, "Picasso and Iberian Sculpture," *The Art Bulletin*, XXIII (New York), pp. 191–98.

10. In the catalogue of the Lyons exhibition, 1953.

11. *Ibid.*

12. Kahnweiler, *Juan Gris: His Life and Work*, trans. by Douglas Cooper (New York, 1947).

13. Sabartés, *Picasso à Antibes* (Paris, 1948), p. 36.

14. Jean Cocteau, *Picasso* (Paris, 1923), p. 20.

15. Jean Cassou, *Picasso* (New York, 1940), p. 27.

16. Sabartés, *Picasso: An Intimate Portrait.*

17. *Minotaure*, I (1933), pp. 30–31.

18. *Neue Zürcher Zeitung* (November 13, 1932). Reprinted in *Cahiers d'art* (1932), pp. 352–54; by C. G. Jung in *Wirklichkeit und Seele*

(1947), pp. 170–79; and in *Pablo Picasso. Wort und Bekenntnis* (1954), pp. 118–26.

19. *Cahiers d'art* (1935), p. 173.

20. Dating from April 24, 1935, reproduced in *Cahiers d'art* (1935) opposite p. 185.

21. *Cahiers d'art* (1935), p. 178.

22. C. G. Seckel, "Picasso und die Insel des Minotaurus," *Das Kunstwerk*, IV (1950), no. 5.

23. Alfred H. Barr, *Picasso: Fifty Years of His Art* (New York, 1946), p. 268.

24. Important drawings relating to this subject in Zervos, *Dessins de Pablo Picasso 1892–1948* (Paris, [1949]).

25. J. P. Hodin, *Edvard Munch* (Stockholm, [1948]), p. 109.

26. Barr, *op. cit.*, p. 202.

27. *Ibid.*, p. 242.

28. *Picasso à Antibes*, p. 21.

29. *Verve* (1951). (Special Picasso section.)

30. Reproduced by Harriet and Sidney Janis, *Picasso. The Recent Years: 1939–46* (New York, 1946), pl. 42.

31. Claude Roy, *Picasso: La guerre et la paix* (Paris, 1954), p. 105.

32. *Verve, op. cit.*

33. Drawings reproduced in *Cahiers d'art* (1951); and in Zervos, *Picasso*, V, no. 265.

34. *Cahiers d'art* (1938). (Special Picasso number.)

35. Gotthard Jedlicka, *Begegnungen mit Künstlern der Gegenwart* (Erlenbach-Zurich, 1945), p. 146.

36. *Picasso à Antibes*, p. 37.

37. Janis, *op. cit.*, text on plate 60.

38. For the ceramics not reproduced in this volume see *Cahiers d'art* (1948), pp. 91, 109, 176.

39. Compare with reproductions in *Verve, op. cit.*

40. Conversation with the author at Vallauris, October 23, 1952.

41. E. de Lorey, "Picasso et l'orient musulman," *Gazette des Beaux-Arts*, LXXIV, 2 (1932), pp. 299–314.

42. *Verve, op. cit.*

43. Quoted by Roy, *op. cit.*, pp. 42, 43, 145.

44. Sabartés, *Picasso à Antibes*, p. 30.

45. Herbert Read, *The Philosophy of Modern Art* (London, [1952]), p. 161.

46. See the articles by R. Jullian, "Humanité de Picasso," and Jean Cassou, "Picasso et l'Espagne," catalogue of the Lyons museum exhibition, *Picasso* (1953).

47. Raynal, *op. cit.*, p. 44.

48. Roy, *op. cit.*, p. 27.

49. Cocteau in *Commentari*, IV (1953), pp. 171–82; or in catalogue of the Geneva exhibition (1955).

50. Sabartés, *Picasso à Antibes*, p. 29.

51. Raynal, *op. cit.*, p. 64.

52. Picasso to Xavier Vilato, who reported it to Gjon Mili in 1950.

53. Cocteau, *Démarche d'un poète* (Munich, 1953), p. 18.

54. Quoted by Roy, *op. cit.*, p. 16.

55. Quoted by Sabartés, *Picasso: An Intimate Portrait*.

56. Picasso to Ernst Jünger, July 22, 1942. See Jünger, *Strahlungen* (1949), pp. 138–39.

57. See the photographs by Gjon Mili in *Paris Match* (1950).

58. Cocteau, *Démarche d'un poète*, pp. 17–18.

59. Sabartés, *Picasso à Antibes*, p. 18.

60. Ramon Gomez de la Serna, *Cahiers d'art* (1932), p. 124.

61. See C. Zervos, *Cahiers d'art* (1935), p. 173.

62. Sabartés, *Picasso à Antibes*, p. 17.

*Triumph of the Dove*
1950

*Study of a Plaster Cast of a Foot* (1894)

*The Artist's Father* (1895)

*Aunt Pepa* (1895)

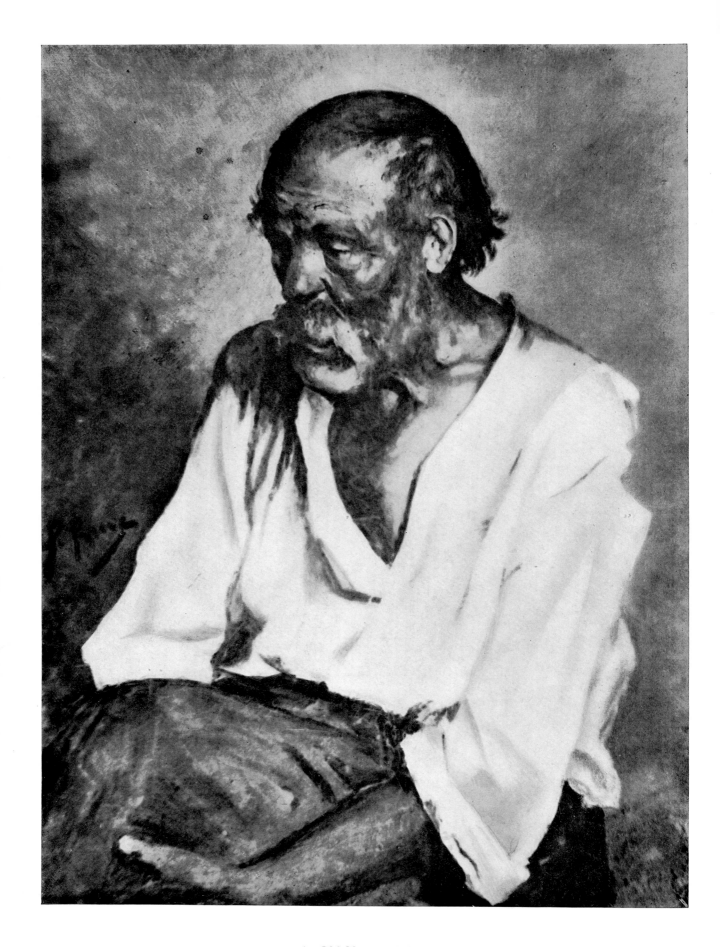

*An Old Man* (1895)

*Promenade* (1897)

*The Divan* (1900)

*Couple on the Street* (1901)

*The Embrace* (1901)

*The Embrace* (1903)

361

*Girl with Pigeon* (1901)

*Mother and Child* (1901)

363

*The Glass of Beer (Jaime Sabartés)* (1901)

*The Blue Room* (1901)

*The Life* (1903)

*The Madman* (1904)

367

*The Frugal Repast* (1904)

*The Saltimbanques* (1905)

*Boy Leading a Horse* (1905)

*Mother and Child* (1905)

371

*Landscape with Figures* (1908)

*Nude with Drapery* (1907)

374

*Seated Man* (1908)

375

*Wilhelm Uhde* (1910)

*The Accordionist* (1911)

377

*Spanish Still Life* (1912)

*Student with a Pipe* (1913)

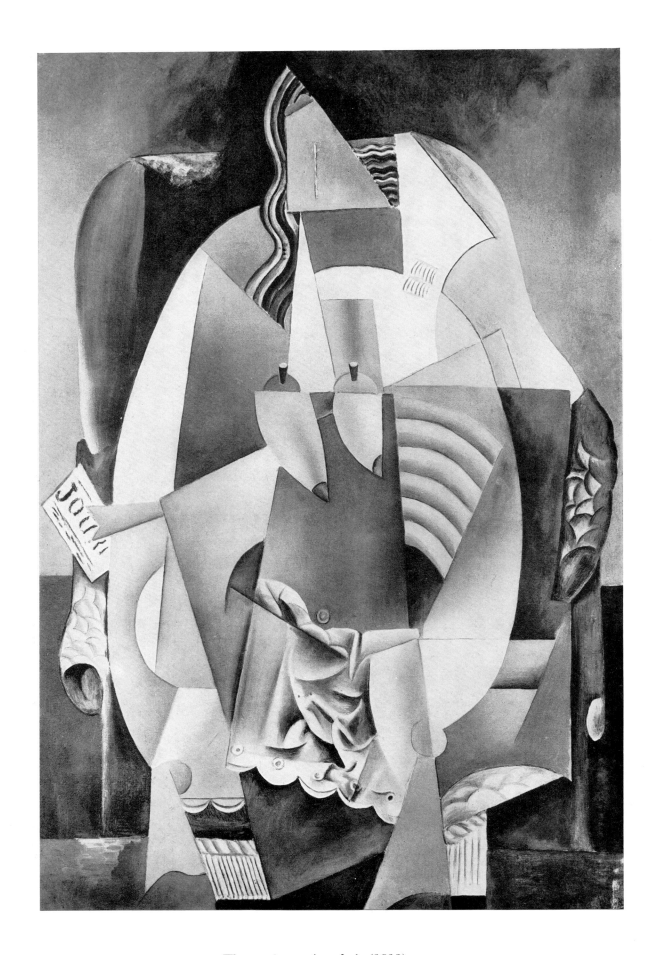

*Woman in an Armchair* (1913)

*Man Leaning on a Table* (1915/16)

*Mandolin (Wood Construction)* (1914)

*Table with Guitar* (1920)

*Landscape* (1920)

*Landscape* (1921)

*Head of a Man* (1921)

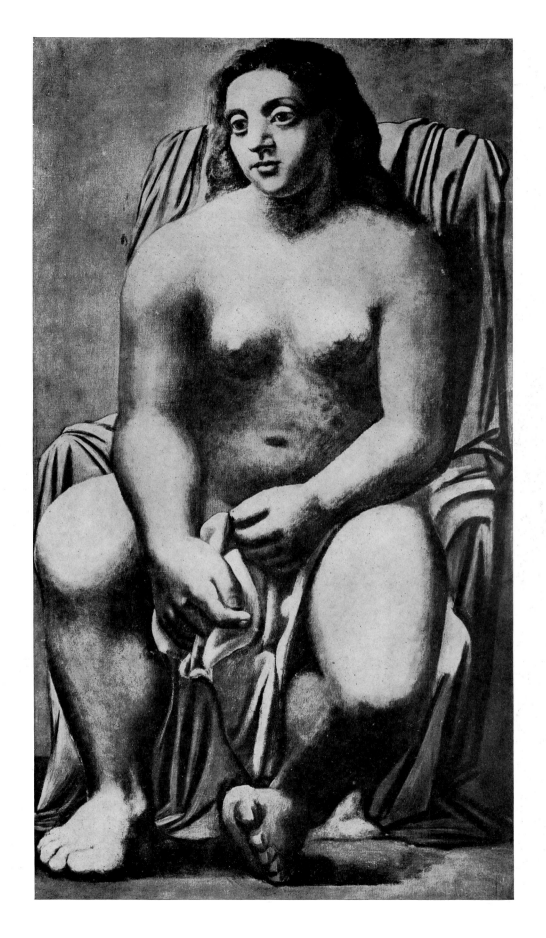

*Seated Nude* (1921)

*Paul, Son of the Artist* (1923)

*The Artist's Mother* (1923)

*Young Girl and Little Boy* (1922/23)

*Landscape* (1924)

391

*Bather* (1927)

*Seated Bather* (1929)

*Bull and Horse* (1927)

*Seated Nude Surrounded by Sketches of Animals and Men* (1927)

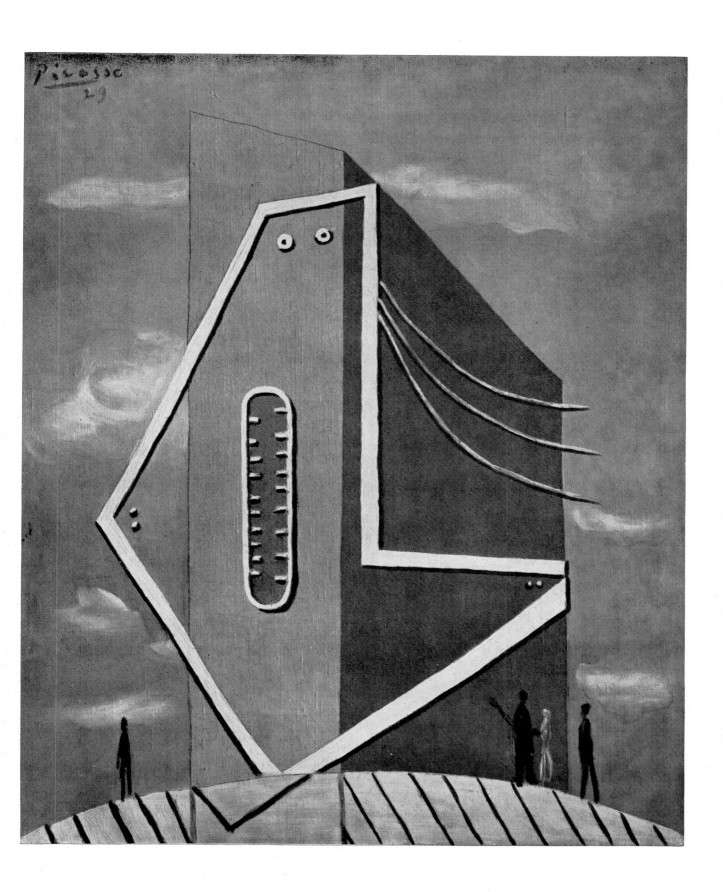

*Monument: Woman's Head* (1929)

*The Picador* (1934)

*The Beast* (1935)

*Young Girl and Minotaur* (1934/35)

*Weeping Woman* (1937)

399

400

*Minotauromachy* (1935)

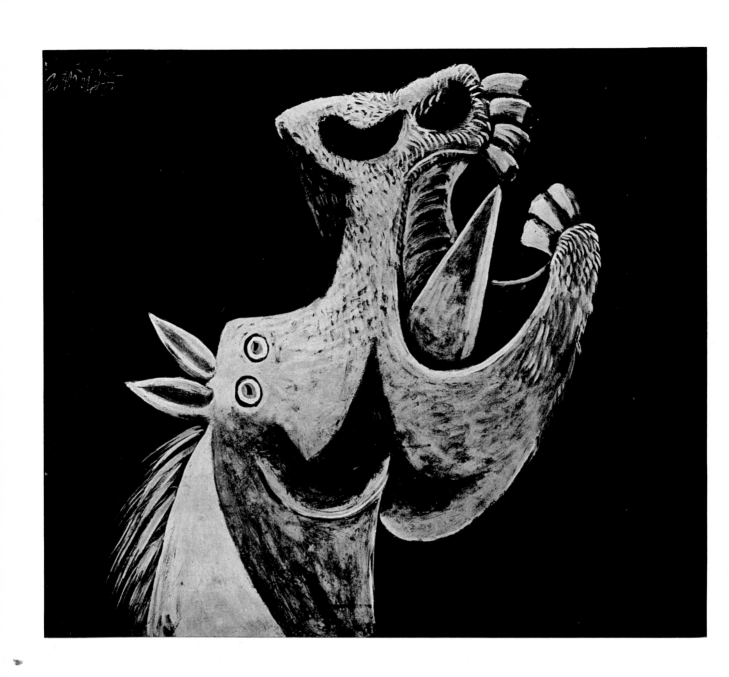

*Head of a Horse* (1937)

*Study for Bull's Head* (1937)

*Composition Study for "Guernica"* (1937)

*Guernica I* (1937)

*Guernica III* (1937)

*Guernica IV* (1937)

*Jaime Sabartés* (1939)

*Nush Eluard* (1938)

**409**

*Dora Maar* (1942)

*Still Life with Blood Sausage* (1941)

*Female Figure* (1946)

*The Studio Window* (1943)

413

*Le Vert-Galant* (1943)

*View of Paris, with Notre-Dame* (1945)

*Still Life with Basket of Fruit* (1942)

*View of Paris, with Notre-Dame* (1945)

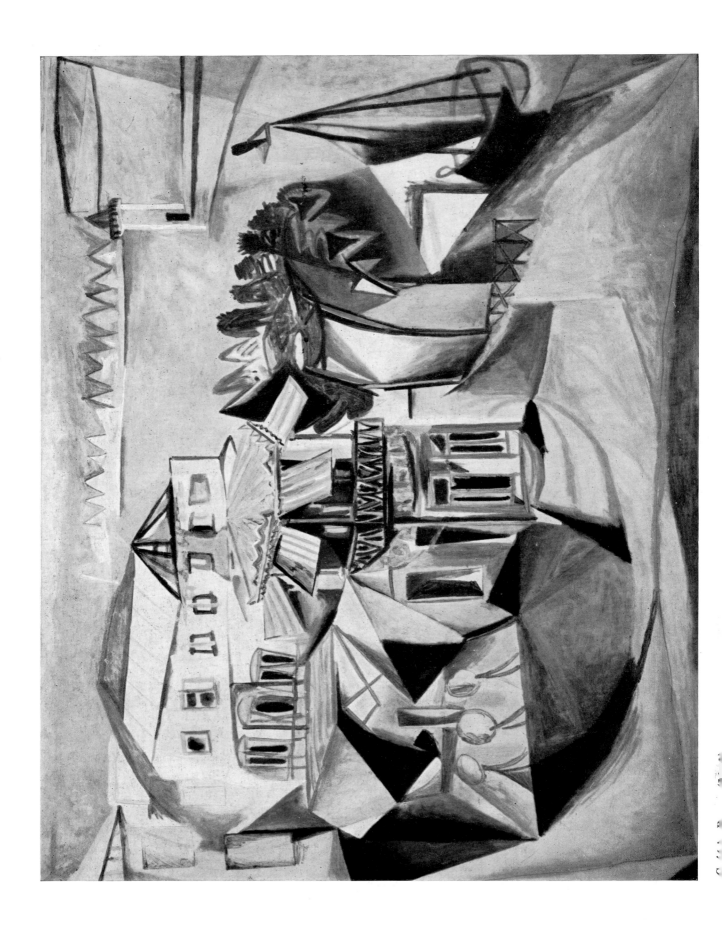

*"Bacchanale," after Poussin* (1944)

*La joie de vivre* (1946), *detail*

*La joie de vivre* (1946), *detail*

419

*View of Ménerbes* (1946)

*Still Life with Knife and Melon* (1946)

*The Rape of Europa* (1946)

*Portrait of a Painter, after El Greco* (1950)

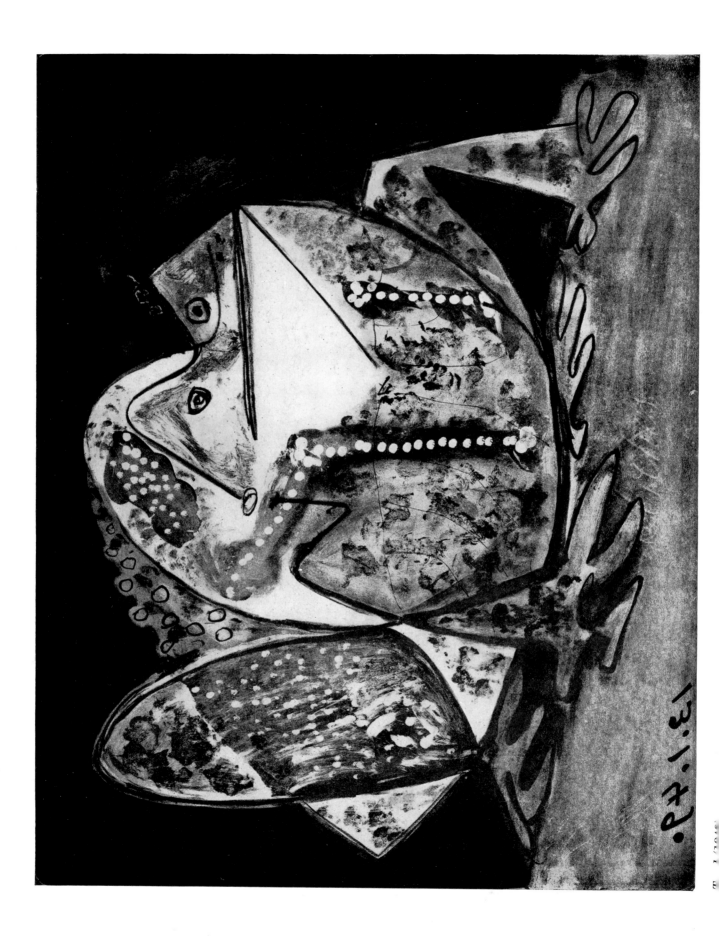

*Winter Landscape* (1950)

*Claude and Paloma* (1950)

*Paloma, the Artist's Daughter* (1951)

*Demoiselles des bords de la Seine, after Courbet* (1950)

*Massacre in Korea* (1951)

*War* (1952)

*Peace* (1952)

*Head of a Woman* (1905)

*Head* (1906)

*Metamorphose* (1928)

*Cock* (1932)

*Death's Head* (1944)

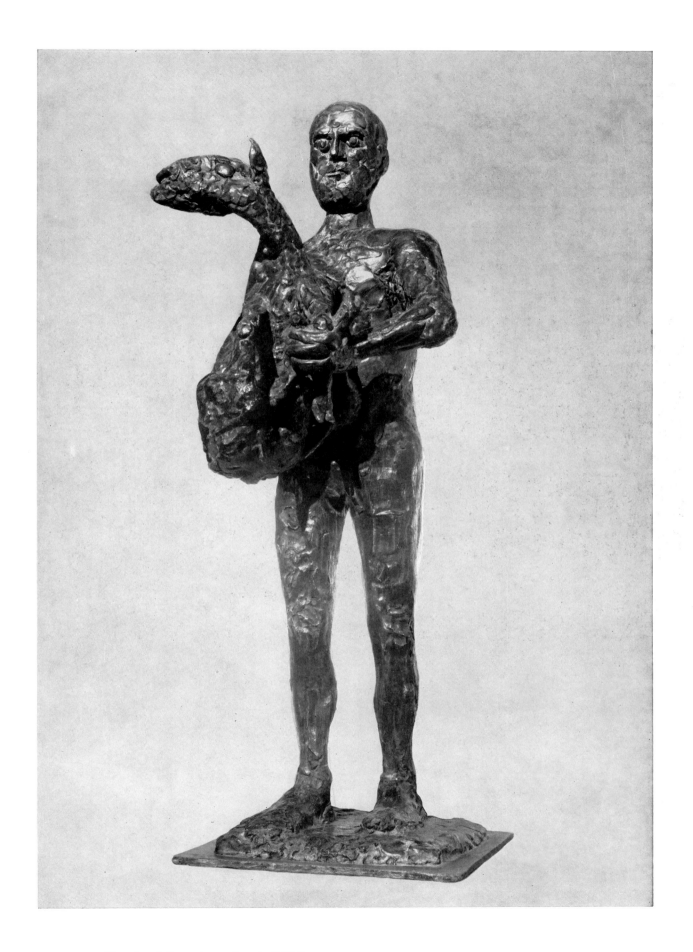

*Shepherd Carrying a Lamb* (1944)

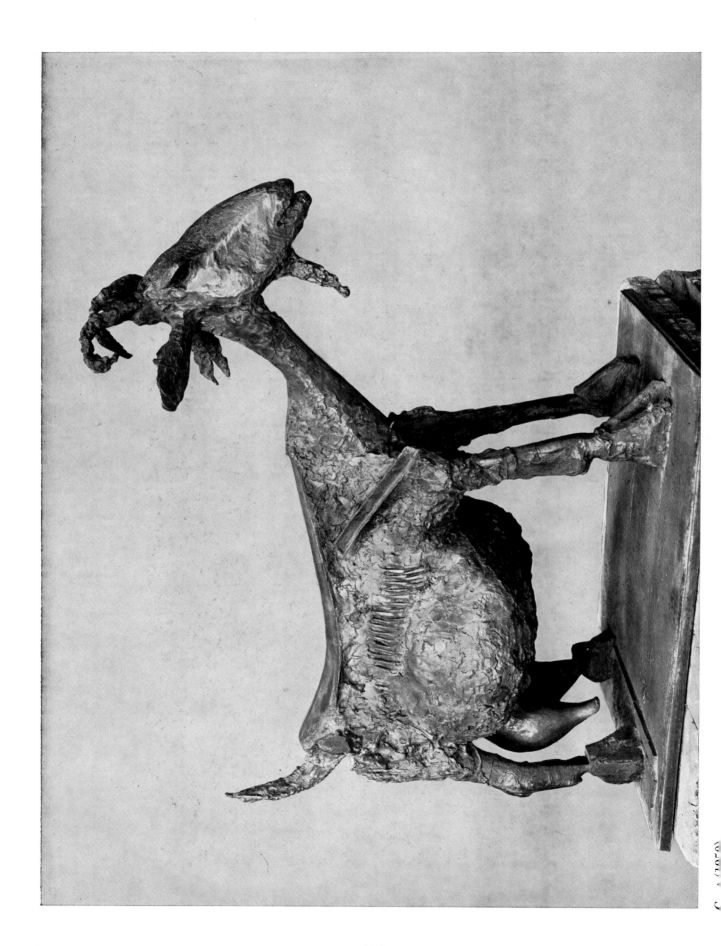

*Crane* (1951)

439

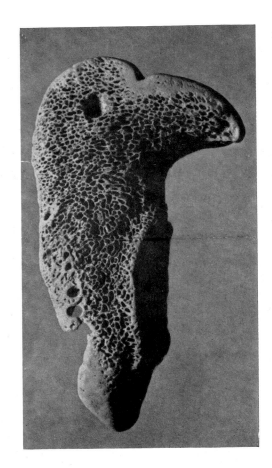

*Bird's Head* (1937)

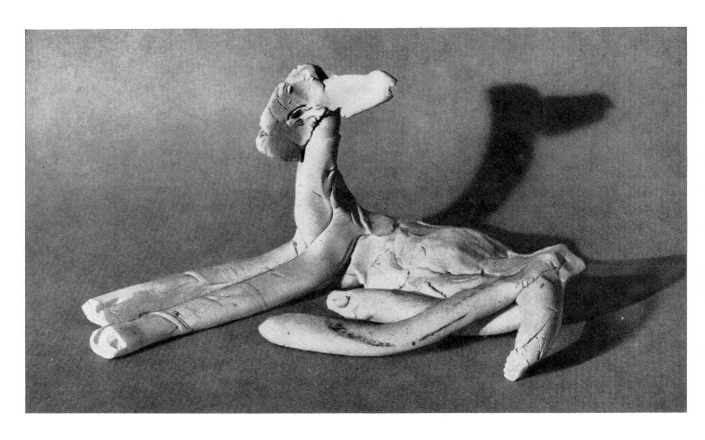

*Goat* (1950)

440

*Pitcher and Figs* (1952)

*Decorated Ceramics* (1947)

*Bird (Vase)* (1948)

*Ibex (Vase)* (1949)

442

*Woman (Vase)* (1948)

443

*Female Figure (Vase)* (1950)

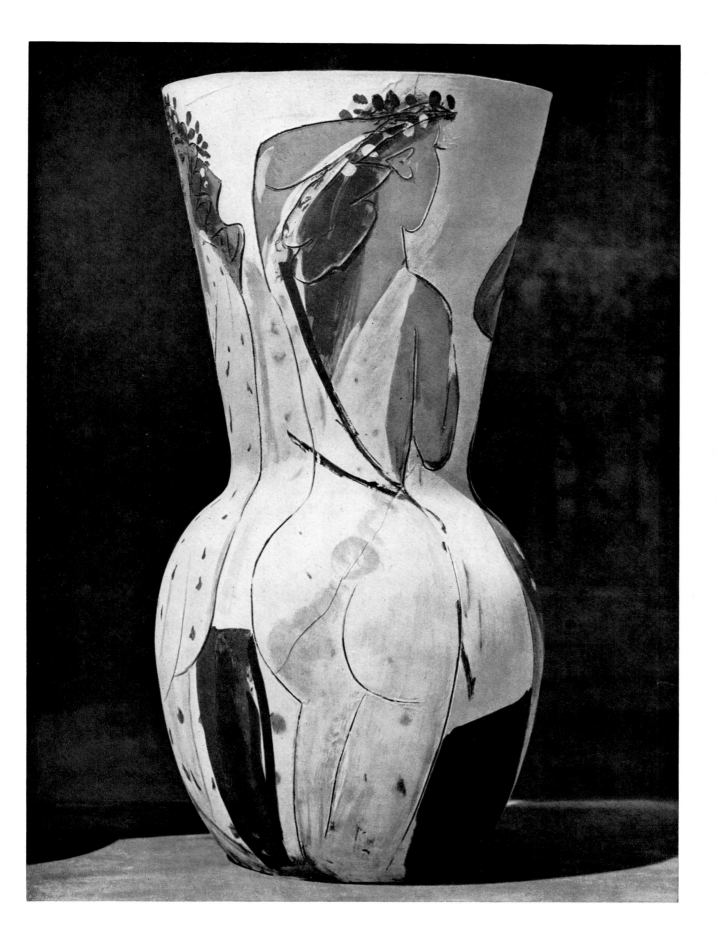

*Nudes Seen from the Rear (Vase)* (1950)

*Faun's Head (Vase)* (1950)

*Owl (Vase)* (1951)

*Decorated Plates* (1948)

*Decorated Plates* (1948)

449

*Decorated Casseroles* (1950)

*Bullfight (Plate)* (1953)

**Classified Catalogue**

*Preliminary note*

This catalogue is intended to enable the reader to survey Picasso's development and the great variety of his artistic production from 1894 to 1955. Each of Picasso's periods is illustrated by separate groups of pictures. For the sake of completeness we have also included some sculptures. Certain special groups make it possible to inform oneself separately about special subjects and techniques such as sculpture, ceramics, or the image of man in Picasso's works. The chronological order of all works and periods has been retained as far as possible. The measurements indicate height and width insofar as it is possible to ascertain them. As for the technique, the medium, the location, or the owner of the works reproduced, see "List of Works Reproduced," page 487.

**1**

1. *Portrait of Uncle Baldomero Chiara*
   (1894)

2. *Portrait of Don Ramon Perez Costalez*
   (1895)  52 : 37 cm – 20 1/2 : 14 1/2″

3. *A Beggar*
   (1895)

4. *Still Life*
   (1895)

5. *Barefoot Girl*
   (1895)  75 : 50 cm – 29 1/2 : 19 5/8″

6. *First Communion*
   (1895)

7. *Mother and Son*
   (1898)  48 : 25.5 cm – 18 7/8 : 10″

8. *The Artist's Mother, Doña Maria Picasso*
   (1895)

9. *The Ballerina*
   (1900)  38 : 31 cm – 15 : 12 1/8″

10. *Portrait of the Painter Murillo Carreras*
    (1901)  24 : 20.5 cm – 9 1/2 : 8″

11. *Portrait of a Woman*
    (1901)  64 : 48 cm – 25 1/4 : 18 7/8″

12. *At the Café*
    (1901)  48 : 64 cm – 18 7/8 : 25 1/4″

13. *Boulevard de Clichy*
    (1901)  61 : 46 cm – 24 : 18 1/8″

14. *Nude*
    (1901)  66.5 : 52 cm – 26 1/4 : 20 1/2″

15. *Portrait of Gustave Coquiot*
    (1901)  46 : 37 cm – 18 1/8 : 14 5/8″

16. *A Boy Drawing*
    (1901)

17. *Mother and Child*
    (1901)  111 : 97 cm – 43 3/4 : 38 1/8″

18. *Self-Portrait at the Seaside*
    (1902)

**2**

**3**

19. *Portrait of a Woman*
    (1902)  27.7 : 20 cm − 10 $^7/_8$ : 7 $^7/_8''$

20. *The Gift*
    (1902)  25 : 26 cm − 9 $^7/_8$ : 10 $^1/_4''$

21. *Seller of Mistletoe*
    (1903)  55 : 38 cm − 21 $^5/_8$ : 15''

22. *Self-Portrait with a Dog*
    (1903)

23. *Portrait of a Child*
    (1904)

24. *Head of a Woman*
    (1904)  42 : 31 cm − 16 $^1/_2$ : 12 $^1/_8''$

**4** 25. *Clown on Horseback*
    (1904)  100 : 69 cm − 39 $^3/_8$ : 27 $^1/_8''$

26. *Woman with a Fan*
    (1905)  101 : 82 cm − 39 $^3/_4$ : 32 $^1/_4''$

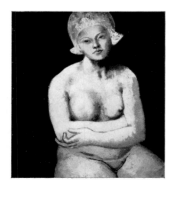

27. *Dutch Girl*
    (1905)

28. *The Troubadours*
    (1905)

29. *Saltimbanque*
    (1905) 23 : 15 cm – 9 : 5 7/8″

30. *Nude Doing Her Hair*
    (1905) 24 : 15 cm – 9 1/2 : 5 7/8″

31. *Man and Woman with a Crow*
    (1905) 69 : 54 cm – 27 1/8 : 21 1/4″

32. *Jester*
    (1905) Height 41 cm – 16 1/8″

33. *Three Nudes*
    (1906) 29.5 : 40.5 cm – 11 5/8 : 16″

34. *Girl on Horseback and Young Man*
    (1906)

35. *Portrait of Gertrude Stein*
    (1906) 99 : 81 cm – 39 1/4 : 32″

36. *Head of a Peasant*
    (1906) 45 : 39 cm – 17 3/4 : 15 5/8″

5

37. *Head of a Woman*
    (1906)

38. *Head of a Man*
    (1907) 33 : 24 cm – 13 : 9 1/2″

39. *Nude*
    (1907)  93 : 43 cm − 36⁵/₈ : 16⁷/₈″

40. *Woman with a Fan*
    (1908)  152 : 100 cm − 59⁵/₈ : 39³/₈″

41. *Small House in a Garden*
    (1908)  73 : 60 cm − 28³/₄ : 21⁵/₈″

42. *Still Life with a Bouquet of Flowers*
    (1908)  38 : 46 cm − 15 : 18¹/₈″

43. *Head of a Man*
    (1908)  27 : 21 cm − 10⁵/₈ : 8¹/₄″

44. *Head of a Man*
    (1908/09)  62 : 45 cm − 24³/₈ : 17³/₄″

**6**  45. *The Fishes*
    (1909)  21 : 27 cm − 8¹/₄ : 10⁵/₈″

46. *Bust of a Woman*
    (1909)  62 : 48 cm − 24³/₈ : 18⁷/₈″

47. *Woman in a Black Hat*
    (1909)  73 : 60 cm − 28³/₄ : 23⁵/₈″

48. *Queen Isabeau*
    (1909)  92.5 : 73 cm − 36¹/₂ : 28³/₄″

49. *The Reservoir of Horta de Ebro*
(1909) 81 : 65 cm – 31 $^7/_8$ : 25 $^5/_8$″

50. *The Beer Glass*
(1909) 81 : 65 cm – 31 $^7/_8$ : 25 $^5/_8$″

51. *Harlequin*
(1909)

52. *Sugar Bowl and Fan*
(1910) 31 : 43 cm – 12 $^1/_4$ : 16 $^7/_8$″

53. *Woman with Mustard Pot*
(1910) 73 : 60 cm – 28 $^3/_4$ : 23 $^5/_8$″

54. *Head of a Woman*
(1910) Height 40 cm – 15 $^7/_8$″

**7**

55. *The Port of Cadaqués*
(1910) 38 : 46 cm – 15 : 18 $^1/_8$″

56. *The Mandolin Player*
(1911) 100 : 69 cm – 39 $^3/_8$ : 27 $^1/_8$″

57. *The Fan*
(1911) 30 : 22 cm – 11 $^3/_4$ : 8 $^5/_8$″

58. *The Bullfighter*
(1911) 46 : 38 cm – 18 $^1/_8$ : 15″

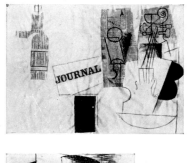

59. *The Pigeon*
    (1912)  46 : 27 cm – 18 1/8 : 10 5/8"

60. *The Brandy Bottle*
    (1912)  49.5 : 31 cm – 19 1/2 : 12 1/8"

61. *Pigeon and Peas*
    (1912)  65 : 54 cm – 25 5/8 : 21 1/4"

62. *Souvenir of Le Havre*
    (1912)  92 : 65 cm – 36 1/4 : 25 5/8"

**8**  63. *Three Instruments*
    (1913)  100 : 81 cm – 39 3/8 : 31 7/8"

64. *Still Life: Ma Jolie*
    (1913)

65. *Violin, Bottle, and Glass*
    (1913)

66. *The Violin Hanging on the Wall*
    (1913)  65 : 46 cm – 25 5/8 : 18 1/8"

67. *Head of a Man*
    (1913)  65 : 50 cm – 25 5/8 : 19 5/8"

68. *Head of a Man*
    (1913/14)  63 : 46 cm – 24 3/4 : 18 1/8"

69. *Head*
   (1914)  44 : 34 cm – 17³/₈ : 13³/₈″

70. *Violin*
   (1914)

71. *Man with a Bowler Hat*
   (1914)  30 : 23 cm – 11³/₄ : 9″

72. *Seated Man*
   (1914)  47 : 33 cm – 18¹/₂ : 13″

73. *The Glass*
   (1915)  12 : 16 cm – 4³/₄ : 6¹/₄″

74. *Fruitbowl and Musical Instruments*
   (1915)  22 : 22 cm – 8⁵/₈ : 8⁵/₈″

**9**

75. *Portrait of Olga*
   (1917)  120 : 75 cm – 47¹/₄ : 29¹/₂″

76. *Portrait of a Woman*
   (1917)  100 : 81 cm – 39³/₈ : 31⁷/₈″

77. *Pierrot*
   (1917)  64 : 46 cm – 25¹/₄ : 18¹/₈″

78. *Harlequin*
   (1918)  143 : 100 cm – 56¹/₄ : 39³/₈″

79. *Woman with a Fan*
   (1917) 20 : 14 cm – 7 7/8 : 5 1/2 ″

80. *Neapolitan Woman*
   (1918) 31.5 : 21.5 cm – 12 1/2 : 8 1/2 ″

**10a** 81. *Woman in an Armchair*
   (1918)

82. *Masks*
   (1920) 22 : 27 cm – 8 5/8 : 10 5/8 ″

83. *Bather*
   (1920) 27 : 21 cm – 10 5/8 : 8 1/4 ″

84. *Girl in a Yellow Hat*
   (1921) 105 : 75 cm – 41 3/8 : 29 1/2 ″

85. *On the Beach*
   (1923) 24 : 31 cm – 9 1/2 : 12 1/4 ″

86. *Reclining Nude and Young Man
   with Pipes of Pan*
   (1923) 24 : 31 cm – 9 1/2 : 12 1/4 ″

**10b** 87. *The Buffet*
   (1919) 81 : 100 cm – 31 7/8 : 39 3/8 ″

88. *Composition*
   (1920)

465

89. *Fish Stranded in the Sun*
   (1922) 14 : 19 cm – 5 1/2 : 7 1/2″

90. *The Fish*
   (1922) 65 : 81 cm – 25 5/8 : 31 7/8″

91. *Fish on a Newspaper*
   (1922) 15 : 11 cm – 5 7/8 : 4 3/8″

92. *Composition with an Apple*
   (1923) 14 : 22 cm – 5 1/2 : 8 5/8″

93. *The Table*
   (1919) 116 : 73 cm – 45 5/8 : 28 3/4″

**10c**

94. *The Open Book*
   (1920) 27.5 : 21.5 cm – 10 7/8 : 8 1/2″

95. *The Table*
   (1921) 28 : 21 cm – 11 : 8 1/4″

96. *The Windows*
   (1922) 23 : 22 cm – 9 : 8 5/8″

97. *Construction: Guitar and Bottle of Bass* **10d**
   (1917)

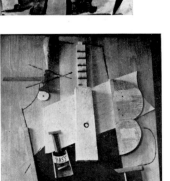

98. *Guitar*
   (1918) 54 : 65 cm – 21 1/4 : 25 5/8″

99. *Guitar*
(1917) 73 : 60 cm − 28 3/8 : 23 5/8″

100. *Guitars–Composition*
(1920)

**11**  101. *Three Bathers*
(1920) 49 : 64 cm − 19 1/4 : 25 1/4″

102. *Bather*
(1920) 32 : 22 cm − 12 5/8 : 8 5/8″

103. *Seated Nude*
(1920)

104. *Mother and Child*
(1921) 162 : 115 cm − 63 3/4 : 45 1/8″

105. *Mother and Child*
(1921) 162 : 97 cm − 63 3/4 : 38 1/8″

106. *Man and Woman*
(1921) 106 : 74 cm − 41 3/4 : 29 1/8″

107. *Head of a Woman*
(1922)

108. *Head of a Woman*
(1922)

109. *Three Women Dancing*
    (1923)  28 : 22 cm – 11 : 8 5/8″

110. *The Pipes of Pan*
    (1923)  24 : 31 cm – 9 1/2 : 12 1/4″

**12**

111. *Paul, Aged Two*
    (1923)  130 : 97 cm – 51 1/8 : 38 1/8″

112. *Paul as Harlequin*
    (1924)  130 : 97 cm – 51 1/8 : 38 1/8″

113. *Paul, Aged Four, Dressed as a Bullfighter*
    (1925)  162 : 97 cm – 63 3/4 : 38 1/8″

114. *Paul as Pierrot*
    (1925)  130 : 97 cm – 51 1/8 : 38 1/8″

115. *Mandolin and Guitar*
    (1924)  143 : 202 cm – 56 1/4 : 79 1/2″

**13**

116. *Fruitbowl and Guitar*
    (1924)  97 : 130 cm – 38 1/8 : 51 1/8″

117. *Still Life with Fish Net*
    (1925)  100 : 81 cm – 39 3/8 : 31 7/8″

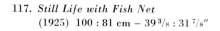

118. *Woman with a Mandolin*
    (1925)  130 : 97 cm – 51 1/8 : 38 1/8″

119. *Composition with Classical Bust*
    (1925)  81 : 100 cm − 31 7/8 : 39 3/8″

120. *The Cage*
    (1925)  81 : 100 cm − 31 7/8 : 39 3/8″

121. *Bowl of Grapes*
    (1926)  97 : 130 cm − 38 1/8 : 51 1/8″

122. *On the Beach*
    (1926)  130 : 97 cm − 51 1/8 : 38 1/8″

 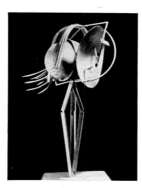

123. *The Painter and His Model*
    (1926)  173 : 255 cm − 68 1/8 : 100 3/8″

124. *The Painter and His Model Knitting*
    (1927)  19.4 : 27.9 cm − 7 5/8 : 11″

**14**

125. *Construction: Head*
    (1931)  Height 81 cm − 31 7/8″

126. *Construction: Head*
    (1931)  Height 100 cm − 39 3/8″

127. *Head of a Woman*
    (1931/32)  Height 57 cm − 22 1/2″

128. *Head*
    (1931/32)  Height 70 cm − 27 5/8″

129. *Head of a Woman*
    (1932)  Height 86 cm — 33 $^{7}/_{8}$"

130. *Cow's Head*
    (1932)  Height 34 cm — 13 $^{3}/_{8}$"

131. *Head of a Woman*
    (1932)  Height 78 cm — 30 $^{3}/_{4}$"

132. *Head of a Helmeted Warrior*
    (1933)  Height 121 cm — 47 $^{5}/_{8}$"

133. *Still Life with Fruits and Leaves*
    (1931)

**15**

134. *The Table*
    (1931)  130 : 195 cm — 51 $^{1}/_{8}$ : 76 $^{3}/_{4}$"

135. *Girl with Flower*
    (1932)  162 : 130 cm — 63 $^{3}/_{8}$ : 51 $^{1}/_{8}$"

136. *The Rescue*
    (1932)  35 : 27 cm — 13 $^{3}/_{4}$ : 10 $^{5}/_{8}$"

137. *Bather Playing with a Ball*
    (1932)  146 : 114 cm — 57 $^{1}/_{2}$ : 44 $^{7}/_{8}$"

138. *Nude in a Landscape*
    (1933)  40 : 48 cm — 15 $^{3}/_{4}$ — 18 $^{7}/_{8}$"

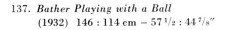

139. *Woman Lying before a Window*
(1934) 26 : 33 cm – 10 1/4 : 13″

140. *Two Women*
(1935) 130 : 162 cm – 51 1/8 : 63 3/4″

141. *The Studio*
(1935) 130 : 194 cm – 51 1/8 : 76 3/8″

142. *Girl before a Window*
(1935) 162 : 130 cm – 63 3/4 : 51 1/8″

**17** 143. *Reclining Nude*
(1936) 130 : 162 cm – 51 1/8 : 63 3/4″

144. *Girl with Red Cap*
(1937) 22 : 16 cm – 8 5/8 : 6 1/4″

145. *Nude with Hat*
(1937) 33.5 : 25.5 cm – 13 1/4 : 10″

146. *Head of a Bull*
(1938) 97 : 130 cm – 38 1/8 : 51 1/8″

147. *Man with a Red Glove*
(1938) 66 : 45 cm – 26 : 17 3/4″

148. *Cat and Bird*
(1939) 81 : 100 cm – 31 7/8 : 39 3/8″

149. *Still Life with Sheep's Skull*
    (1939)  50 : 61 cm – 19 5/8 : 24″

150. *Face*
    (1939)  55 : 46 cm – 21 5/8 : 18 1/4″

151. *Head with a Hood*
    (1940)  46 : 38 cm – 18 1/4 : 15″

152. *Faun and Woman*
    (1940)

153. *Boy with a Lobster*
    (1941) 130 : 97 cm – 51 1/8 : 38 1/8″

154. *Still Life with Flowers*
    (1941)  73 : 97 cm – 28 3/4 : 38 1/8″

155. *Seated Woman*
    (1941) 130 : 97 cm – 51 1/8 : 38 1/8″

156. *Seated Woman*
    (1941) 100 : 81 cm – 39 3/8 : 31 7/8″

157. *Sketches*
    (1941)  21 : 27 cm – 8 1/4 : 10 5/8″

158. *Nude*
    (1941)  65 : 92 cm – 25 5/8 : 36 1/4″

159. *Head of a Woman*
     (1942)  63 : 44 cm – 24 3/4 : 17 3/8″

160. *Mother and Child*
     (1942)

161. *Still Life with Bull's Skull*
     (1942)  130 : 97 cm – 51 1/8 : 38 1/8″

162. *Woman in an Armchair*
     (1942)  81 : 65 cm – 31 7/8 : 25 1/4″

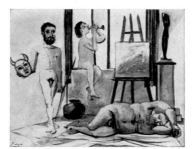

163. *Reclining Nude*
     (1942)  130 : 75 cm – 51 1/8 : 29 1/2″

164. *The Painter Asleep in His Studio*
     (1942)  54 : 65 cm – 21 1/4 : 25 1/4″

165. *Head of a Bull*
     (1943)  Height 41 cm – 16 1/8″

166. *Woman with Orange*
     (1943)  Height 180 cm – 70 7/8″

167. *Young Boy with Pigeons*
     (1943)  100 : 81 cm – 39 3/8 : 31 7/8″

168. *Still Life with Spikes of Flowers*
     (1943)  92 : 73 cm – 36 1/4 : 28 3/4″

169. *Seated Woman*
    (1943)  146 : 89 cm – 57 1/2 : 35"

170. *Woman's Face*
    (1943)  81 : 65 cm – 31 7/8 : 25 1/4"

171. *Still Life with a Vase*
    (1943)  81 : 100 cm – 31 7/8 : 39 3/8"

172. *Still Life*
    (1943)  81 : 130 cm – 31 7/8 : 51 1/8"

173. *Bust of a Woman*
    (1943)  100 : 81 cm – 39 3/8 : 31 7/8"

174. *Head*
    (1943)  Height 58 cm – 22 7/8"

175. *Woman*
    (1943/44)  Height 161 cm – 63 3/8"

176. *Coffee Pot*
    (1944)  81 : 60 cm – 31 7/8 : 23 5/8"

177. *Woman in a Blue Hat*
    (1944)  92 : 60 cm – 36 1/4 : 23 5/8"

178. *Female Face*
    (1944)  35 : 22 cm – 13 3/4 : 8 5/8"

179. *Still Life with Candlestick*
     (1944)  65 : 92 cm – 25 5/8 : 36 1/4″

180. *Interior*
     (1944)  73 : 92 cm – 28 3/4 : 36 1/4″

181. *Still Life*
     (1944)  22 : 27 cm – 8 5/8 : 10 5/8″

182. *Still Life with Tomato Plant*
     (1944)  92 : 73 cm – 36 1/4 : 28 3/4″

**20**  183. *Reclining Nude*
           (1944)  97 : 130 cm – 38 1/8 : 51 1/8″

184. *The Charnel House*
     (1944–1948)  175 : 250 cm – 68 7/8 : 98 3/8″

185. *Cock and Hen*
     (1944)

186. *To the Spaniards Who Died for France*
     (1945)

187. *Still Life with Candlestick*
     (1945)  46 : 55 cm – 18 1/8 : 21 5/8″

188. *View of Paris with Notre-Dame*
     (1945)  73 : 92 cm – 28 3/4 : 36 1/4″

189. *Still Life with Skull*
(1945)  73 : 116 cm – 28 3/4 : 45 5/8″

190. *Little Girl*
(1945)  130 : 89 cm – 51 1/8 : 35″

191. *Standing Woman*
(1945)  Height 20 cm – 7 7/8″

   *Seated Woman*
(1945)  Height 16.5 cm – 6 1/2″

192. *Standing Woman*
(1945)  Height 24 cm – 9 1/2″

   *Nude*
(1945)  Height 22 cm – 8 5/8″

193. *Faun and Centaur*
(1946)  54 : 65 cm – 21 1/4 : 25 5/8″

**21**

194. *She-Goat*
(1946)

195. *Portrait of a Woman*
(1946)

196. *Seated Woman*
(1946)

197. *The Turkish Coffeepot*
(1946)  66 : 51 cm – 26 : 20 1/8″

198. *Faun on a White Ground*
(1946)  65.5 : 50.5 cm – 25 7/8 : 20″

209. *Dove*
(1949)  54.5 : 76 cm – 21 1/2 : 29 7/8″

210. *Venus and Eros, Black Ground*
(1949)  76 : 56.5 cm – 29 7/8 : 22 1/4″

211. *Lady in Blue*
(1949)  100 : 81 cm – 39 3/8 : 31 7/8″

212. *Claude, Aged Two*
(1949)  130 : 97 cm – 51 1/8 : 38 1/8″

213. *Nude*
(1949)  130 : 97 cm – 51 1/8 : 38 1/8″

214. *Woman Drawing, and Children*
(1950)  208 : 130 cm – 81 7/8 : 51 1/8″

215. *Panorama of Vallauris*
(1950)  100 : 200 cm – 39 3/8 : 78 3/4″

216. *Pregnant Woman*
(1950)  Height 110 cm – 43 1/4″

217. *Villa with Palm Tree*
(1951)  89 : 116 cm – 35 : 45 5/8″

**23**

218. *House at Vallauris*
(1951)  50.5 : 66 cm – 20 : 26″

478

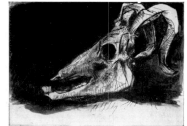

219. *Page-Boys at Play*
    (1951)  38 : 52 cm – 15 : 20 1/2″

220. *Skull of a Goat*
    (1951)  50.5 : 65.5 cm – 20 : 25 3/4″

221. *Vallauris Smoke*
    (1951)  60 : 73 cm – 23 5/8 : 28 3/4″

222. *The Reservoir*
    (1952)  80 : 124 cm – 31 1/2 : 48 7/8″

223. *Goat's Skull and Bottle*
    (1952)  89 : 116 cm – 35 : 45 5/8″

224. *Hen*
    (1952)  50 : 65 cm – 19 5/8 : 25 5/8″

225. *Teapot and Cup*
    (1953)  27 : 35 cm – 10 5/8 : 13 3/4″

226. *Woman's Head, Inclined*
    (1953)  27 : 22 cm – 10 5/8 : 8 5/8″

227. *Female Torso*
    (1953)  91 : 64 cm – 35 7/8 : 25 1/4″

228. *Seated Woman*
    (1953)  27 : 22 cm – 10 5/8 : 8 5/8″

229. *Portrait of Sylvette*
    (1954) 81 : 65 cm – 31 $^7/_8$ : 25 $^5/_8$″

230. *Woman and Monkey*
    (1954)

231. *Dances*
    (1954) 50 : 65 cm – 19 $^5/_8$ : 25 $^5/_8$″

232. *Women of Algiers*
    (1955)

233. *Clothed Woman (Vase)*
    (1948) Height 37.5 cm – 14 $^7/_8$″

234. *Pitcher with Nude*
    (1948) Height 34 cm – 13 $^3/_8$″

**24**

235. *Plate with Horseman*
    (1948) 31 : 37.5 cm – 12 $^1/_4$ : 14 $^7/_8$″

236. *Plate with Head of a Faun*
    (1949) 38 : 32 cm – 15 : 12 $^5/_8$″

237. *Head of a Woman*
    (1951) Height 53 cm – 20 $^7/_8$″

238. *Goat's Skull and Candle*
    (1951/52) 80 : 68 : 36 cm – 31 $^3/_8$ : 26 $^7/_8$ : 14″

239. *The White Owl*
(1952)  Height 33 cm – 13″

240. *Monkey and Her Young*
(1952)  Height 55 cm – 21 5/8″

241. *A Bouquet*
(1953)  Height 61 cm – 24″

242. *The Ruffled Pigeon*
(1953)  20 : 21 cm – 7 7/8 : 8 1/4″

243. *Plate with Picador*
(1953)  33 : 32 cm – 13 : 12 5/8″

244. *The Circus Vase*
(1954)  Height 58 cm – 22 7/8″

**25**  245. *Lola, Sister of the Artist*
(1898)

246. *Seated Woman*
(1900)

247. *Portrait of Jaime Sabartés*
(1904)  49.5 : 38 cm – 19 1/2 : 15″

248. *Head of a Boy*
(1905)  40 : 30 cm – 15 3/4 : 11 7/8″

249. *Beggar*
     (1906)  17 : 12 cm − 6³/₄ : 4³/₄″

250. *Seated Man*
     (1908)  63 : 46 cm − 24³/₄ : 18¹/₈″

251. *Female Torso*
     (1908)  73 : 60 cm − 28³/₄ : 23⁵/₈″

252. *Portrait of Georges Braque*
     (1909)  61 : 50 cm − 24 : 19⁵/₈″

253. *Head of a Man*
     (1912)  64 : 49 cm − 25¹/₄ : 19¹/₄″

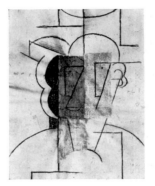

254. *Masked Man with a Palette*
     (1914)  49.7 : 38 cm − 19¹/₂ : 15″

255. *Female Head*
     (1921)

256. *Seated Woman*
     (1923)  92 : 73 cm − 36⁵/₈ : 28³/₄″

257. *Harlequin*
     (1923)  130 : 97 cm − 51¹/₈ : 38¹/₈′

258. *The Pipes of Pan*
     (1923)  25 : 32 cm − 9⁷/₈ : 12⁵/₈″

259. *Two Dancers*
(1925)  35.5 : 25.5 cm – 13 $^7/_8$ : 10"

260. *Head of a Woman*
(1926)  27 : 17 cm – 10 $^5/_8$ : 6 $^3/_4$"

261. *Woman in an Armchair*
(1927)  81 : 65 cm – 31 $^7/_8$ : 25 $^5/_8$"

262. *Woman's Head*
(1932)  Height 65 cm – 25 $^5/_8$"

263. *Woman in a Yellow Armchair*
(1932)  130 : 97 cm – 51 $^1/_8$ : 38 $^1/_8$"

264. *Seated Nude*
(1937)  130 : 97 cm – 51 $^1/_8$ : 38 $^1/_8$"

265. *Maïa, Aged Two*
(1938)  73 : 54 cm – 28 $^3/_4$ : 21 $^1/_4$"

266. *Woman Doing Her Hair*
(1939)  46 : 38 cm – 18 $^1/_8$ : 15"

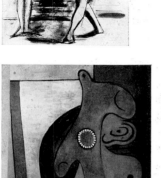

267. *Reclining Nude*
(1941)  21 : 27 cm – 8 $^1/_4$ : 10 $^5/_8$"

268. *Bust of a Woman*
(1942)  100 : 81 cm – 39 $^3/_8$ : 31 $^7/_8$"

269. *Head of a Woman*
    (1943)  92 : 73 cm – 36 1/4 : 28 3/4"

270. *Woman*
    (1943)  73 : 60 cm – 28 3/4 : 23 5/8"

271. *Head of a Young Girl*
    (1946)  44 : 33 cm – 17 3/4 : 13"

272. *Seated Woman*
    (1948)  100 : 81 cm – 39 3/8 : 31 7/8"

273. *Claude on His Bed*
    (1948)  130 : 97 cm – 51 1/8 : 38 1/8"

274. *Woman at the Window*
    (1952)  90 : 65 cm – 35 3/8 : 25 5/8"

275. *Woman with a Hat*
    (1953)  100 : 81 cm – 39 3/8 : 31 7/8"

276. *Portrait in the Manner of the School
    of Lyons*
    (1953)  65 : 50 cm – 25 5/8 : 19 5/8"

277. *Woman Playing with a Cat*
    (1954)  32 : 24 cm – 12 5/8 : 9 1/2"

278. *People and Dove*
    (1954)  50 : 65 cm – 19 5/8 : 25 5/8"

Picasso's Signatures
1898–1923

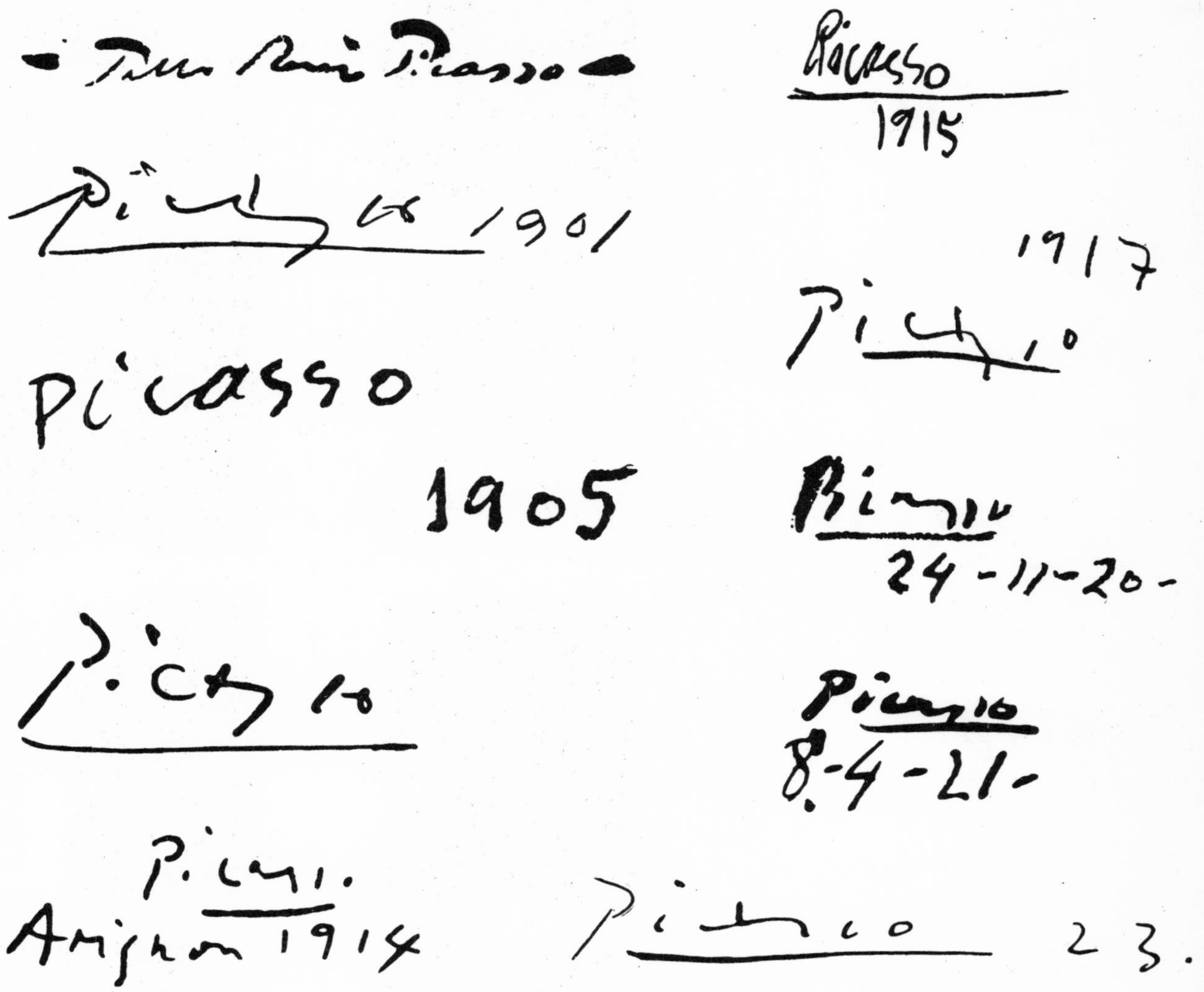

The signatures reproduced appear on the following works:

(left)

1. *Lola, Sister of the Artist;* water color (1898); Cl. Cat. 245
2. *At the Café;* water color (1901); Cl. Cat. 12
3. *The Saltimbanque;* water color and ink wash (1905); Cl. Cat. 29
4. *Nude;* pencil drawing (1907)
5. *Masked Man with a Palette;* water color and pencil (1914); Cl. Cat. 254

(right)

6. *Man with a Pipe;* pencil drawing (1915)
7. *Woman with a Fan;* charcoal drawing (1917); Cl. Cat. 79
8. *Seated Nude;* charcoal drawing (1920); Cl. Cat. 103
9. *Man and Woman;* pastel (1921); Cl. Cat. 106
10. *The Three Graces;* pen drawing (1923)

**The Catalogue numbers refer to the "Classified Catalogue," page 457.**

The signatures reproduced appear on the following works:

(left)

1. *Guitar;* brush drawing (1926)
2. *Minotaur and Maiden;* pen drawing (1936); page 53
3. *Portrait of a Woman;* pen drawing (1938); page 55
4. *Woman Doing Her Hair;* gouache (1939); Cl. Cat. 266
5. *Reclining Nude;* chalk drawing (1941); Cl. Cat. 267

(right)

6. *Head of a Woman;* pen drawing (1942); Cl. Cat. 159
7. *Cock and Hen;* oil (1944); Cl. Cat. 185
8. *Vase of Flowers;* wash drawing (1948); Cl. Cat. 205
9. *The Picador;* aquatint (1952)
10. *Woman Playing with a Cat;* wash drawing (1954); Cl. Cat. 277

The page references give the place where the pictures are reproduced.
The Catalogue numbers refer to the "Classified Catalogue," page 457.

## List of Works Reproduced

All the works reproduced are arranged by year, and within each year, according to medium. When two dates are given, the first is preferred. Measurements and owners' names are supplied wherever the information was available. Information for each reproduction is given in the following sequence: title, measurements (height before width), medium or technique, collection, page reference to reproduction or number in Classified Catalogue. The bold numbers refer to color plates.

*Abbreviations and Explanations:*

| | |
|---|---|
| Oil | = oil painting on canvas, wood, fiberboard, cardboard, or paper |
| D. | = drawing |
| D. wash | = a drawing that has been worked over by the brush in one or more tones |
| D. pen | = a drawing in ink or India ink and done exclusively with pen |
| D. brush | = a drawing in ink or India ink and done in part or exclusively with the brush |
| Lithograph | = includes prints done on zinc plates |
| Etching | = also includes dry point |
| Watercolor, Aquatint, Gouache, Pastel | = denote works in which these techniques predominate |
| S. | = Sculpture |
| C. | = Ceramics |

1. *Portrait of Uncle Baldomero Chiara;* Oil, Cl. Cat. 1       **1894**
2. *Study of a Plaster Cast of a Foot;* 20 : 14³/₈″; D. chalk, page 353

3. *Aunt Pepa;* Oil, page 355       **1895**
4. *An Old Man;* Oil; Sala, Barcelona, page 356
5. *Portrait of Don Ramón Pérez Costalez;* 20¹/₂ : 14¹/₂″; Oil, Cl. Cat. 2
6. *A Beggar;* Oil, Cl. Cat. 3
7. *Still Life;* Oil, Cl. Cat. 4
8. *Barefoot Girl;* 29¹/₂ : 19⁵/₈″; Oil; owned by the artist, Cl. Cat. 5
9. *First Communion;* Oil, Cl. Cat. 6
10. *The Artist's Father;* Watercolor, page 354
11. *The Artist's Mother, Doña Maria Picasso;* Pastel, Cl. Cat. 8

| 1897 | 12. *Promenade;* 13 : 3¹/₄″; D. chalk, page 357 |

1898
13. *Lola, Sister of the Artist;* Watercolor, Cl. Cat. 245
14. *Mother and Son;* 18⁷/₈ : 10″; D. charcoal and wash; Josef Stransky, New York, Cl. Cat. 7

1900
15. *The Divan;* 9⁷/₈ : 11³/₈″; Pastel; Museo de Arte Moderno, Barcelona, page 358
16. *The Ballerina;* 15 :12¹/₈″; Pastel, Cl. Cat. 9
17. *Seated Woman;* Pastel, Cl. Cat. 246

1901
18. *Bibi la Purée,* 19¹/₄ : 15³/₈″; Oil; Max Pellequer, Paris, page 111
19. *Bullfight;* 18¹/₈ : 21⁵/₈″; Oil; Max Pellequer, Paris, page 115
20. *Girl with Pigeon;* 28³/₄ : 21¹/₄″; Oil; Private collection, London, page 362
21. *Mother and Child;* 36¹/₄ : 23⁵/₈″; Oil; Bernheim Jeune, Paris, page 363
22. *The Glass of Beer (Jaime Sabartés);* 31⁷/₈ : 25¹/₄″; Oil ,Museum of Western Modern Art, Moscow, page 364
23. *The Blue Room;* 20 : 24¹/₂″; Oil; Phillips Memorial Gallery, Washington, page 365
24. *Boulevard de Clichy;* 24 : 18¹/₈″; Oil; Max Pellequer, Paris, Cl. Cat. 13
25. *Nude;* 26¹/₄ : 20¹/₂″; Oil; Private collection, Paris, Cl. Cat. 14
26. *Portrait of Gustave Coquiot;* 18¹/₈ : 14⁵/₈″; Oil; E. Bührle, Zurich, Cl. Cat. 15
27. *Mother and Child;* 43³/₄ : 38¹/₈″; Oil; **Mrs. Maurice Wertheim, New York,** Cl. Cat. 17
28. *Portrait of a Woman;* 25¹/₄ : 18⁷/₈″; Watercolor, Cl. Cat. 11
29. *At the Café;* 18⁷/₈ : 25¹/₄″; Watercolor, Cl. Cat. 12
30. *Couple on the Street;* D. pen, page 359
31. *The Embrace;* 7 : 5¹/₈″; D. charcoal, page 360
32. *Portrait of the Painter Murillo Carreras;* 9¹/₂ : 8″; D. charcoal; Museum, Málaga, Cl. Cat. 10
33. *A Boy Drawing;* D. pencil, Cl. Cat. 16

1902
34. *Portrait of a Woman;* 10⁷/₈ : 7⁷/₈″; Watercolor; A. Schoeller, Paris, Cl. Cat. 19
35. *The Amateur;* D. pen, page 318
36. *Self-Portrait at the Seaside;* D. pen and colored crayon; Private collection, Barcelona, Cl. Cat. 18
37. *The Gift;* 9⁷/₈ : 10¹/₄″; D. pen; H. Berggruen, Paris, Cl. Cat. 20
38. *Letter to Max Jacob from Barcelona;* D. pen, page 6

1903
39. *Célestine;* 31⁷/₈ : 23⁵/₈″; Oil; owned by the artist, page 121
40. *La Vie;* 77³/₈ : 50⁷/₈″; Oil; Cleveland Museum of Art (Gift of Hanna Fund), page 366
41. *The Embrace;* Gouache, page 361
42. *Seller of Mistletoe;* 21⁵/₈ : 15″; Gouache; Max Pellequer, Paris, Cl. Cat. 21
43. *Self-Portrait with a Dog;* D. pen; E. Bonnet, Paris, Cl. Cat. 22

1904
44. *Clown on Horseback;* 39³/₈ : 27¹/₈″; Oil; M. Level, Paris, Cl. Cat. 25
45. *Portrait of Jaime Sabartés;* 19¹/₂ : 15″; Oil, Cl. Cat. 247
46. *The Madman;* 33¹/₂ : 13³/₄″; Watercolor; Museo de Arte Moderno, Barcelona, page 367
47. *Head of a Woman;* 16¹/₂ : 12¹/₈″; Gouache; Mr. and Mrs. Walter S. Brewster, Chicago, Cl. Cat. 24
48. *The Frugal Repast;* 18¹/₄ : 14³/₄″; Etching; several proofs, page 368
49. *"La belle qui passe";* 11³/₈ : 15³/₄″; D. pen; reproduced in "Le manuscrit trouvé dans un chapeau," by André Salmon, Paris, page 10
50. *Portrait of a Child;* D. pen, Cl. Cat. 23

1905
51. *The Saltimbanques;* 84 : 90³/₈″; Oil; National Gallery of Art, Washington (Chester Dale Collection, Loan), page 369

**1909**

98. *Still Life with Gourd;* 28³/₄ : 23⁵/₈"; Oil; formerly collection Gertrude Stein, Paris, page 149

99. *The Fishes;* 8¹/₄ : 10⁵/₈"; Oil; R. Dutilleul, Paris, Cl. Cat. 45

100. *Woman in a Black Hat;* 28³/₄ : 23⁵/₈"; Oil; Ida Bienert, Munich, Cl. Cat. 47

101. *Queen Isabeau;* 36¹/₂ : 28³/₄"; Oil; Museum of Western Modern Art, Moscow, Cl. Cat. 48

102. *The Reservoir of Horta de Ebro;* 31⁷/₈ : 25¹/₄"; Oil; formerly collection Gertrude Stein, Paris, Cl. Cat. 49

103. *The Beer Glass;* 31⁷/₈ : 25⁵/₈"; Oil, Cl. Cat. 50

104. *Harlequin;* Oil, Cl. Cat. 51

105. *Portrait of Georges Braque;* 24 : 19⁵/₈"; Oil; Edward A. Bragaline, Cl. Cat. 252

106. *Bust of a Woman;* 24³/₈ : 18⁷/₈"; Gouache, Cl. Cat. 46

**1910**

107. *Daniel-Henry Kahnweiler;* 39³/₈ : 28³/₄"; Oil; The Art Institute, Chicago (Mrs. Charles B. Goodspeed Collection), page 241

108. *Wilhelm Uhde;* 31⁷/₈ : 23⁵/₈"; Oil; Mrs. Lee Miller Penrose, London, page 376

109. *Woman with Mustard Pot;* 28³/₄ : 23⁵/₈"; Oil; S. Rosengart, Lucerne, Cl. Cat. 53

110. *The Port of Cadaqués;* 15 : 18¹/₈"; Oil; Cl. Cat. 55

111. *Sugar Bowl and Fan;* 12¹/₄ : 16⁷/₈"; Watercolor, Cl. Cat. 52

112. *Head of a Woman;* Height 15⁷/₈"; S. bronze: Museum of Modern Art, New York, Cl. Cat. 54

**1911**

113. *The Accordionist;* 51¹/₈ : 35"; Oil; Museum of Non-Objective Paintings, New York, page 377

114. *The Mandolin Player;* 39³/₈ : 27¹/₈"; Oil, Cl. Cat. 56

115. *The Bullfighter;* 18¹/₈ : 15"; Oil; P. Eluard, Paris, Cl. Cat. 58

116. *The Fan;* 11³/₄ : 8⁵/₈"; Watercolor, Cl. Cat. 57

**1912**

117. *Spanish Still Life;* 18¹/₈ : 13"; Oil; R. Dutilleul, Paris, page 378

118. *The Pigeon;* 18¹/₈ : 10⁵/₈"; Oil; P. Chadourne, Paris, Cl. Cat. 59

119. *Pigeon and Peas;* 25⁵/₈ : 21¹/₄"; Oil, Cl. Cat. 61

120. *Souvenir of Le Havre;* 36¹/₄ : 25⁵/₈"; Oil; R. La Roche, Paris, Cl. Cat. 62

121. *Head of a Man;* 25¹/₄ : 19¹/₄"; D. charcoal, ink, and pasted paper, Cl. Cat. 253

122. *The Brandy Bottle;* 19¹/₂ : 11¹/₈"; Etching; several proofs; Museum of Modern Art, New York, Cl. Cat. 60

123. *Construction;* 6¹/₈ : 4⁷/₈"; D. pen; Museum of Modern Art, New York, page 18

**1913**

124. *Card Player;* 42¹/₂ : 35⁷/₄"; Oil; Museum of Modern Art, New York (Lillie P. Bliss Bequest), page 153

125. *The Roast Goose;* 18¹/₂ : 23¹/₄"; Pasted paper, page 160

126. *Student with a Pipe;* 29¹/₈ : 23¹/₂"; Oil and pasted paper; formerly collection Gertrude Stein, Paris, page 379

127. *Woman in an Armchair;* 57¹/₂ : 38¹/₈"; Oil; Ingeborg Eichmann, Zurich, page 380

128. *Three Instruments;* 39³/₈ : 31⁷/₈"; Oil, Cl. Cat. 63

129. *Still Life: Ma Jolie;* Oil, Cl. Cat. 64

130. *The Violin Hanging on the Wall;* 25⁵/₈ : 18¹/₈"; Oil mixed with sand; H. Rupf, Bern, Cl. Cat. 66

131. *Head of a Man;* 24³/₄ : 18¹/₈"; Oil; H. Berggruen, Paris, Cl. Cat. 68

132. *Violin, Bottle, and Glass;* 18¹/₂ : 24⁵/₈"; D. charcoal and pasted paper; Tristan Tzara, Paris, Cl. Cat. 65

133. *Head of a Man;* 25⁵/₈ : 19⁵/₈"; D. colored chalk; Mrs. Lee Miller Penrose, London, Cl. Cat. 67

134. *Vive la France;* 21¼ : 25⅝″; Oil; L. B. Block, Chicago, page 155                1914
135. *Masked Man with a Palette;* 19½ : 15″; Watercolor and pencil,
     Cl. Cat. 254
136. *Still Life with Death's Head;* 6 : 4½″; Etching; illustration for "Le Siège
     de Jérusalem," by Max Jacob, page 19
137. *Head;* 17⅜ : 13⅜″; D. charcoal and pasted paper; Mrs. Lee Miller Pen-
     rose, London, Cl. Cat. 69
138. *Man with a Bowler Hat;* 11¾ : 9″; D. chalk; H. Berggruen, Paris,
     Cl. Cat. 71
139. *Decanter and Glasses;* 14 : 19⅝″; D. pencil, page 158
140. *Studies of Glasses;* 9¾ : 12½″; D. pencil, page 159
141. *Plate with Wafers;* 11¾ : 18⅞″; D. pencil, page 161
142. *Seated Man;* 18½ : 13″; D. pencil; H. Berggruen, Paris, Cl. Cat. 72
143. *Mandolin;* Height 23⅝″; S. wood construction; owned by the artist,
     page 382
144. *Violin;* S. painted sheet metal; owned by the artist, Cl. Cat. 70

145. *Still Life in Landscape;* 24½ : 29½″; Oil; H. Berggruen, Paris, page 167     1915
146. *Man Leaning on a Table;* 78¾ : 39⅜″; Oil; formerly Mrs. Errazuriz,
     Paris, page 381
147. *The Glass;* 4¾ : 6¼″; Watercolor, Cl. Cat. 73
148. *Fruitbowl and Musical Instruments;* 8⅝ : 8⅝″; Watercolor, Cl. Cat. 74
149. *Reclining Woman;* 12⅝ : 9¾″; D. pencil, page 157
150. *Violin;* 5¼ : 3⅜″; D. pen and pencil, page 162
151. *Violin;* 5¼ : 3⅜″; D. pencil, page 152
152. *Max Jacob;* 13 : 9¾″; D. pencil; Dora Maar, Paris, page 182

153. *Woman in an Armchair;* 12¼ : 9⅛″; D. pencil, page 163               1916

154. *Italian Woman;* 58¾ : 39¾″; Oil; E. Bührle, Zurich, page 171          1917
155. *Portrait of Olga;* 47¼ : 29½″; Oil; Picasso, Cl. Cat. 75
156. *Portrait of a Woman;* 39⅜ : 31⅞″; Oil, Cl. Cat. 76
157. *Guitar;* 28⅜ : 23⅝″; Oil, Cl. Cat. 99
158. *Pierrot;* 25¼ : 18½″; D. brush; Private collection, U. S. A., Cl. Cat. 77
159. *Dying Horse;* D. crayon, page 236
160. *Woman with a Fan;* 7⅞ : 5½″; D. charcoal; H. Berggruen, Paris,
     Cl. Cat. 79
161. *Guitar and Bottle of Bass;* S. painted wood construction, Cl. Cat. 97

162. *Harlequin ("Si tu veux");* 56¼ : 39⅜″; Oil; Private collection, Cl. Cat. 78    1918
163. *Guitar;* 21¼ : 25⅝″; Oil mixed with sand; Maurice Raynal, Paris,
     Cl. Cat. 98
164. *Woman in an Armchair;* D. wash, Cl. Cat. 81
165. *Harlequin;* 4⅜ : 3¾″; D. pen, page 20
166. *Neapolitan Woman;* 12½ : 8½″; D. chalk, Cl. Cat. 80

167. *The Buffet;* 31⅞ : 39⅜″; Oil; owned by the artist, Cl. Cat. 87         1919
168. *The Table;* 45⅝ : 28¾″; Oil; owned by the artist, Cl. Cat. 93
169. *Study for the Curtain of the Ballet "Le Tricorne";* D. chalk, page 181
170. *Pitcher and Bowl of Apples;* 29½ : 39⅜″; D. chalk, page 78
171. *Neapolitan Woman;* 8⅝ : 6¾″; D. pencil, page 184

172. *Still Life with Dead Bird;* 24⅜ : 18½″; Pastel; Mme. Cuttoli, Paris,      1920
     page 175
173. *Landscape;* 20⅛ : 26¾″; Oil; owned by the artist, page 384
174. *Table with Guitar;* 8¼ : 8¼″; Gouache, page 383
175. *Masks;* 8⅝ : 10⅝″; Gouache, Cl. Cat. 82
176. *Bather;* 10⅝ : 8¼″; Gouache, Cl. Cat. 83
177. *Composition;* Gouache and chalk; Saidenberg Gallery, New York,
     Cl. Cat. 88
178. *The Open Book;* 10⅞ : 8½″; Gouache, Cl. Cat. 94

179. *Guitars—Composition;* Pastel, Cl. Cat. 100
180. *Three Bathers;* 19¼ : 25¼"; Pastel, Cl. Cat. 101
181. *Reclining Woman;* 8¼ : 10⅝"; D. pen, page 313
182. *Bather;* 12⅝ : 8⅝"; D. chalk, Cl. Cat. 102
183. *Seated Nude;* D. charcoal, Cl. Cat. 103
184. *Igor Stravinsky;* 24¼ : 18¾"; D. pencil; Private collection, U.S.A., page 183
185. *On the Beach;* 10⅝ : 16½"; D. pencil, page 21
186. *Conversation;* 12⅝ : 8⅝"; D. pencil, page 21
187. *Reclining Woman;* 8⅝ : 12¼"; D. pencil, page 22

1921

188. **Three Musicians;** 80 : 74"; Oil; Philadelphia Museum of Art (A. E. Gallatin Collection), page 179
189. *Seated Nude;* 71¾ : 39⅜"; Oil, page 387
190. *Mother and Child;* 63¾ : 45⅛"; Oil; owned by the artist, Cl. Cat. 104
191. *Mother and Child;* 63¾ : 38⅛"; Oil, Cl. Cat. 105
192. *Landscape;* 19¾ : 25⅝"; Pastel; Private collection, U.S.A., page 385
193. *The Table;* 11 : 8¼"; Gouache, Cl. Cat. 95
194. *Head of a Man;* 30¼ : 23⅝"; Pastel; Mme. Cuttoli, Paris, page 386
195. *Girl in a Yellow Hat;* 41⅜ : 29½"; Pastel; Private collection, U.S.A., Cl. Cat. 84
196. *Man and Woman;* 41¾ : 29⅛"; Pastel, Cl. Cat. 106
197. *Female Head;* Pastel, Cl. Cat. 255

1922

198. *Still Life with a Bottle and Bowl of Pears;* 25⅝ : 21¼"; Oil, page 79
199. **Mother and Child;** 38⅛ : 27"; Oil; Alex L. Hillman, New York, page 189
200. *Young Girl and Little Boy;* 51¼ : 38⅛"; Oil; P. Matisse, New York, page 390
201. *Fish Stranded in the Sun;* 5½ : 7½"; Oil, Cl. Cat. 89
202. *The Fish;* 25⅝ : 31⅞"; Oil, Cl. Cat. 90
203. *Fish on a Newspaper;* 5⅞ : 4⅜"; Oil, Cl. Cat. 91
204. *Head of a Woman;* Oil, Cl. Cat. 107
205. *Head of a Woman;* Oil, Cl. Cat. 108
206. *The Windows;* 9 : 8⅝"; Gouache, Cl. Cat. 96

1923

207. *The Sigh;* 24 : 19⅝"; Oil and charcoal; James Thrall Soby, Farmington, page 185
208. **Paul Sketching;** 51⅛ : 38⅛"; Oil; owned by the artist, page 191
209. *Paul, Son of the Artist;* 39⅜ : 31⅞"; Oil; owned by the artist, page 388
210. *The Artist's Mother;* 28¾ : 23⅝"; Oil; owned by the artist, page 389
211. *Composition with an Apple;* 5½ : 8⅝"; Oil mixed with sand, Cl. Cat. 92
212. *Paul, Aged Two;* 51⅛ : 38⅛"; Oil; owned by the artist, Cl. Cat. 111
213. *Seated Woman;* 36⅝ : 28¾"; Oil; Frank Stoop, London, Cl. Cat. 256
214. *Harlequin;* 51⅛ : 38⅛"; Oil; Jacques Seligman, New York, Cl. Cat. 257
215. *Three Bathing Women;* 5⅛ : 4¾"; D. pen, page 23
216. *Nude on a couch;* 9¾ : 12¼"; D. pen, page 314
217. *On the Beach;* 9½ : 12¼"; D. pen, Cl. Cat. 85
218. *Reclining Nude and Young Man with Pipes of Pan;* 9½ : 12¼"; D. pen; Saidenberg Gallery, New York, Cl. Cat. 86
219. *Three Women Dancing;* 11 : 8⅝"; D. pen; Saidenberg Gallery, New York, Cl. Cat. 109
220. *The Pipes of Pan;* 9½ : 12¼"; D. pen, Cl. Cat. 110
221. *Two Nudes and Youth Playing the Pipes of Pan;* 9⅞ : 12¼"; D. brush, page 186
222. *The Pipes of Pan;* 9⅞ : 12½"; D. chalk, Cl. Cat. 258

1924

223. *Landscape;* 14 : 18⅛"; Oil, page 391
224. *Paul as Harlequin;* 51⅛ : 38⅛"; Oil; owned by the artist, Cl. Cat. 112
225. *Mandolin and Guitar;* 56¼ : 79½"; Oil; Solomon R. Guggenheim Museum, New York, Cl. Cat. 115
226. *Fruitbowl and Guitar;* 38⅛ : 51⅛"; Oil, Cl. Cat. 116

| | |
|---|---|
| 1931 | 263. *Still Life on a Table;* 76³/₈ : 51¹/₈″; Oil; owned by the artist, page 217 |
| | 264. *Still Life with Fruits and Leaves;* Oil, Cl. Cat. 133 |
| | 265. *The Table;* 51¹/₈ : 76³/₄″; Oil, Cl. Cat. 134 |
| | **266. *Nude;* 5¹/₈ : 4³/₄″; Etching, page 316** |
| | 267. *Construction: Head;* Height 31⁷/₈″; S. bronze; owned by the artist, Cl. Cat. 125 |
| | 268. *Construction: Head;* Height 39³/₈″; S. wrought iron; owned by the artist, Cl. Cat. 126 |
| | 269. *Head of a Woman;* Height 22¹/₂″; S. bronze; owned by the artist, Cl. Cat. 127 |
| | 270. *Head;* Height 27⁵/₈″; S. bronze; owned by the artist, Cl. Cat. 128 |

| | |
|---|---|
| 1932 | 271. *Dream;* 51¹/₈ : 38¹/₈″; Oil; Victor W. Ganz, New York, page 221 |
| | 272. *Girl with Flower;* 63³/₈ : 51¹/₈″; Oil, Cl. Cat. 135 |
| | 273. *The Rescue;* 13³/₄ : 10⁵/₈″; Oil, Cl. Cat. 136 |
| | 274. *Bather Playing with a Ball;* 57¹/₂ : 44⁷/₈″; Oil, Cl. Cat. 137 |
| | 275. *Woman in a Yellow Armchair;* 51⁵/₈ : 38¹/₈″; Oil, Cl. Cat. 263 |
| | 276. *Playing on the Beach;* 9⁷/₈ : 13³/₄″; D. pen, page 39 |
| | 277. *Figures on Dark Background;* 13⁵/₈ : 19³/₄″; D. brush, page 195 |
| | 278. *Cock;* Height 26″; S. bronze; owned by the artist, page 435 |
| | 279. *Head of a Woman;* Height 33⁷/₈″; S. bronze; owned by the artist, Cl. Cat. 129 |
| | 280. *Cow's Head;* Height 13³/₈″; S. bronze; owned by the artist, Cl. Cat. 130 |
| | 281. *Head of a Woman;* Height 30³/₄″; S. bronze; owned by the artist, Cl. Cat. 131 |
| | 282. *Woman's Head;* Height 25⁵/₈″; S. bronze; owned by the artist, Cl. Cat. 262 |

| | |
|---|---|
| 1933 | 283. *On the Beach;* 15³/₄ : 20¹/₈″; Watercolor, page 197 |
| | 284. *Nude in a Landscape;* 15³/₄ : 18⁷/₈″; Watercolor, Cl. Cat. 138 |
| | 285. *Farmer's Wife on Stepladder;* 76³/₈ : 67¹/₄″; Pastel; Mme. Cuttoli, Paris, page 223 |
| | 286. *Torso;* 15³/₄ : 20¹/₈″; D. pen, page 196 |
| | 287. *An Anatomy;* D. pencil, page 199 |
| | 288. *Head of a Helmeted Warrior;* Height 47⁵/₈″; S. bronze; owned by the artist, Cl. Cat. 132 |

| | |
|---|---|
| 1934 | 289. *The Picador;* 19¹/₂ : 27³/₈″; Etching; several proofs, page 396 |
| | 290. *Illustration for "Lysistrata," by Aristophanes;* D.; published 1934, page 50 |
| | 291. *Illustration for "Lysistrata," by Aristophanes;* D.; published 1934, page 51 |
| | 292. *Surrealistic Still Life;* 28 : 38″; D. pen, page 200 |
| | 293. *Young Girl and Minotaur;* 38 : 24″; D. brush, page 398 |
| | 294. *Woman Lying before a Window;* 10¹/₄ : 12″; D. brush, Cl. Cat. 139 |

| | |
|---|---|
| 1935 | 295. *Woman with a Hat;* Oil; Georges Salles, Paris. page 82 |
| | 296. *Two Women;* 51¹/₈ : 63³/₄″; Oil; N. A. Rockefeller, New York, Cl. Cat. 140 |
| | 297. *The Studio;* 51¹/₈ : 76³/₈″; Oil; Musée National d'Art Moderne, Paris, Cl. Cat. 141 |
| | 298. *Girl before a Window;* 63³/₄ : 51¹/₈″; Oil, Cl. Cat. 142 |
| | 299. *The Beast;* 13³/₈ : 20¹/₈″; D. brush and pastel, page 397 |
| | 300. *Minotauromachy;* 19¹/₂ : 27¹/₄″; Etching; several proofs, page 401 |

| | |
|---|---|
| 1936 | 301. *Reclining Nude;* 51¹/₈ : 63³/₄″; Oil; owned by the artist, Cl. Cat. 143 |
| | 302. *Minotaur and Maiden;* 13³/₄ : 10¹/₄″; D. pen; H. Berggruen, Paris, page 53 |

| | |
|---|---|
| 1937 | 303. *Woman in an Armchair;* 39³/₈ : 31⁷/₈″; Oil; owned by the artist, page 227 |
| | **304. *Guernica;* 11 ft. 6″ : 25 ft. 8″; Oil; Museum of Modern Art, New York, pages 233/34** |

353. *Still Life with Bull's Skull;* $51\frac{1}{8} : 38\frac{1}{8}''$; Oil; Private collection, Paris, Cl. Cat. 161

354. *Woman in an Armchair;* $31\frac{7}{8} : 25\frac{1}{4}''$; Oil, Cl. Cat. 162

355. *Reclining Nude;* $29\frac{1}{2} : 51\frac{1}{8}''$; Oil, Cl. Cat. 163

356. *The Painter Asleep in His Studio;* $21\frac{1}{4} : 25\frac{1}{4}''$; Oil, Cl. Cat. 164

357. *Bust of a Woman;* $39\frac{3}{8} : 31\frac{7}{8}''$; Oil, Cl. Cat. 268

358. *Two Women;* $11\frac{3}{4} : 15''$; Gouache, page 74

359. *Bull and Horse;* $11\frac{3}{4} : 15''$; D. pen, page 345

360. *Head of a Woman;* $24\frac{3}{4} : 17\frac{3}{8}''$; D. pen, Cl. Cat. 159

361. *Mother and Child;* D. pen, Cl. Cat. 160

**1943**

362. *The Studio Window;* $51\frac{1}{8} : 38\frac{1}{8}''$; Oil; Galerie Louis Carré, Paris, page 413

363. *Le Vert-Galant;* $25\frac{5}{8} : 36''$; Oil; owned by the artist, page 414

364. *Young Boy with Pigeons;* $39\frac{3}{8} : 31\frac{7}{8}''$; Oil, Cl. Cat. 167

365. *Still Life with Spikes of Flowers;* $36\frac{1}{4} : 28\frac{3}{4}''$; Oil, Cl. Cat. 168

366. *Seated Woman;* $57\frac{1}{2} : 35''$; Oil, Cl. Cat. 169

367. *Woman's Face;* $31\frac{7}{8} : 25\frac{1}{4}''$; Oil, Cl. Cat. 170

368. *Still Life with a Vase;* $31\frac{7}{8} : 39\frac{3}{8}''$; Oil, Cl. Cat. 171

369. *Still Life;* $31\frac{7}{8} : 51\frac{1}{8}''$; Oil, Cl. Cat. 172

370. *Bust of a Woman;* $39\frac{3}{8} : 31\frac{7}{8}''$; Oil; Galerie Louis Carré, Paris, Cl. Cat. 173

371. *Head of a Woman;* $36\frac{1}{4} : 28\frac{3}{4}''$; Oil, Cl. Cat. 269

372. *Woman;* $28\frac{3}{4} : 23\frac{5}{8}''$; Oil, Cl. Cat. 270

373. *The Toilette;* $19\frac{3}{4} : 15\frac{3}{4}''$; D. pencil, page 249

374. *Head of a Bull;* Height $16\frac{1}{8}''$; S. handle bars and seat of a bicycle; owned by the artist, Cl. Cat. 165

375. *Woman with Orange;* Height $70\frac{7}{8}''$; S. bronze; owned by the artist, Cl. Cat. 166

376. *Head;* Height $22\frac{7}{8}''$; S. bronze; owned by the artist, Cl. Cat. 174

377. *Woman;* Height $63\frac{3}{8}''$; S. bronze; owned by the artist, Cl. Cat. 175

**1944**

378. *Tomato Plant and Decanter;* $28\frac{3}{4} : 36\frac{1}{4}''$; Oil; owned by the artist, page 257

379. *Coffee Pot;* $31\frac{7}{8} : 23\frac{5}{8}''$; Oil, Cl. Cat. 176

380. *Woman in a Blue Hat;* $36\frac{1}{4} : 23\frac{5}{8}''$; Oil; owned by the artist, Cl. Cat. 177

381. *Female Face;* $13\frac{3}{4} : 8\frac{5}{8}''$; Oil, Cl. Cat. 178

382. *Still Life with Candlestick;* $25\frac{5}{8} : 36\frac{1}{4}''$; Oil, Cl. Cat. 179

383. *Interior;* $28\frac{3}{4} : 36\frac{1}{4}''$; Oil, Cl. Cat. 180

384. *Still Life;* $8\frac{5}{8} : 10\frac{5}{8}''$; Oil, Cl. Cat. 181

385. *Still Life with Tomato Plant;* $36\frac{1}{4} : 28\frac{3}{4}''$; Oil, Cl. Cat. 182

386. *Reclining Nude;* $38\frac{1}{8} : 51\frac{1}{8}''$; Oil, Cl. Cat. 183

387. *The Charnel House* (finished 1948); $68\frac{7}{8} : 98\frac{3}{8}''$; Oil; Collection Art and Resistance, Paris, Cl. Cat. 184

388. *Cock and Hen;* Oil, Cl. Cat. 185

389. *Portrait of a Girl* (Daughter of the artist); $11 : 15\frac{7}{8}''$; Watercolor; owned by the artist, page 238

390. *"Bacchanale," after Poussin;* $11 : 16''$; Watercolor and gouache; owned by the artist, page 417

391. *Woman Washing Her Feet;* $20\frac{1}{8} : 15\frac{1}{8}''$; D. pencil, page 312

392. *Girl with Necklace;* $19\frac{1}{8} : 12\frac{3}{4}''$; D. pencil, page 331

393. *Death's Head;* Height $11\frac{3}{8}''$; S. bronze; owned by the artist, page 436

394. *Shepherd Carrying a Lamb;* Height $81\frac{1}{4}''$; S. bronze; owned by the artist, page 437

**1945**

395. *Still Life with Casserole;* $32\frac{5}{8} : 41\frac{3}{8}''$; Oil; Musée National d'Art Moderne, Paris, page 80

396. *View of Paris, with Notre-Dame;* $28\frac{3}{4} : 36\frac{1}{4}''$; Oil; owned by the artist, page 259 and Cl. Cat. 188

397. *View of Paris, with Notre-Dame;* 6¹/₂ : 10¹/₂″; Oil; owned by the artist, page 414

398. *View of Paris, with Notre-Dame;* 20⁷/₈ : 31⁷/₈″; Oil; owned by the artist, page 415

399. *To the Spaniards Who Died for France;* Oil, Cl. Cat. 186

400. *Still Life with Candlestick;* 18¹/₈ : 21⁵/₈″; Oil, Cl. Cat. 187

401. *Still Life with Skull;* 28³/₄ : 45⁵/₈″; Oil; owned by the artist, Cl. Cat. 189

402. *Little Girl;* 51¹/₈ : 35″; Oil, Cl. Cat. 190

403. *Sketches of Bulls;* 12¹/₄ : 16⁷/₈″; Lithograph; several proofs, page 59

404. *The Bull, I;* 11³/₈ : 16¹/₂″; Lithograph; several proofs, page 100

405. *The Bull, III;* 11³/₈ : 16¹/₂″; Lithograph; several proofs, page 100

406. *The Bull, IV;* 11³/₈ : 16¹/₂″; Lithograph; several proofs, page 101

407. *The Bull, V;* 11³/₈ : 16¹/₂″; Lithograph; several proofs, page 101

408. *The Bull, VI;* 11³/₈ : 16¹/₂″; Lithograph; several proofs, page 102

409. *Portrait of Mallarmé,* with inscription imitating the autograph of Edgar Allan Poe; D. brush, page 247

410. *Standing Woman;* Height 7⁷/₈″; S. bronze, Cl. Cat. 191

411. *Seated Woman;* Height 6¹/₂″; S. bronze, Cl. Cat. 191

412. *Standing Woman;* Height 9¹/₂″; S. bronze, Cl. Cat. 192

413. *Nude;* Height 8⁵/₈″; S. bronze, Cl. Cat. 192

414. *Sleeping Nude;* 21⁵/₈ : 47¹/₄″; Oil; Musée Grimaldi, Antibes, page 75       **1946**

415. *Reclining Nude;* 47¹/₄ : 98¹/₂″; Oil; Musée Grimaldi, Antibes, page 76

416. *La joie de vivre;* 47¹/₄ : 98¹/₂″; Oil; Musée Grimaldi, Antibes, pages 267/68

417. *Triptych;* 98¹/₂ : 141¹/₈; Oil; Musée Grimaldi, Antibes, page 275

418. *Female Figure;* 57¹/₂ : 35″; Oil; Galerie Louis Carré, Paris, page 412

419. *La joie de vivre,* Detail, page 418

420. *La joie de vivre,* Detail, page 419

421. *Still Life with Knife and Melon;* 37³/₈ : 68⁷/₈″; Oil; Musée Grimaldi, Antibes, page 421

422. *The Rape of Europa;* 77 : 51¹/₈″; Oil, page 422

423. *The Turkish Coffeepot;* 26 : 20¹/₈″; Oil, Cl. Cat. 197

424. *Faun on a White Ground;* 25⁷/₈ : 20″; Oil, Cl. Cat. 198

425. *Sea Urchins;* 19⁵/₈ : 25⁵/₈″; Oil, Cl. Cat. 199

426. *The Dance on the Beach;* 19⁵/₈ : 25⁵/₈″; D. wash, page 274

427. *The Dance on the Beach;* 19⁵/₈ : 25⁵/₈″; Watercolor, page 274

428. *View of Ménerbes;* 13 : 19⁷/₈″; Gouache, page 420

429. *Pastorale;* 20 : 25⁵/₈″; Gouache, Cl. Cat. 200

430. *Two Pigeons;* 13³/₄ : 17³/₈″; Colored lithograph; several proofs, page 501

431. *Eight Silhouettes;* 12⁵/₈ : 16⁷/₈″; Lithograph; several proofs, page 61

432. *The Bull, VIII;* 11³/₈ : 16¹/₂″; Lithograph; several proofs, page 102

433. *The Bull, IX;* 11³/₈ : 16¹/₂″; Lithograph; several proofs, page 103

434. *The Bull, XI;* 11³/₈ : 16¹/₂″; Lithograph; several proofs, page 103

435. *Two Nudes* (tenth state); 9⁷/₈ : 12″; Lithograph; several proofs, page 250

436. *Head of a Young Girl;* 17³/₄ : 13″; Lithograph; several proofs, Cl. Cat. 271

437. *Combat of Centaurs;* 19³/₄ : 25⁵/₈″; D. pen, page 99

438. *Combat of Centaurs;* 19³/₄ : 25⁵/₈″; D. pen, page 99

439. *Maenad;* 26 : 20¹/₈″; D. colored chalk, page 273

440. *Faun and Centaur;* 21¹/₄ : 25⁵/₈″; D. colored chalk; H. Berggruen, Paris, Cl. Cat. 193

441. *Head of a Girl;* 25⁵/₈ : 19³/₄″; D. pencil, page 57

442. *Family of Centaurs with Doves;* D. pencil, page 60

443. *The Owl;* 25⁵/₈ : 19³/₄″; D. pencil, page 91

444. *Two Nudes;* 12³/₄ : 19³/₄″; D. pencil, page 250

445. *Nudes in Profile;* D. pencil, page 273

446. *Studies for a Vase in the Shape of a Bull;* 12³/₄ : 19³/₄″; D. pencil, page 309

447. *She-Goat;* D. pencil and pen; Musée Grimaldi, Antibes, Cl. Cat. 194

448. *Portrait of a Woman;* D. pencil, Cl. Cat. 195

449. *Seated Woman;* D. pencil, Cl. Cat. 196

**1947**

450. *Seated Woman;* 51¹/₈ : 38¹/₈"; Oil; owned by the artist, page 329
451. *Owl on a Chair;* 28³/₄ : 23⁵/₈"; Oil, Cl. Cat. 201
452. *The Birth of the Last Centaur;* 12 : 10"; Etching; illustration for "Dos Contes," by Reventos, published 1947, page 63
453. *Owl on a Chair;* 25⁵/₈ : 19³/₄"; Colored lithograph; several proofs, Cl. Cat. 202
454. *The Black Owl;* 24³/₄ : 18⁷/₈"; Lithograph; several proofs, page 92
455. *Flower in a Glass;* 9 : 5⁷/₈"; Lithograph; several proofs, page 104
456. *Flower in a Glass;* 9¹/₂ : 6¹/₄"; Lithograph; several proofs, page 105
457. *The Black Bull;* 15³/₄ : 25⁵/₈"; Lithograph; several proofs, page 106
548. *Two Women at the Beach;* 19⁵/₈ : 25⁵/₈"; Lithograph; several proofs, Cl. Cat. 203
459. *Centaur and Bacchante;* 19⁵/₈ : 25⁵/₈"; Lithograph; several proofs, Cl. Cat. 204
460. *Studies of Owls;* 25⁵/₈ : 19³/₄"; D. pencil and colored crayon, page 90
461. *Decorated Ceramic (with Nude);* Height 3¹/₂"; C. painted; Mme. Cuttoli, Paris, page 441
462. *Decorated Ceramic (with Woman's Head);* Height 3¹/₂"; C. painted; Mme. Cuttoli, Paris, page 441

**1948**

463. *Seated Woman with a Picture;* 51¹/₈ : 38¹/₈"; Oil, Cl. Cat. 206
464. *Lobster and Bottle;* 19⁵/₈ : 24"; Oil, Cl. Cat. 207
465. *The Kitchen;* 68⁷/₈ : 98³/₈"; Oil, Cl. Cat. 208
466. *Seated Woman;* 39³/₈ : 31⁷/₈"; Oil, Cl. Cat. 272
467. *Claude on His Bed;* 51¹/₈ : 38¹/₈"; Oil; owned by the artist, Cl. Cat. 273
468. *Illustration for "Vingt Poèmes,"* by Góngora; 14 : 10⁵/₈"; Etching, page 84
469. *Al sepulcro de Dominico Greco,* poem in Picasso's handwriting, from "Vingt Poèmes," by Góngora; 14 : 10⁵/₈"; Etching; several proofs, page 343
470. *Head of a Faun;* 19³/₄ : 25⁵/₈"; Lithograph for a poster, page 341
471. *Musical Faun;* 25¹/₄ : 20⁷/₈"; Lithograph; several proofs, page 276
472. *The Great Owl;* 26³/₄ : 20⁷/₈"; Lithograph; several proofs, page 311
473. *Vase of Flowers;* 27⁵/₈ : 20¹/₈"; D. wash, Cl. Cat. 205
474. *Decorated Plate* (Faun and Goat); 12⁵/₈ : 14"; C. painted, page 281
475. *Decorated Plate* (Face) 12⁵/₈ : 14"; C. painted, page 281
476. *Bird (Vase);* Height 15³/₈"; C. painted, page 442
477. *Woman (Vase);* Height 14³/₈"; C. painted, page 443
478. *Decorated Plate* (Face); 12⁵/₈ : 14"; C. painted, page 448
479. *Decorated Plate* (Glass and Lemon); 12⁵/₈ : 14"; C. painted, page 448
480. *Decorated Plate* (Combat of Centaurs); 12⁵/₈ : 14"; C. painted, page 449
481. *Decorated Plate* (Fishes); 12⁵/₈ : 14"; C. painted, page 449
482. *Clothed Woman* (Vase); Height 14⁷/₈"; C. painted, Cl. Cat. 233
483. *Pitcher with Nude;* Height 13³/₈"; C. painted, Cl. Cat. 234
484. *Plate with Horseman;* 12¹/₄ : 14⁷/₈"; C. painted, Cl. Cat. 235

**1949**

485. *Lady in Blue;* 39³/₈ : 31⁷/₈"; Oil, Cl. Cat. 211
486. *Claude, Aged Two;* 51¹/₈ : 38¹/₈"; Oil; owned by the artist, Cl. Cat. 212
487. *Nude;* 51¹/₈ : 38¹/₈"; Oil, Cl. Cat. 213
488. *Illustration from "Carmen,"* by Mérimée; 4 : 7¹/₈"; Etching, page 346
489. *"Peinture écrite";* Lithograph; several proofs, page 349
490. *Toad;* 19¹/₂ : 25¹/₄"; Lithograph; several proofs, page 424
491. *Dove;* 21¹/₂ : 29⁷/₈"; Lithograph; several proofs, Cl. Cat. 209
492. *Venus and Eros, Black Ground;* 29⁷/₈ : 22¹/₄"; Lithograph; several proofs, Cl. Cat. 210
493. *Owl;* D. pencil, page 89
494. *Ibex (Vase);* Height 15"; C. painted, page 442
495. *Plate with Head of a Faun;* 15 : 12⁵/₈"; C. painted, Cl. Cat. 236

**1950**

496. *Claude and Paloma at Play;* 57¹/₈ : 46¹/₂"; Oil; owned by the artist, page 307

497. *Portrait of a Painter, after El Greco;* 39³/₄ : 31³/₄″; Oil; S. Rosengart, Lucerne, page 423

498. *Winter Landscape;* 39³/₄ : 48³/₄″; Oil; Victor W. Ganz, New York, page 425

499. *Claude and Paloma;* 45⁵/₈ : 35″; Oil; owned by the artist, page 426

500. *Les demoiselles des bords de la Seine, after Courbet;* 78³/₄ : 39³/₈″; Oil; Kunstmuseum Basel, page 428

501. *Woman Drawing, and Children;* 81⁷/₈ : 51¹/₈″; Oil, Cl. Cat. 214

502. *Panorama of Vallauris;* 39³/₈ : 78³/₄″; Oil, Cl. Cat. 215

503. *Face;* illustration for "Corps perdu," by Césaire, published 1950; 15¹/₂ : 11″; Etching, page 70

504. *Figural Composition;* illustration for "Corps perdu," by Césaire, published 1950; 15¹/₂ : 11″; Etching, page 344

505. *Triumph of the Dove;* 8¹/₄ : 10⁵/₈″; D. brush, page 352

506. *Owl;* Height 7¹/₈″; S. C. painted; owned by the artist, page 73

507. *Goat;* 47¹/₄ : 55¹/₈″; S. bronze; owned by the artist, page 438

508. *Goat;* S. plasticine, page 440

509. *Pregnant Woman;* Height 43¹/₄″; S. bronze; owned by the artist, Cl. Cat. 216

510. *Female Figure (Vase);* Height 19³/₄″; C. painted, page 444

511. *Nudes Seen from the Rear (Vase);* Height 27¹/₂″; C. painted, page 445

512. *Faun's Head (Vase);* Height 17³/₄″; C. painted, page 446

513. *Decorated Casseroles;* 7⁷/₈ : 8⁵/₈″; C. painted, page 450


514. *Night Landscape;* 57¹/₂ : 44⁷/₈″; Oil; owned by the artist, page 289 1951

515. *Paloma, the Artist's Daughter;* 21⁵/₈ : 18¹/₈″; Oil; owned by the artist, page 427

516. *Massacre in Korea;* 43¹/₄ : 82³/₄″; Oil; owned by the artist, page 429

517. *Villa with Palm Tree;* 35 : 45⁵/₈″; Oil, Cl. Cat. 217

518. *Vallauris Smoke;* 23⁵/₈ : 28³/₄″; Oil, Cl. Cat. 221

519. *Page-Boys at Play;* 15 : 20¹/₂″; Lithograph; several proofs, Cl. Cat. 219

520. *Mother and Child;* 10⁵/₈ : 8¹/₂″; D. pen, page 326

521. *Knight and Page-Boy;* 26 : 19⁵/₈″; D. brush, page 248

522. *House at Vallauris;* 19⁷/₈ : 26″; D. brush, Cl. Cat. 218

523. *Skull of a Goat;* 19⁷/₈ : 25³/₄″; D. brush, Cl. Cat. 220

524. *Crane;* Height 29¹/₂″; S. painted bronze; owned by the artist, page 439

525. *Head of a Woman;* Height 20⁷/₈″; S. bronze; owned by the artist, Cl. Cat. 237

526. *Goat's Skull and Candle;* 31¹/₂ : 26³/₄ : 14¹/₈″; S. painted bronze; owned by the artist, Cl. Cat. 238

527. *Bullfight (Plate);* 11³/₈ : 25⁵/₈″; C. painted; owned by the artist, page 451

528. *Owl (Vase);* Height 21⁵/₈″; C. painted; Mme. Cuttoli, Paris, page 447


529. *Portrait of Mrs. H. P.;* 57³/₄ : 37³/₄″; Oil; owned by the artist, page 253 1952

530. *War;* 185 : 403″; Oil; Chapel "Temple de la Paix," Vallauris, page 430

531. *Peace;* 185 : 403″; Oil; Chapel "Temple de la Paix," Vallauris, page 431

532. *Paloma, Asleep;* 44⁷/₈ : 57¹/₂″; Oil; owned by the artist, page 452

533. *The Reservoir;* 31¹/₂ : 48³/₄″; Oil; Cl. Cat. 222

534. *Goat's Skull and Bottle;* 35 : 45⁵/₈″; Oil; Galerie Louise Leiris, Paris, Cl. Cat. 223

535. *Hen;* 19³/₄ : 25⁵/₈″; Aquatint, Cl. Cat. 224

536. *Woman at the Window;* 35³/₈ : 25⁵/₈″; Aquatint, Cl. Cat. 274

537. *Balzac, II;* 29⁷/₈ : 22¹/₂″; Lithograph, page 67

538. *Round Dance;* 9 : 5⁷/₈″; D. pen, page 65

539. *Nursing Mother;* 5⁷/₈ : 9″; D. pen, page 332

540. *Musical Faun;* 26 : 19⁷/₈″; D. brush; S. Rosengart, Lucerne, page 1

541. *Man in Owl's Figure;* 5⁷/₈ : 9″; D. brush, page 297

542. *Nude with Raised Arms;* 26 : 20¹/₈″; D. brush, page 317

543. *Composition Study;* 5⁷/₈ : 9″; D. pencil, page 297

544. *Composition Study;* 5⁷/₈ : 9″; D. pencil, page 297

545. *Round Dance;* 5⁷/₈ : 9″; D. pencil, page 297

546. *Hearse Horses*; page from a school-copybook; D. pencil, page 298
547. *Horse's Hoofs*; D. pencil, page 298
548. *Man in Owl's Figure*; D. pencil, page 298
549. *Composition Study*; $5^7/_8 : 9''$; D. pencil, page 298
550. *Horse's Head*; D. pencil, page 299
551. *Horse with Pigeon and Owl*; D. pencil, page 299
552. *Hoofs of a Camel*; D. pencil, page 299
553. *Skeleton*; D. pencil, page 299
554. *Boar*; D. pencil, page 64
555. *Pig as Camel-Driver*; D. pencil, page 300
556. *Distorted Houses*; D. pencil, page 300
557. *Composition Study for "War"*; page from a school-copybook; D. pencil, page 300
558. *Imprisoned Fishes and Birds*; D. pencil, page 300
559. *Pitcher and Figs*; $11^3/_8 : 18^3/_4''$; S. painted bronze; owned by the artist, page 441
560. *The White Owl*; Height 13''; S. painted plaster, Cl. Cat. 239
561. *Monkey and Her Young*; Height $21^5/_8''$; S. bronze; owned by the artist, Cl. Cat. 240

1953

562. *The Meal*; $38^1/_4 : 51^1/_8''$; Oil; owned by the artist, page 293
563. *Teapot and Cup*; $10^5/_8 : 13^3/_4''$; Oil, Cl. Cat. 225
564. *Woman's Head, Inclined*; $10^5/_8 : 8^5/_8''$; Oil, Cl. Cat. 226
565. *Seated Woman*; $10^5/_8 : 8^5/_8''$; Oil, Cl. Cat. 228
566. *Woman with a Hat*; $39^3/_8 : 31^7/_8''$; Oil, Cl. Cat. 275
567. *Female Torso*; $35^7/_8 : 25^1/_4''$; Etching; several proofs, Cl. Cat. 227
568. *Gardens in Vallauris*; $22^1/_2 : 29^7/_8''$; Lithograph; several proofs, page 68
569. *Portrait in the Manner of the School of Lyons*; $25^5/_8 : 19^5/_8''$; Lithograph, Cl. Cat. 276
570. *Dwarf and Girl*; page from a sketchbook; D. brush, page 319
571. *A Bouquet*; Height 24''; S. bronze, Cl. Cat. 241
572. *The Ruffled Pigeon*; $7^7/_8 : 8^1/_4''$; S. ceramic, Cl. Cat. 242
573. *Plate with Picador*; $13 : 12^5/_8''$; C. painted, Cl. Cat. 243

1954

574. *Sylvette, XIII*; $45^5/_8 : 35''$; Oil, page 333
575. *Portrait of Sylvette*; $31^7/_8 : 25^5/_8''$; Oil, Cl. Cat. 229
576. *The Studio*; $9^7/_8 : 19^3/_4''$; Colored lithograph; several proofs, page 507
577. *Composition with Clowns*; Colored lithograph, several proofs, page 508
578. *The Rehearsal*; $19^3/_4 : 25^5/_8''$; Lithograph, page 336
579. *Dance with Banderillas*; $19^3/_4 : 25^5/_8''$; Lithograph, page 339
580. *Dances*; $19^3/_4 : 25^5/_8''$; Lithograph; several proofs, Cl. Cat. 231
581. *People and Dove*; $19^3/_4 : 25^5/_8''$; Lithograph; several proofs, Cl. Cat. 278
582. *Old Man and Girl*; D. colored chalk, page 502
583. *Woman and Monkey*; D. wash, Cl. Cat. 230
584. *Woman Playing with a Cat*; $12^5/_8 : 9^1/_2''$; D. wash, Cl. Cat. 277
585. *Old Painter and Model*; page from a sketchbook; D. brush, page 321
586. *Girl and Masked Cupid*; page from a sketchbook; D. brush, page 320
587. *Old Man and Young Girl*; page from a sketchbook; D. brush, page 322
588. *Nude and Male Heads*; page from a sketchbook; D. brush, page 323
589. *Monkey as Painter*; page from a sketchbook; D. brush, page 324
590. *Nude with Hat in the Studio*; page from a sketchbook; D. brush, page 335
591. *Woman with Monkey and Clown*; page from a sketchbook; D. brush, page 337
592. *Visitors in the Studio*; page from a sketchbook; D. brush, page 338
593. *The Circus Vase*; Height $22^7/_8''$; C. painted, Cl. Cat. 244

1955

594. *Women of Algiers XIV, after Delacroix*; $44^7/_8 : 57^1/_2''$; Oil; owned by the artist, page 347
595. *Women of Algiers X*; $51^1/_8 : 63^3/_4''$; Oil; owned by the artist, Cl. Cat. 232
596. *Two Heads*; $11^3/_4 : 18^7/_8''$; D. brush; K. Flinker, Paris, Cover

500

*Two Pigeons* (1946)

*Old Man and Girl* (1954)

## Documents

When Picasso was once asked to approve certain written versions of his conversations, he said that he found it unnecessary, that the only important thing was to create enthusiasm. The passages that follow have not necessarily been translated literally; they aim, instead, to preserve the immediacy and spirit of observations and statements which Picasso has made through the years.

*Editor*

### Conversation with Marius de Zayas                           1923

First published in *The Arts* (New York), May 26, 1923, based on an interview given by Picasso in Spanish, and checked by him after it was written down. The excerpts printed here are from *Picasso: Fifty Years of His Art* by Alfred H. Barr, Jr., with the permission of the Museum of Modern Art, New York.

In my opinion to search means nothing in painting. To find is the thing.

We all know that Art is not truth. Art is a lie that makes us realize truth, at least the truth that is given us to understand. The artist must know the manner whereby to convince others of the truthfulness of his lies.

The several manners I have used in my art must not be considered as an evolution, or as steps toward an unknown ideal of painting. All I have ever made was made for the present and with the hope that it will always remain in the present.

### Conversation with E. Tériade                           1932

(While Picasso was supervising the hanging of his pictures in the retrospective exhibition in that year.)
First published in the newspaper *L'Intransigeant* (Paris), June 15, 1932.

The other day I visited the retrospective at the Salon. Here is something I noticed. A good picture hanging among bad pictures becomes a bad picture. And a bad one hanging among good ones ends up by becoming good.

Somebody asked me how I was going to arrange this exhibition. I told him: "Badly." For an exhibition is like a painting; if it is "arranged" —well or badly—it comes to the same thing. What counts is the spirit of the thing. If the right spirit is there, everything comes out well—even in an affair that has gone sour.

How often, as I was on the point of putting blue into a picture, I suddenly realized that I didn't have any more. So I used red instead. So much for our creative vanity!

When you come right down to it, all you have is your self. Your self is a sun with a thousand rays in your belly. The rest is nothing. It's only because of this, for example, that Matisse is Matisse. It's because he carries the sun in his belly that he can accomplish something from time to time.

The work that one does is another way of keeping a diary.

When you see some of your early pictures come back, as I have today at this exhibition, it's like the return of prodigal children—only now dressed in robes of gold.

Painters beget pictures as princes beget children—not with princesses, but with country girls. One never paints the Parthenon, or a Louis XV chair. One makes pictures out of a hovel, a tobacco pack, or an old stool.

At bottom, there is nothing but love. No matter what kind. One ought to put out the eyes of painters as they put out the eyes of goldfinches to improve their singing.

One of the ugliest things in art is the "I-beg-to-remain-sir-Yours-Faithfully" kind of polite convention that spoils even the best of pictures because it shows compliance with public taste.

A friend who is writing a book on my sculptures starts it like this: "Picasso told me one day that a straight line is the shortest distance between two points." Obviously I was very surprised and asked him: "Are you quite sure it was I who found this out?"

If you start out with a portrait and eliminate more and more in your search for pure form—the clean, basic volume—you can't help ending up with an egg. On the other hand, if you start out with an egg and follow the same path in the opposite direction, you can arrive at a portrait. But art, I think, must avoid this over-simplified approach which consists of going from one extreme to the other. One always has to be able to stop in time.

Everything interesting in art happens right at the start. Once past the beginning, you're already at the end.

I don't work *after* nature, but *before* nature—and with her.

Nothing can be accomplished without solitude. I have made a kind of solitude for myself which nobody is aware of. Today it's very difficult to be alone because we have watches. Have you ever seen a saint wearing a watch? I've searched for one all over—even among the patron saints of watchmakers. Here we are right now, talking. We could go on like this for years, and still find something to say. Ten years later we'd still be here, perfectly happy, talking and talking . . .

(And with that Picasso took out his watch and said: "Good-by now, see you soon, I'm expected for lunch.")

## Conversation with Christian Zervos

First published in *Cahiers d'art* (Paris), 1935.

Previously, pictures moved toward completion in progressive stages. Each day brought something new. A picture used to be a sum of additions. With me, a picture is a sum of destructions. I make a picture, then I destroy it. But in the end nothing is lost: the red I took away from one place turns up in another place.

There is no abstract art. One must always begin with something. Then all traces of reality can be removed. There isn't any danger then, because the idea of the object has left an indelible mark.

One cannot go contrary to nature. She is stronger than the strongest men! It is wholly to our interest to be on good terms with her. We may permit ourselves certain liberties, but only in details.

One should take the good where one finds it—except from one's own work. I have a horror of copying myself . . .

It is not what the artist does that counts, but what he is.

Everyone wants to understand painting. Why don't they try to understand the singing of the birds? Why do people love the night, a flower, everything that surrounds them, without trying to understand them? But painting—that they must *understand*.

## Written statement for Simone Téry

First published in *Lettres françaises* (Paris), March 24, 1945.

What do you think an artist is? An imbecile who has nothing but eyes if he is a painter, or ears if he is a musician, or a lyre at every level of his heart if he is a poet, or nothing but muscles if he is a boxer? Quite the contrary, he is at the same time a political being, constantly aware of what goes on in the world, whether it be harrowing, bitter, or sweet, and he cannot help being shaped by it. How would it be possible not to take an interest in other people, and to withdraw into an ivory tower from participation in their existence? No, painting is not interior decoration. It is an instrument of war for attack and defense against the enemy.

## Four conversations with Daniel-Henry Kahnweiler

First published in *Le point* (Souillac), 1952.

### October 2, 1933

Picasso tells me that in order to avoid casting from the model, at Boisgeloup (his château, near Gisors) he is going to make concave sculptures in clay. Then he will pour the plaster into these "molds." Result: plaster sculpture in relief.

"And," he says, "I should like to paint these sculptures. You see, painting will never be anything but an art of illusion. If you put down a black, the observer thinks of it as a shadow, and indeed this is the way you do show volume. But if you paint a piece of sculpture pink, it stays pink."

### February 6, 1934

Picasso: "For example, that portrait of Rembrandt. It's the same old story of trouble with the wax ground. I had a plate where this happened. I said to myself: 'It's ruined, I'll make any old thing over it.' I started to doodle. It became Rembrandt. It began to please me and so I developed it. I even made another one right away, with his turban, his furs, his eye—you know what I mean, his elephant's eye. I'm still working on this plate to get his blacks. You don't get them right away."

### February 13, 1934

It's as though I've never been able to build up a painting myself. I begin with an idea, and then it becomes something else. After all, what is a painter? He's a collector who gets what he likes in others by painting them himself. This is how I begin, and then it becomes something else.

### Vallauris, March 10–13, 1951

He speaks with a certain fear of old age. He mimics an old man who moves with difficulty. "This is what is terrible! Right now we can still do everything we want. But to want and no longer be able to, this is what is terrible! I must make my 'Temple of Peace' now, while I can still climb the ladder." (He began this work in the summer of 1952.)

I find in my notebook: "I am a Communist so that there will be less misery." But I can no longer remember the context in which he said it.

1948                    **Prose poem by Picasso, of May 13, 1941**

Published in *Cahiers d'art* (Paris), 1948.

Chasuble of blood cast over the naked shoulders of the green wheat shivering between the wet sheets symphonic orchestra of the slashed flesh hung from flowering trees of the ocher-painted wall flapping its great apple-green and white-lavender wings tearing its beak against the architectural window panes of congealed fat on the waves of earthy perfumes of music of birds baskets full of provisions among rambling roses pinned up like swarms of bees in the disheveled hair of landscape stretched out in the sun, the four paws of the mountain of rice of the rocks planted in the sunken stones up to their ankles in the mud of the sky—the hanging tongue of the plough stuck to the tilled land sweating lead from the weight of the effort perpetrated at the center of the bouquet twisted by the chains of teeth of surprised flowers in the middle of the tough skin of their eyes fixed from top to bottom of the dress in its broken pleats, its rents, the worn fabric covered with stains the thousand and one patches, its vermin, the gilt arches of stone fanning out and the distant closed windows on the houses encrusted by fine sands of the trees of the forest and the yawning of white feathers flown from the glass of water neck raised the great lit tapers of the big barges resting at the edge of the pit listening to the perfume of the rain which breathes through the flute the fingers of green olives.

*The Studio* (1954)

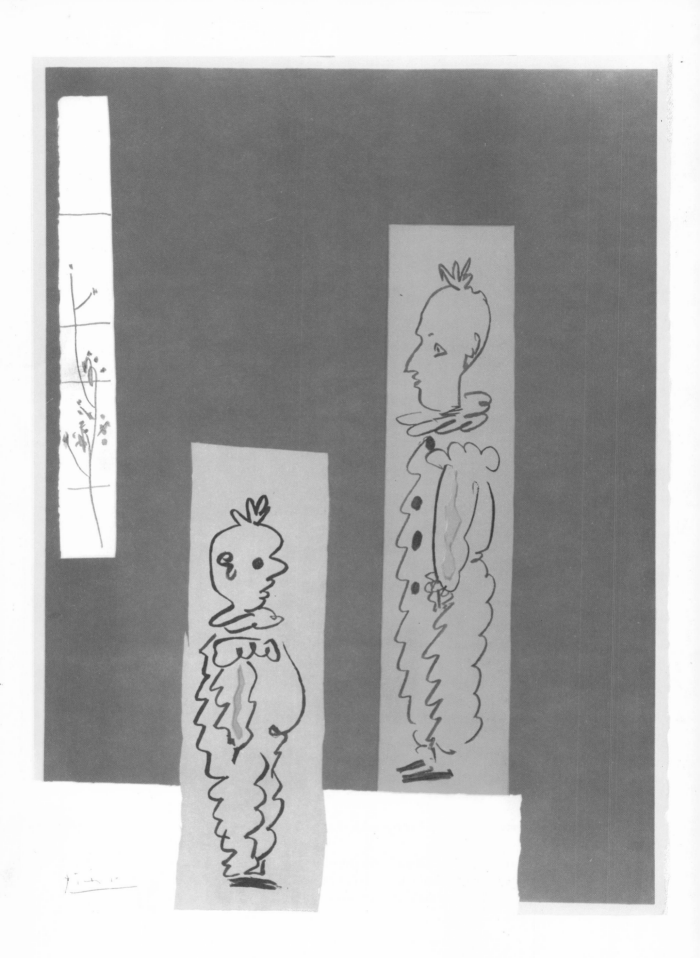

*Composition with Clowns* (1954)

# Graphological Analysis

(By M. Raymond Trillat, based on a letter of September 14, 1936, from Picasso to Paul Eluard, and written down by Eluard on May 21, 1942.)

First published in *Le point* (Souillac), 1952.

Eluard's notes of the analysis.

May 21, 1942

I was visited today by M. Raymond Trillat, graphologist. I showed him the following letter (the first page), taking care to hide from him the back of the envelope [with its signature]. As I did not absent myself for a single moment, no fraud was possible.

I gave no sign of approval during the analysis. I neither encouraged nor contradicted it in any way.

"He handles trees ... no, arms. He defends his poor ego which batters against others, and is penetrated by others. He does not want others to be his ruin. He is influenced by banal forces, and receptive to waves that act on him strangely.

"Exaltation: a flight that is too vast in scope, not to be put in words— trances.

"The desire to rush toward others, the desire for a bridge—unrealizable. He is of another time, another world: chivalrous, childish, mad.

"He is afraid to give free rein to his nerves and has to resort, to keep his equilibrium, to measures whose brutality and intense force would, in others, yield the opposite results.

"His life is crisscrossed with catastrophes which he himself creates by his lack of 'bourgeoisism' and of care.

"The question of money does not count for him, but he is forced to grant it a vital importance, since it takes him by the throat.

"Very sweet and very hard, he disregards the average and moderation.

"His sensuality is instantaneous in certain matters, and victorious after having been seductive and complicated. He seeks an impulsion upward, but abandons it at the moment he could profit by it.

"He loves intensely and kills what he loves.

"He is sad. Seeks a way out and issues from his sadness by a pure creation. Joy, happiness, harm him. Sadness serves him.

"CREATOR, creator, mad for some, sublime for others. First rate.

"One must not try to get something out of him by flattery, for then he becomes false.

"Temperament: sanguine, bilious. Nerves subject to great discharges followed by apathy.

"Glandular system influenced by fatigue: hypophyseal, thyroidism.

"Vision: when looking far off, through the left eye: weak. Adjusted but blurred when looking close-up through both eyes."

———

For those who know Picasso, this analysis is impressive. M. Trillat spoke quite rapidly, without pause, without hesitation. I give here the notes I was able to take, unchanged.

*Paul Eluard*

## Biographical Summary

Pablo Ruiz Picasso born on October 25 at 9:30 p.m. in 36 (now 15) Plaza de la Merced, Málaga. First child of Maria Picasso Lopez and Don José Ruiz Blasco, art teacher in San Telmo, school of arts and industries.

1881

Family moves to La Coruña (Galicia). Picasso a student at Da Guarda, school of arts and industries, where his father teaches art. Picasso's first pictures are painted under his father's instruction.

1891

Don José gives his paints and brushes to his son, retires from painting.

1894

In the summer, brief visit to Madrid. Family settles in Barcelona. Picasso enters the art school La Llonja where his father again teaches art. Picasso accepted in the advanced class in drawing after taking only one day to complete the examination for which a month is ordinarily allotted.

1895

First studio in Barcelona, in Calle de la Plata.

1896

Awarded Honorable Mention at the Exhibition of Fine Arts in Madrid for his painting *Science and Charity (Ciencia y Caridad)*. Belongs to the Bohemian group which centers around the café Els Quatre Gats (The Four Cats); paints his friends' portraits on the walls of the café; beginning of friendship with Jaime Sabartés. First exhibition in Barcelona at Els Quatre Gats.
Spends the summer in Málaga.
In October successfully applies to, and is accepted for the advanced classes in, the Royal Academy of San Fernando, Madrid.

1897

Has scarlet fever; leaves Madrid in the spring to convalesce at Horta de Ebro (sometimes said to be Horta de San Juan). Wins medals in Madrid and Málaga for his painting *Customs of Aragon*.

1898

In Barcelona; paints and also works as an illustrator for periodicals. Works in Cardona's studio, 1 Calle Escudillers Blanchs.

1899

First drawings published in the magazine *Joventut*.
October-December, first trip to Paris with Carlos Casagemas; studio at 49 Rue Gabrielle.
The dealer Berthe Weill buys three sketches.

1900

511

| 1901 | In the spring, in Madrid; art editor and illustrator of the magazine *Arte Joven*. |
| | Exhibition of pastels in the Salon Parés, Barcelona, arranged by the magazine *Pel y Ploma*. |
| | At the end of May, second trip to Paris; studio at 130ter Boulevard de Clichy. |
| | In June, first Paris exhibition by Ambroise Vollard. |
| | Now signs his paintings "Picasso" (heretofore "P. Ruiz Picasso," etc.). |
| | At the end of the year returns to Barcelona. |
| | |
| 1902 | Exhibition at Galerie Berthe Weill, Paris. |
| | In October, third trip to Paris with Sebastián Junyer. |
| | Shares a room with Max Jacob on the Boulevard Voltaire. |
| | |
| 1903 | Returns to Barcelona early in the year. |
| | |
| 1904 | In April, again with Sebastián Junyer, to Paris to settle permanently. |
| | Moves into the *Bateau-lavoir*, 13 Rue de Ravignan (now 13 Place Émile-Goudeau), where he lives until 1909. |
| | Meets the French writers Maurice Raynal, André Salmon, etc. |
| | |
| 1905 | Meets Guillaume Apollinaire. |
| | In summer, trip to Holland. |
| | The Americans Leo and Gertrude Stein and the Russian Shchukine begin to buy his pictures. |
| | Becomes acquainted with Fernande Olivier. |
| | |
| 1906 | Meets Matisse. |
| | Summer in Gosol with Fernande Olivier, who remains his constant companion until 1911. |
| | Meets Georges Braque, André Derain, Daniel-Henry Kahnweiler, who opens a gallery. |
| | |
| 1908 | Picasso gives a banquet to honor the *Douanier* Henri Rousseau. |
| | End of summer in La Rue-des-Bois (Oise). |
| | |
| 1909 | Moves to 11 Boulevard de Clichy. |
| | Summer in Horta de Ebro (Horta de San Juan). |
| | First exhibition in Germany (Galerie Thannhauser, Munich) |
| | |
| 1910 | Summer in Cadaqués (Spain) with Derain. |
| | |
| 1911 | Summer in Céret (French Pyrenees) with Braque and his old friend, the sculptor Manolo. First exhibition in the United States (Photo-Secession Gallery, New York). |
| | Kahnweiler publishes Max Jacob's *Saint Matorel* with etchings by Picasso, the artist's first venture in book illustration. |
| | |
| 1912 | Becomes acquainted with "Eva" (Marcelle Humbert). |
| | Summer in Avignon, Céret, and with Braque in Sorgues (Vaucluse). |
| | Moves from Montmartre to Montparnasse. |
| | First exhibition in England (Stafford Gallery, London). |

| | |
|---|---|
| Summer in Céret with Braque, Juan Gris, and Max Jacob. | 1913 |
| Father dies in Barcelona. | |
| Occupies a studio in 5bis Rue Schoelcher. | |
| | |
| Summer in Avignon with Braque and Derain. | 1914 |
| His painting *The Jugglers* brings 11,500 francs at the Hôtel Drouot. | |
| | |
| Remains in Paris after the outbreak of war. | 1915 |
| | |
| Moves to Montrouge (Seine). | 1916 |
| | |
| In February, to Rome with Jean Cocteau. Designs scenery and costumes for Serge Diaghilev's Ballet Russe production of *Parade* (book by Cocteau, music by Erik Satie; performed May 18 in Paris). | 1917 |
| In Rome, meets Igor Stravinsky, becomes acquainted with Olga Koklova, a dancer in the Ballet Russe. | |
| Visits Naples, Pompeii, and Florence. | |
| Summer in Barcelona and Madrid. | |
| | |
| Marries Olga Koklova. | 1918 |
| Takes an apartment at 23 Rue de la Boétie (which he keeps until 1951). | |
| Trip to Barcelona. Summer in Biarritz. | |
| | |
| In London with the Ballet Russe. Designs for the ballet *Le tricorne* (book by Martinez Sierra, music by Manuel de Falla; performed on July 22 in London). Summer in Saint-Raphaël (Côte d'Azur). Meets Joan Miró. | 1919 |
| | |
| Designs for the ballet *Pulcinella* (music by Stravinsky; performed May 15 in Paris). | 1920 |
| Summer in Juan-les-Pins. | |
| | |
| Birth of son Paul. | 1921 |
| Designs the ballet *Cuadro flamenco* (music by Manuel de Falla; performed May 22 in Paris). | |
| Summer in Fontainebleau. | |
| | |
| Summer in Dinard (Brittany). | 1922 |
| Participates in the designs for Cocteau's *Antigone* (performed December 20 in Paris). | |
| | |
| Summer in Cap d'Antibes. | 1923 |
| | |
| Designs for the ballet *Mercure* (music by Satie; performed June 14 in Paris). | 1924 |
| Curtain for the ballet *Le train bleu* (book by Cocteau, music by Darius Milhaud, scenery by Henri Laurens; performed June 20 in Paris). | |
| Summer in Juan-les-Pins. | |
| | |
| Spring in Monte Carlo. | 1925 |
| Summer in Juan-les-Pins. | |
| Participates in the first exhibition of Surrealist painting in Paris. | |
| | |
| Summer in Juan-les-Pins. | 1926 |

| 1927 | Summer in Cannes. |
|------|-------------------|
| 1928 | Summer in Dinard.<br>Begins to work at sculpture again (for the first time since 1914). |
| 1929 | Summer in Dinard. |
| 1930 | Summer in Juan-les-Pins.<br>Awarded First Prize, Carnegie Institute (Pittsburgh) for his 1918 painting "Portrait of Mme. Picasso." |
| 1931 | Publication by Vollard of Honoré de Balzac, *Le chef-d'œuvre inconnu*, with illustrations by Picasso.<br>Publication by Albert Skira of Ovid, *Métamorphoses*, with 30 etchings by Picasso.<br>Summer in Juan-les-Pins. |
| 1932 | Establishes a studio in the Château du Boisgeloup (bought in 1930) at Gisors (Eure).<br>Great retrospective exhibitions in Paris and Zurich. |
| 1933 | Trip to Cannes and Barcelona. |
| 1934 | Lives at Boisgeloup.<br>Extended trip to Spain (San Sebastián, Madrid, Toledo, Escorial, and Barcelona).<br>Lives in Cannes.<br>Publication of Aristophanes, *Lysistrata*, with illustrations by Picasso. |
| 1935 | Separation from Olga Koklova.<br>Lives at Boisgeloup.<br>Birth of daughter Maïa. |
| 1936 | Summer in Juan-les-Pins and Mougins (Alpes-Maritimes).<br>Traveling exhibition of his work in Spain.<br>After outbreak of the Spanish Civil War, named Director of the Prado.<br>Rents a house in Le Tremblay-sur-Mauldre from Vollard (until 1939).<br>Association with Dora Maar. |
| 1937 | Publishes *Sueño y mentira de Franco (Dream and Lie of Franco)*.<br>Takes a studio at 7 Rue des Grands-Augustins (still in use), where he paints *Guernica*, which is exhibited in June in the Spanish Pavilion at the Paris World's Fair.<br>Summer in Mougins. |
| 1938 | Summer in Mougins and Le Tremblay. |
| 1939 | Great, comprehensive retrospective exhibition at The Museum of Modern Art, New York.<br>Mother dies in Barcelona.<br>Summer in Antibes, later in Royan near Bordeaux. |
| 1940 | Mainly in Royan, with frequent trips to Paris. |

Unable to leave Paris until the end of the Occupation. Writes the play *Le désir attrapé par la queue (Desire Caught by the Tail).*  — 1941

Publication by Fabiani of Buffon, *Histoire naturelle*, with 31 aquatints by Picasso (project originally undertaken for Vollard).  — 1942

Facsimile edition of *Le désir attrapé par la queue.*  — 1943

After the Liberation, participates in the Salon d'Automne.
Joins the French Communist Party.  — 1944

Late summer in Golfe Juan.
November 2 takes up lithography in the workshop of Fernand Mourlot.  — 1945

Association with Françoise Gilot.
Summer in Golfe Juan.
Autumn in Antibes. Gives numerous new works to the Musée Grimaldi.  — 1946

Continues his lithographic work with Mourlot.
Birth of son Claude.
From August in Golfe Juan, then in Vallauris. Takes up ceramics in the workshop of Suzanne and Georges Ramié in Vallauris.  — 1947

Settles in Vallauris, in the villa La Galloise.
Trip to Poland.
Publication of Góngora, *Vingt poèmes*, with 41 aquatints and dry points by Picasso.
Publication of Pierre Reverdy, *Le chant des morts*, with 6 lithographs by Picasso.  — 1948

Trip to Italy (Rome, Florence).
Birth of daughter Paloma.
Publication of Prosper Mérimée, *Carmen*, with 38 burin engravings and 4 aquatints by Picasso.  — 1949

Exhibition at the Venice Biennale.
Named honorary citizen of Vallauris.
Publication of Aimé Césaire, *Corps perdu*, with 31 engravings done by Picasso.  — 1950

Lives in Paris briefly at 9 Rue Gay-Lussac.  — 1951

Publication of Adrian de Monluc, *La maigre*, with 10 dry points by Picasso.  — 1952

Great retrospective exhibitions in Rome, Milan, Lyons, and São Paulo (Brazil).
Separation from Françoise Gilot.  — 1953

Summer in Collioure and Perpignan (French Pyrenees).  — 1954

Winter in Paris.
To Vallauris for a few days in early spring, then moves to his new villa in Cannes.  — 1955

# Bibliography

This selected bibliography is intended as a guide to specific areas of Picasso's artistic activity. It is suggested that the reader also consult the bibliography – the first truly comprehensive one – published by Alfred H. Barr, Jr. in *Picasso: Fifty Years of His Art*, New York: The Museum of Modern Art, 1946, and the lists in the catalogues of the exhibitions at Milan (1954) and Paris (1955).

## General Works on Modern Painting

Salmon, André. *La jeune peinture française.* Paris: Société des Trente, 1912.

Meier-Graefe, J. *Entwicklungsgeschichte der modernen Kunst*, Vol. III. Munich: R. Piper, 1914.

Kahnweiler, D.-H. *The Rise of Cubism.* Translation by Henry Aronson of the 1920 German edition. New York: Wittenborn, Schultz, 1949.

Salmon, André. *L'art vivant.* Paris: G. Crès & Cⁱᵉ, 1920.

Einstein, Carl. *Die Kunst des 20. Jahrhunderts.* Berlin: Propyläen-Verlag, 1926.

Huyghe, René. *La peinture française: les contemporains.* Biographical notes by G. Bazin. Paris: P. Tisné, [1939].

Breton, André. *Le surréalisme et la peinture.* Paris: Librairie Gallimard, 1928; New York: Brentano's, 1945.

Kahnweiler, D.-H. *Juan Gris: His Life and Work.* Translated from the French and revised by Douglas Cooper. London: Lund Humphries, 1947.

Dorival, Bernard. *Les étapes de la peinture française contemporaine.* 18th ed., Vol. II. Paris: Gallimard, 1948, pp. 215–46.

Kahnweiler, D. H. "Ursprung und Entwicklung des Kubismus," in *Die Meister französischer Malerei der Gegenwart.* Edited by M. Jardot and K. Martin. Baden-Baden: Woldemar Klein, 1948. (Issued in connection with an exhibition in Freiburg, 1947.)

Raynal, Maurice. *From Picasso to Surrealism (History of Modern Painting*, Vol. III). Translated by Stuart Gilbert. Geneva: A. Skira, [1949–50].

Haftmann, Werner. *Malerei im 20. Jahrhundert.* Munich: Prestel-Verlag, [1954].

## Memorabilia

Apollinaire, Guillaume. *The Cubist Painters.* Translation by Lionel Abel of the 1913 French edition. New York: Wittenborn, 1944.

Däubler, Theodor. *Der neue Standpunkt*. Dresden-Hellerau: Hellerauer Verlag, 1916, pp. 145–63.

Raynal, Maurice. *Picasso*. Munich: Delphin Verlag, 1921; Paris: G. Crès et C$^{ie}$, 1922.

Cocteau, Jean. *Picasso*. Paris: Stock, 1923.

Reverdy, Pierre. *Pablo Picasso*. Paris: Éditions de la Nouvelle Revue Française, 1924.

Cocteau, Jean. *A Call to Order*. London: Faber & Gwyer, 1926, pp. 223 to 248.

Jacob, Max. "Souvenirs sur Picasso," in *Cahiers d'art* (Paris), 1927, No. 2, pp. 199–202.

Uhde, Wilhelm. *Picasso and the French Tradition*. Translated by F. M. Loving. New York: E. Weyhe, 1929.

Olivier, Fernande. *Picasso et ses amis*. Paris: Stock, [1933].

Stein, Gertrude. *Autobiography of Alice B. Toklas*. New York: Harcourt, Brace and Company, 1933; Modern Library, 1955.

Stein, Gertrude. *Picasso*. Paris: 1938.

Jedlicka, Gotthard. *Begegnungen mit Künstlern der Gegenwart*. Erlenbach-Zurich: E. Rentsch, 1945.

Sabartés, Jaime. *Picasso: An Intimate Portrait*. Translated by Angel Flores. New York: Prentice-Hall, 1948.

Sabartés, Jaime. *Picasso: documents iconographiques*. Geneva: Pierre Cailler, 1954.

Monographs and Articles

Level, André. *Picasso*. Paris: G. Crès & C$^{ie}$, [1928].

*Documents* (Paris), 1930, II, No. 3. (Special Picasso number).

D'Ors, Eugenio. *Pablo Picasso*. London: A. Zwemmer, [1930].

Grohmann, Will. "Picasso." (*Allgemeines Lexikon der bildenden Künstler*. Edited by Ulrich Thieme and Felix Becker. Vol. XXVI). Leipzig: E. A. Seamann, 1932, pp. 576–78.

*Cahiers d'art* (Paris), 1938, XIII, No. 3–10. (Special Picasso number).

Cassou, Jean. *Picasso*. New York: Hyperion Press, 1940.

Merli, Joan. *Picasso*. Buenos Aires: "El Ateneo," 1942; new ed. 1948.

Barr, Alfred H., Jr. *Picasso: Fifty Years of His Art*. New York: The Museum of Modern Art, 1946. (Basic scholarly work.)

*Le point* (Souillac), 1952, XLII. (Picasso number: articles by M. Raynal, D.-H. Kahnweiler, P. Reverdy, G. Besson, T. Tzara, P. Gay, E. Pignon, C. Roy; photographs taken at Vallauris by R. Doisneau).

Raynal, Maurice. *Picasso*. Translated by James Emmons. Geneva: Skira, [1953].

*Commentari* (Rome), 1953, No. 3. (Picasso number: articles by J. Cocteau, T. Tzara, D. Valeri, L. Venturi).

Interpretations of Work and Personality

Raphael, Max. *Von Monet zu Picasso*. Munich: Delphin Verlag, 1919.

Raphael, Max. *Proudhon, Marx, Picasso: trois études sur la sociologie de l'art.* Paris: Excelsior, 1933, pp. 187–237. (Picasso seen as the artistic representative of the middle class.)

Brandi, Cesare. *Carmine o della pittura con due saggi e su Duccio e Picasso.* Florence: Vallecchi, 1947, pp. 243–326.

Erben, Walter. *Picasso und die Schwermut: Versuch einer Deutung.* Heidelberg: Lambert Schneider, 1947.

Hartlaub, G. F. "Das Phänomen Picasso," in *Fragen an die Kunst* (Stuttgart), n.d.

Sedlmayr, Hans. "Kierkegaard über Picasso," in *Wort und Wahrheit* (Vienna), 1950, V, pp. 356–70. (Picasso, in analogy to Kierkegaard's "seducer," described as the "interesting" artist of modern times.)

Gieure, Maurice. *Initiation à l'œuvre de Picasso.* Paris: Éditions des Deux-Mondes, 1951.

Gullón, Ricardo. *De Goya al arte abstracto.* Madrid: [Ediciones Cultura hispánica], 1952, pp. 71–98. (Characterization of his personality as "Picasso Andaluz universal.")

Tzara, Tristan. *Picasso et la poésie.* Rome: De Luca, 1953.


Catalogues

*Cahiers d'art* (Paris), 1932, VII, No. 3–5. (Special number devoted to the Paris Exhibition.)

*Exposition Picasso.* Edited by Ch. Vrancken. Exhibition at Galeries Georges Petit, Paris: 1932. (Also the basis for the catalogue of the exhibition at the Kunsthaus in Zurich, 1932.)

Zervos, Christian. *Pablo Picasso.* (7 vols. in 8 parts.) Paris: Éditions Cahiers d'art, 1932–55. Vol. I published in English, New York: E. Weyhe, 1932.

*Picasso: Forty Years of His Art.* Edited by Alfred H. Barr, Jr. New York: The Museum of Modern Art, 1939. (Exhibition catalogue.)

*Picasso.* Exhibition at the museum in Lyons: 1953. Articles by J. Cassou, D. H. Kahnweiler, C. Zervos, R. Jullian, M. Michaud.

*Pablo Picasso.* Edited by Franco Russoli. Exhibition at the Palazzo Reale, Milan: 1953. (Published as a book, Milan: Amilcare Pizzi, 1954.)

*Pablo Picasso.* Edited by Lionello Venturi. Exhibition at Galleria nazionale d'arte moderna, Rome: 1953.

*Exposição Picasso.* Edited by M. Jardot. Exhibition at São Paulo, Brazil: 1953–54.

*Picasso.* Edited by M. Jardot. Exhibition at the Musée des arts décoratifs, Paris: 1955.


Interpretations of Individual Periods

Zervos, C. "Dernières œuvres de Picasso," in *Cahiers d'art* (Paris), 1927, No. 2, pp. 189–98.

Zervos, C. "Picasso à Dinard," in *Cahiers d'art* (Paris), 1929, No. 4, pp. 5–20.

Zervos, C. "Projets de Picasso pour un monument," in *Cahiers d'art* (Paris), 1929, No. 4, pp. 341–54.

Leiris, Michel. "Toiles récentes de Picasso," in *Documents* (Paris), 1930, No. 2, pp. 57–71. (Surrealist representations of women.)

*Cahiers d'art* (Paris), 1935, No. 7–10. (Special Picasso number devoted to, among others, the 1932 series of reclining nudes, the 1933 series of circus paintings, the 1933–34 matador series, the 1935 series of interiors with girls sleeping or drawing.)

Zervos, C. "Histoire d'un tableau de Picasso (Guernica)," in *Cahiers d'art* (Paris), 1937, No. 4–5. (Special Picasso number.)

*Cahiers d'art* (Paris), 1940–44, No. 15–19. (Special Picasso number with numerous illustrations of his work during these years.)

*Picasso libre: 21 peintures 1940–45*. Exhibition at the Galerie Louis Carée, Paris: 1945. (With articles by various authors.)

Cirici-Pellicer, Alexandre. *Picasso antes de Picasso*. Barcelona: Iberia-Joaquin Gil, [1946]. Revised edition: *Picasso avant Picasso*. Translated by M. de Floris and V. Gasol. Geneva: Pierre Cailler, 1950. (Discusses the years up to 1904.)

Janis, Harriet and Sidney. *Picasso. The Recent Years: 1939–46*. New York: Doubleday & Co., Inc., 1946.

Larrea, Juan. *Pablo Picasso: Guernica*. Preface by Alfred H. Barr, Jr. New York: Curt Valentin, 1947.

Sabartés, Jaime. "Antipolis 1946," in *Verve* (Paris), 1948, Vol. V, No. 19–20.

*Picasso à Antibes*. "Picasso au travail," by Jaime Sabartés; "Picasso bon maître de la liberté," by Paul Eluard; photographs by Michel Sima. Paris: René Drouin, [1948].

De la Souchère, R. "Picasso au Musée d'Antibes," in *Cahiers d'art* (Paris), 1948, [No.] 1, pp. 11–68.

Zervos, C. "Œuvres récentes de Picasso exposées à la Maison de la Pensée Française," in *Cahiers d'art* (Paris), 1949, No. 2, pp. 237–72. (Work of 1946–49.)

Zervos, C. "Œuvres et images inédites de la jeunesse de Picasso," in *Cahiers d'art* (Paris), 1950, No. 2, pp. 277–333. (Work of 1892 to 1906.)

Verdet, André. *Pablo Picasso au Musée d'Antibes*. Paris: Falaize, 1951. (Work of 1946.)

*Verve* (Paris), 1951, No. 25–26. (Special section: "Picasso à Vallauris" with articles by D.-H. Kahnweiler ["Le sujet chez Picasso"], O. Elytis, G. Ramié.)

*Picasso, 2 périodes: 1900–14, 1950–54*. Exhibition at Maison de la Pensée Française. Paris: 1954.

*Cahiers d'art* (Paris), 1954, 29th year, pp. 71–91. (Reproductions of the series of portraits of Sylvette and of his children, from the exhibition at the Maison de la Pensée Française.)

Roy, Claude. *Picasso: La guerre et la paix*. Paris: Éditions Cercle d'Art, 1954. (Contains the drawings from the sketchbook.)

## Publications of Color Reproductions

Desnos, Robert. *Picasso: Seize peintures, 1939–1943.* Paris: Les Éditions du Chêne, 1943.

Sabartés, Jaime. *Picasso.* (Couleurs des Maîtres.) Paris: Braun & Cⁱᵉ; New York: Tudor Publishing Co., 1946.

Sutton, Denys. *Picasso. Peintures: époques bleue et rose.* Paris: Les Éditions du Chêne, 1948.

Lieberman, William S. *Pablo Picasso: Blue and Rose Periods.* New York: Harry N. Abrams, Inc., 1954.

Wittgens, Fernanda. *Picasso.* Milan: "Silvana" Editoriale D'Arte, 1954.

*Du* (Zurich), 1954, No. 7. (Special Picasso number.)

## Drawings

George, Waldemar. *Picasso: dessins.* Paris: Éditions des Quatre Chemins, 1926.

Zervos, C. "Projets de Picasso pour un monument," in *Cahiers d'art* (Paris), 1929, No. 4, pp. 341–53. (Pen drawings of summer, 1928.)

Kitahara, Yoshio. *Picasso: 54 dessins.* Tokyo: Atelier-Sha, 1937.

*Cinquanta disegni di Pablo Picasso.* Text by C. Carrà, E. Prampolini, A. Savinio, G. Severini, A. Soffici. Novara: Posizione, 1943. (A selection designed to point up the Classical element in Picasso's work.)

*Picasso: Fifteen Drawings.* New York: Pantheon, 1946. (Facsimile reproductions of practically all drawings in color made between 1903–37 now in American collections.)

Tzara, Tristan. *Pablo Picasso.* Geneva: Albert Skira, 1948.

*Carnet de dessins de Picasso (1940–42).* Paris: Éditions Cahiers d'art, 1948. (Primarily women, half-lengths, and heads of the Royan period.)

Zervos, C. *Dessins de Pablo Picasso 1892–1948.* Paris: Éditions Cahiers d'art, [1949].

Bouret, Jean. *Picasso: dessins.* Paris: Éditions des Deux-Mondes, 1950.

*Homage to Picasso: Drawings and Watercolors since 1893.* London: Lund Humphries, 1951. ("Drawings of Picasso," by Roland Penrose; "Picasso, Good Master of Liberty," by Paul Eluard, translated by Roland Penrose.)

Zambrano, Maria. "L'amour et la mort dans les dessins de Picasso," in *Cahiers d'art* (Paris), 26th year, pp. 29–56. (Drawings of 1942–43.)

Eluard, Paul. *Picasso: dessins.* Paris: Braun & Cⁱᵉ, [1952].

*Vallauris 1954: A Suite of 180 Drawings by Picasso, November 28, 1953 to February 3, 1954.* New York: Harcourt, Brace and Company, 1954. (The English edition of *Verve* [Paris], 1954, No. 29–30. Preface by Tériade; "Picasso and the Human Comedy," by Michel Leiris; and an appreciation by Rebecca West.)

## Graphic Work

Geiser, Bernhard. *Picasso peintre-graveur (1899–1931).* Bern: Published by the author, 1933; new ed. 1955.

Geiser, Bernhard. *Pablo Picasso: Lithographs 1945–48.* New York: Curt Valentin, 1948.

Mourlot, Fernand. *Picasso lithographe.* 2 vols., I: 1919–47, II: 1947–49. Monte Carlo: André Sauret, 1949–50.

*Pablo Picasso: das graphische Werk.* Edited by B. Geiser. Catalogue of the exhibition at the Kunsthaus, Zurich: 1954.

Geiser, Bernhard. *Picasso: Fifty-Five Years of His Graphic Work.* Translated by L. Gombrich. New York: Harry N. Abrams, Inc., 1955. (168 plates.)

*L'œuvre gravée de Pablo Picasso.* Articles by Jean Cocteau, B. Geiser, P. Cailler. Exhibition at the Musée Rath, Geneva: 1955.

*Picasso: l'œuvre gravée.* Edited by Jean Adhémar and C. Pérussaux. Exhibition at the Bibliothèque nationale, Paris: 1955.

Sculpture

Breton, André. "Picasso dans son élément," in *Minotaure* (Paris), 1933, I, pp. 2–37. (Photographs by Brassai of Picasso's sculpture and his studio.)

Prampolini, E. *Picasso scultore.* (Anticipazioni serie Arti 2.) Rome: Fratelli Bocca, 1943.

Zervos, C. "L'homme à l'agneau de Picasso," in *Cahiers d'art* (Paris), 1945–46, pp. 85–113. (Genesis of the statue and the preliminary studies of Juli 1942–October 1943.)

Kahnweiler, D.-H. *Sculptures de Picasso.* Paris: Les Éditions du Chêne, 1948. (Fundamental work.)

Verdet, André. *La chèvre de Picasso.* Paris: Éditions de Beaune, 1952.

Argan, G. C. *Scultura di Picasso.* Venice: Alfieri, 1953. (Text in Italian and English.)

Zervos, C. "L'arrière-saison de Picasso," in *Picasso.* Catalogue of exhibition at the museum in Lyons, 1953. (Appraisal of Picasso's sculpture since 1945.)

Ceramics

"Céramiques de Picasso," in *Cahiers d'art* (Paris), 1948, [No.] 1, pp. 73 to 208.

Ramié, Suzanne and Georges, *Céramiques de Picasso.* Paris: A. Skira, 1948.

Sabartés, Jaime. *Picasso ceramista.* Milan: All'Insegna del Pesce d'Oro, 1953.

Ballet

Picasso, Pablo. *Trente-deux reproductions des maquettes en couleur d'après les originaux des costumes et décor pour le ballet "Le tricorne."* Paris: Paul Rosenberg, 1920.

Lieberman, William S. "Picasso and the Ballet," in *Dance Index* (New York), 1946, pp. 261–308.

Breton, André. "Picasso poète," in *Cahiers d'art* (Paris), 1935, No. 7–10, pp. 185–91.

Sabartés, Jaime. "La littérature de Picasso," in *Cahiers d'art* (Paris), 1935, No. 7–10, pp. 225–38. (Reproduction of a Spanish poem ["Lengue de fuego . . ."] of November 28, 1935, and his "Métamorphoses" of December 5, 6, 24, 1935, with translations into French.)

Picasso, Pablo. *Le désir attrapé par la queue.* (Collections Métamorphoses XXIII. Paris: Gallimard, 1945. (Play written in January 1941. German translation in *Pablo Picasso. Wort und Bekenntnis.* Zurich: Die Arche, 1954, pp. 59–98.)

*Picasso: poemas y declaraciones.* Mexico: Darro y Genil, 1944.

Zervos, C. (ed.). "Textes de Picasso," in *Cahiers d'art* (Paris), 1948, [No.] 1, pp. 50–60. (Prose of the years 1941–43 from a notebook which Picasso kept between February 11, 1941, and February 4, 1944.)

Picasso, Pablo. *Tout le fatras immonde. . . .* Paris: Galerie Louise Leiris, 1954. (Prose of February 11, 1941, and also writings of 1949 illustrated with lithographs and bound in a portfolio.)

Tzara, Tristan. *Picasso et sa poésie.* Rome: De Luca, 1953.

*Pablo Picasso. Wort und Bekenntnis.* Zurich: Die Arche, 1954. (Pp. 46 to 57: German translation of his collected poems and statements first published by André Breton in French in *Cahiers d'art* [Paris], 1935, No. 7–10, pp. 185–91.)

# Index of Names

The numbers in italics refer to reproductions

## Photo Credits

Bibliothèque Nationale, Paris; Galerie Louis Carré, Paris; Cauvin, Paris; Chevojon, Paris; Gilbert, Paris; Lanièpce, Paris; Galerie Louise Leiris, Paris; MAS-Photo, Barcelona; Musée Grimaldi, Antibes; S. Ohana, Paris; Perls Galleries, New York; S. Rosengart, Lucerne; Routhier, Paris; J. Sabartés, Paris; M. Vaux, Paris; Württemberg State's Galleries, Stuttgart; Archives.

## Publication Credits

*Art and Decoration* – Alfred H. Barr Jr., *Picasso, Fifty Years of His Art*, New York 1946 – *Cahiers d'Art*, Paris – J. Cocteau, B. Geiser, P. Cailler, *The Graphic Œuvre of Pablo Picasso*, Geneva 1955 – Harriet and Sidney Janis, *Picasso, The Recent Years (1939–1946)*, New York 1946 – Daniel-Henry Kahnweiler, *Sculptures of Picasso*, Paris 1948 – Jean Larrea, *Pablo Picasso, Guernica*, New York 1947 – *Minotaure I*, Paris 1933 – Fernand Mourlot, *Picasso lithographe (1919–1949)*, Monte Carlo 1949 and 1950 – Alejandro Cirici-Pellicer, *Picasso before Picasso*, Barcelona 1946 – *Picasso in Antibes*, Paris 1948 – *Picasso-Portefolio* of the Éditions du Chêne, Paris – Suzanne and Georges Ramié, *Ceramics of Picasso*, Geneva 1948 – *DU* (Zurich), 1954, No. 7 (Special Picasso Number) *Verve*, Paris – Christian Zervos, *Pablo Picasso I–VI*; Paris 1932–1954.

## Credits for the colored photographs

Lanièpce, Paris; Dräyer, Zurich; Museum of Modern Art, New York; Publishers Conzett & Huber, Zurich.